MY MEMOIRS

MAJEED MEMON
Senior Advocate

BLUEROSE PUBLISHERS
India | U.K.

Copyright © Majeed Memon - Sr.Advocate 2025

All rights reserved by author. No part of this publication may be reproduced, stored in a retrieval system or transmitted in any form or by any means, electronic, mechanical, photocopying, recording or otherwise, without the prior permission of the author. Although every precaution has been taken to verify the accuracy of the information contained herein, the publisher assumes no responsibility for any errors or omissions. No liability is assumed for damages that may result from the use of information contained within.

BlueRose Publishers takes no responsibility for any damages, losses, or liabilities that may arise from the use or misuse of the information, products, or services provided in this publication.

For permissions requests or inquiries regarding this publication,
please contact:

BLUEROSE PUBLISHERS
www.BlueRoseONE.com
info@bluerosepublishers.com
+91 8882 898 898
+4407342408967

ISBN: 978-93-6783-671-2

First Edition: January 2025

This book is dedicated to my late mother Ayesha who raised me in difficult times and my beloved wife Saeeda who stood by my side all along and tolerated my whimsical and errant ways with patience. But for her support I could not have achieved all that I did.

Acknowledgment

I am greatly indebted to my colleague advocate Ms. Katherine Joseph in compiling this book. She has taken out her valuable time along with her legal practice to scan the records and choose selected cases as cited in this book from among hundreds of cases which I have conducted over the years. I am also thankful to her for going through the Parliamentary records and choosing selected speeches delivered by me in Parliament during my term as a Member of Parliament (Rajya Sabha) from 2014-2020 to enable me to incorporate them in this book.

My gratitude is also due to my longtime close friend and well wisher Shri Hafizullah Baig for encouraging me to compile this book and getting it published in time.

Foreword

When I was requested by Majeed Memon to write a foreword to his book 'MY MEMOIRS' I felt honoured and considered it to be a privilege conferred on me.

I went through the manuscript almost at one stretch as I found it quite interesting and engrossing. Many of my memories were revived by the references from the account of the cases discussed by him in the book.

I met Majeed Memon first in January, 1980 when I, as a just enrolled Advocate, used to go to the Metropolitan Magistrates' Courts at Bandra. The courts were then situated in a private building near Bandra lake. The government had taken the premises on rent. A number of Advocates used to practice in those courts. A few of them who were seniors were very good and had a good practice, but there were many who did not have much work. Consequently, the atmosphere in the court corridor and the bar room was such that there was more jealousy and gossip rather than any serious discussion about law. In the scenario, Majeed Memon, though a junior advocate distinguished himself by concentrating on his work. My first impression about him was that of being a stern, serious and studious personality who preferred to keep himself aloof from the bar politics and gossip.

I became a Metropolitan Magistrate; later, rose to become a Session Judge and ultimately a High Court Judge. Though Majeed Memon did appear before me at all these levels, there was naturally no personal interaction between us at any time. It is only after my retirement that we really came in contact with each other in connection with professional and social work.

The book is divided by the author in two parts - the first part deals with his role as an Advocate and the second part with his role as a Member of Parliament.

Part I of the book opens with a brief account of the author's family, his career as a student and the acquaintances and friendships that he developed in his college days – including the Government Law College. A facet of his personality – as an Urdu poet – was unknown to me till I read the manuscript. A chapter in the book is devoted to the author's memories of the Hon'ble Shri Justice Krishna Iyer – one of the greatest jurists of all time. When I was on the bench, I was not aware that Majeed Memon was so close to Justice Krishna Iyer. This chapter shows how privileged the author was to have got the affection of such a legendary personality.

In MY MEMOIRS the author has given an account of selected 24 cases/trials in which he was concerned. Most of the trials mentioned by him had attracted media attention and gathered publicity due to the personalities involved in those cases, or the enormity of the crime. Among these cases is one where a soldier from the Central Industrial Security Force had gunned down his superior–being infuriated by the superior's refusal to grant leave to him. Another interesting case is that of the 'Dalals' which I am sure many would remember because of the unexpected turn of events that took place in the case which had attracted much publicity at that time. One Mr. V.H. Dalal and his wife Tara Dalal had committed suicide by jumping down from the window of their flat on eighth floor. On the basis of a suicide note left by them, their son Balkrishna Dalal and his wife Sonal Dalal were prosecuted for abetting the suicide which is punishable under section 306 of the Indian Penal Code. The author was appearing for Balkrishna and Sonal Dalal in the trial. The case took a strange and absolutely unexpected turn when Balkrishna Dalal and Sonal Dalal alongwith their only daughter Pooja themselves committed suicide by jumping from the same window just a day before the judgment of the Sessions

Court was expected! Then there are cases of Milind Vaidya attack and the Ghatkopar bomb blast where the disappearance of the accused Khwaja Yunus remained a mystery (the disappearance of Khwaja Yunus again attracted media attention recently due to some other reasons). Then there is the 1993 bomb blast case, diamond merchant Bharat Shah's case (in which three stars of Bollywood gave evidence) and the Gulshan Kumar murder case. All the 24 cases mentioned by the author are interesting and the graphic account of these cases given by the author shows the range of the author's experience as a lawyer. The last case mentioned by the author is remarkable being in stark contrast with our experience of the witnesses in India, where perjury is rampant and common.

The selection of the cases has not been done on the basis whether the author ultimately succeeded therein. Even the cases where the author did not succeed have been included. When one goes through the account of these cases, the author's personality as an intelligent, hardworking, persuasive Advocate, capable of going on an aggressive footing when needed, is revealed. More particularly, the cases of the midnight order (case 4), Rashida Banu's case (case 23) are remarkable.

The author has inserted anecdotes between the accounts of two cases terming the same under the title 'In a Lighter Vein'. These anecdotes are equally interesting and some of them are quite humorous.

Part II of the book deals with the author as a parliamentarian. I cannot profess to have the same authority in judging his merit as a parliamentarian as I have in assessing his merit as an advocate – having seen him in that capacity. However, after my retirement and while the author was a member of the Rajya Sabha, he had occasions to discuss with me some of the legal issues that were arising out of the bills pending before the parliament. This, and the account of the speeches made by him in the parliament leave no manner of doubt that this job too he took seriously.

To be successful as a lawyer one requires several qualities apart from legal knowledge, hard work, good health and sincerity. The author has acquired name and fame and a status among the leading criminal law practitioners though he started his career in a humble way. Among the lawyers who are considered as experts in criminal law, not all can do the trial work. There are many stalwarts in criminal law whose practice is confined only to the appeals, revisions and criminal writs. Similarly, there are excellent lawyers who never appear in appeals, revisions or criminal writs and keep their practice confined to the trial courts only. Majeed Memon is one of the few advocates who do trial work as well as appellate and writ work. The trial advocate, inter alia, must possess the ability to effectively cross-examine the witnesses, which in turn depends not only on his knowledge of law but also of his understanding of human beings and their nature. He needs to be shrewd and possess a personality that will overawe the witnesses so as to put them on guard if intending to narrate facts incorrectly or falsely. The author possesses all these qualities.

The book makes an interesting reading. The author must be complimented for bringing out, through MY MEMOIRS an account of some of the famous cases that have taken place in last thirty years. I am sure the book will be widely circulated and appreciated by the legal community at all levels, including the law students. I wish the author good luck and expect to have many more books written by him in future – including, perhaps a new collection of Urdu poems.

JUSTICE ABHAY M. THIPSAY
(Former Judge Bombay High Court and Allahabad High Court)

Table of Contents

A. My Humble Beginnings 1
B. Justice V. R. Krishna Iyer: My mentor, My motivator 6
C. Sixth Justice V. R. Krishna Iyer Memorial Lecture 12

PART 1

As Advocate

1. The Killer Cop of CISF 25
   In A Lighter Vein 34
2. The Grand Tragedy of Grand Paradi 36
   In A Lighter Vein 42
3. The Terrible Tuesday and The Bitter Pil 44
   In A Lighter Vein 49
4. A Motor Accident and The Historic Midnight Order 50
   In A Lighter Vein 59
5. The Paedophile Case 61
   In A Lighter Vein 64
6. Anupam Kher Vs Surjeet 65
   In A Lighter Vein 71
7. A Fiancee's Brutal Murder 73
   In A Lighter Vein 79
8. Shootout At Mahim 82
   In A Lighter Vein 87
9. A Messy Missing Mystery 89
   In A Lighter Vein 100

10. The Murky Rape of a Swedish National 101
    In A Lighter Vein 105
11. Crusader Anna Hazare V/S Abdul Karim Telgi 106
    In A Lighter Vein 123
12. The Horrific End of an Infant and His Granny 124
    In A Lighter Vein 132
13. The Controversial IPS Officer and The Court-Room Drama ... 133
    In A Lighter Vein 138
14. Sunil Dutt V/S Sanjay Nirupam 139
    In A Lighter Vein 142
15. Sahil Zaroo and The Shahtoosh Shawls 144
    In A Lighter Vein 148
16. Bollywood and Its U-Turn 151
    In A Lighter Vein 159
17. Biwi No. 1 and Biwi No. 2 160
    In A Lighter Vein 164
18. The 2G Scam 166
    In A Lighter Vein 171
19. Gulshan Kumar Murder 174
    In A Lighter Vein 187
20. Extradition Proceedings in London 188
    In A Lighter Vein 206
21. The Case of Anand Jon in The United States 208
    In A Lighter Vein 216
22. The Bombay Bomb Blasts 217
    In A Lighter Vein 231

23. The Aged Maid and The Stolen Gold 232
    In A Lighter Vein 235
24. The Truthful Lover 236
    In A Lighter Vein 240

PART 2

As People's Representative

    A Parliamentarian 247
1. On the Israel-Palestine Conflict 249
2. On Our Constitution 252
3. Law and Justice 257
4. Atrocities Against Dalits 260
5. The Powerloom Industry 265
6. Problems of Railway Commuters 269
7. Onion Farmers in Maharashtra 271
8. Judicial Vacancies 273
9. Electoral Reforms 277

The Orientation Programme 279

Acting Chairman of The Parliamentary Standing Committee on Personnel, Public Grievances and Law & Justice 281

Positions Held In Rajya Sabha 284

A
MY HUMBLE BEGINNINGS

The dust of the independence struggle of the country had barely settled, and the dawn of freedom was shining with its nascent glory, when I was born, in December of that year, into Memon family. My father, Ahmed, was a small-time merchant, who had done his schooling in Gujarati, and it ended there. My mother, Ayesha, though not formally educated, was quite intelligent and clever. Both were determined to provide good education for their children. My father wanted his two sons to become advocates. He was always attired in a black sherwani, to look a bit like an advocate.

After completing primary education in a local school in Mahim, Bombay in 1955, I joined Anjuman-e-Islam Urdu High School, at Victoria Terminus, Bombay. When I was in the 5th standard, the dreaded disease, cancer, struck my father, who was hardly in his fifties, and took him away from us. I distinctly remember the day. I was in my classroom when my elder brother came to the school, broke the news of my father's death, and took me home. An important chapter in my life ended there.

Unfortunately, we were not financially well off. My father left us little by way of inheritance. He was survived by his widow, six daughters and two sons. I was the younger son, and the sixth child of my parents. After the untimely demise of my father, despite our straitened circumstances, my mother's resolve to educate her children never waned. In my education I was supported considerably by the Memon Education and Welfare Society.

I recall that I used to secure the first rank in the class throughout school so that I could claim a full scholarship, which meant free education.

It was with a strong desire to acquire the highest possible level of education that I joined the Arts faculty at R.D. National College, Bandra, Bombay. I was much ahead of my classmates in my studies. Once, I asked my professor, Shri Shakir Gaya, whether I could directly take the Master of Arts examination, without waiting for six years, as was the norm. He smiled and said, "Not possible".

I remember my class-fellows seeking my assistance and guidance. I used to enjoy teaching them and helping them get over their difficulties. They respected me for this, and I felt elated when they expressed their gratitude. In the second year of college, for the Intermediate Arts course we had two papers on Logic - Inductive and Deductive Logic. Each paper had a hundred marks. These were my favourite subjects in which I scored high marks. It was the subject, Logic, that made me very popular amongst the teachers and class-fellows. When the examination results of Inter Arts were out, I found that I had narrowly missed a first class at the University level. Obtaining a first class in Inter Arts was no piece of cake, as everyone knew.

For the Bachelor of Arts course, my subjects were Economics and Political Science. I graduated in 1969, after four long years of college education. During this time in National College, some of my classmates and friends played important roles in shaping my personality. Amjad Khan (Gabbar Singh, of Sholay fame), Aejaz (the nephew of star actress Waheeda Rehman), Mutiur Rehman (son of music director, Naushad Ali), Hafizullah Baig (later, a business executive overseas) and Krishna Nair (we go back a long way) among others, were my intimate friends. In those days, the music maestro Naushad Saheb lived near our college in Bandra. Because of my friendship with his son Rehman, I would often visit his house. There, I came in contact with Dilip Kumar, Sunil Dutt, Majrooh Sultanpuri, Ali Sardar Jafri, Hasrat Jaipuri - stalwarts of the Indian film industry. Since I had a flair for writing Urdu poems, I was drawn close to these eminent personalities. They appreciated my poems, and I received great encouragement from them, especially Naushad Saheb. Also, these poems would be displayed on the college walls and made me popular among professors and students alike.

I was fortunate to earn praise from even Sahir Ludhianvi Saheb, whom I had given my collection of poems to read. While he expressed appreciation for my thoughts and compositions, he counseled me not to make poetry-writing a profession, or means of earning a livelihood, but to keep it as a hobby. I was grateful to him for his guidance. The compilation of my poems and ghazals (the most popular form of Urdu poetry) was published in the form of a book with a preface by Naushad Saheb titled 'Saya-e-gul'. Later, its Hindi translation was released in New Delhi, at the hands of the Vice-President of India, Shri Hamid Ansari Saheb. It might appear strange that a criminal lawyer is a published poet. But there is a clear dichotomy: my legal practice is my profession whereas poetry is my hobby.

Upon completion of graduation in 1969, I sought admission for the Law degree course at the Government Law College, Bombay; I had to fulfill the dreams of my parents by donning the Advocate's black coat. An illustrious personality, Shri T.K. Tope was the principal of the college and among the lecturers were eminent academics who taught different aspects of law. I was excited to be a student of the most reputed Law College in Bombay. I enjoyed my time there; my closest classmates in law college were Yaseen Momin, Zameer Khan and J.P. Varma, (who was later recruited as a Probationary Officer in the State Bank of India). Incidentally, some of my classmates later rose to high positions in the Indian judiciary: Gulam Vahanvati was appointed Attorney General of India, Ajit Shah rose to be Chief Justice of Delhi High Court and thereafter Chairman of the Law Commission of India, Ranjana Sawant and Hemant Gokhale were Supreme Court judges.

Near the college, opposite Churchgate railway station, was a popular restaurant, called Satkar. My friends and I were regulars there and spent considerable time chatting over cups of tea.

It was in the second week of August 1973 that I applied for registration as an Advocate in the Bar Council of Maharashtra and Goa.

On the 23rd of August that same year, within days of my applying, I was enrolled as an Advocate and member of the Bar Council. That was a special day for me as my parents' dream had turned into reality.

With very little financial support, and practically no guidance, I was beginning a new chapter in my life. As a fledgling in the legal profession, I ventured to set up a small office in a suburb of Bombay, with merely a table and two chairs - the bare essentials that define an office. I remember in the evening of the very first day, an elderly person walked in to get some legal work done. This was encouraging. I attended to the client, and he left quite satisfied. Whatever fees I received, I gave away in charity.

I distinctly recall the following weeks and months and must confess that destiny was very kind to me. Within a short time, I was flooded with clients, so much so that I needed the assistance of junior advocates in the very first year of practice.

Since there was fierce professional competition and jealousy among lawyers in local courts, I was confronted with all kinds of impediments and obstacles in my relentless march towards the name and fame I enjoy now. During the couple of years of my practice at the Magistrates' courts level, I was ranked among the established senior advocates. The judicial officers respected me for my merit and hard work, while litigants found their way to my office.

It did not take long for me to learn the tricks of the trade and soon I started getting difficult and challenging assignments which I accepted willingly. Since the lower courts had limited jurisdiction and power, I felt my growth would be stunted and so shifted my base to the District Court and the High Court, which had jurisdiction to try serious cases punishable with death, or imprisonment for life. During the early years of my practice at this level, I had the opportunity to take up defence in many cases involving murder charges. This was challenging and I used to enjoy cross-examination of difficult witnesses. Not once in my career have I deviated from the basic principles of professionalism, client loyalty and a forthright approach. The litigants never had an occasion to doubt their trust in my work. In the inner circle, at the bar, I was popularly known as MM. Some of my close friends at the bar would say that the acronym MM did not denote Majeed Memon; it stood for 'Master Mind'. I would accept the compliment in good humor.

Both my sons Zulfiquar and Zaheer are lawyers and are doing fairly well. Incidentally, both my daughters-in-law are also law graduates. My grand son Mikaeel has recently graduated in law from Warwick University in the U.K.

During the course of my legal practice over the years I have conducted umpteen criminal cases all over the country, and in various foreign countries. To sum it up all I reminisce countable few important cases to form part of this book.

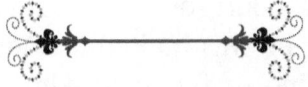

B
.....

JUSTICE V. R. KRISHNA IYER: MY MENTOR, MY MOTIVATOR

It was in the beginning of the 80s when I first came across the great jurist, late Justice V.R.Krishna Iyer. Justice Iyer had finished his term as Supreme Court Judge, in the year 1980, after serving the highest court for 7 years. It was by chance that I met him in Mumbai, where he was invited to address the legal fraternity. He had a huge following of fans and admirers, wherever he went. Among them, in Bombay, were judges of Bombay High Court, Justice P.B.Sawant, Justice H.H.Kantharia and Justice Pratap. Each one of them, and many others, were keen to spend some time with this great visionary, discussing various legal issues. At that point in time, I was a total stranger to him. I had been introduced to him as an advocate practising criminal law in Bombay. I remember my first interaction with him in his hotel room, at Ritz Hotel in Churchgate. On that day, a crowd had gathered inside and outside his room, eager to talk to him. When my turn came, I asked him a question about some aspects of criminal law which got him very involved. He answered my query, but it was apparent that he felt that he had not fully convinced me. He, therefore, asked me to wait while he attended to the others. I sat quietly on a sofa, hearing him talk. After he had finished with them, he turned to me and again addressed my query. He spoke for a few minutes, but his explanation remained inconclusive, and he showed signs of restlessness. He then held my hand and asked me if I could accompany him to the airport in his car, so that he could continue the discussion. I gladly accepted his offer as it was a godsend opportunity for me. I could spend almost an hour in his precious company during our journey from Churchgate to Santa Cruz airport. His conversation with me, during this time, brought me closer to him. This was the beginning of my long association with the great jurist.

During the next few weeks and months, I became closer to him for another reason. My wife belonged to his native city, Ernakulam, in Kerala. Every time I visited Kerala, I made it a practice to visit Justice Iyer at his residence Satgamaya (a highly symbolic name that means 'come towards the truth') on M.G. Road, Ernakulam, which became a regular destination for me. We spent a lot of quality time together and discussed different aspects of law, justice, human rights, the Constitution of India, and other related subjects in great detail. We used to go for walks together, in the evenings, on Ernakulam beach, up to Maharaja's College. Occasionally, judges of the Kerala High Court, and other dignitaries joined us in these walks and discussions.

Whenever Justice Iyer had to visit Mumbai, he would tell his secretary, Shri Nambiar, to inform me of his programme and flight details well in advance. On almost all occasions, I would receive him at the airport and be with him, till he departed from Mumbai.

At times, he not only visited my house, but preferred to stay with me and enjoy South Indian dishes like 'idli sambar' and 'rasam', with unpolished, cooked rice. I had a great time in his company, receiving legal education from a Master and these stays were instrumental in broadening my horizon of humanism and principles of 'natural justice'. No academic qualification, from the most reputed university in the world, could have given a student such an education as was gifted to me by Justice Iyer.

This great man lived in a ground floor flat, consisting of one bedroom, a dining room, and a kitchen. His wife, Sharda, passed away while he was still a sitting judge. He was so attached to her that he longed to converse with her, even after her death, through persons who claimed they could communicate with the dead.

One incident that Justice Iyer revealed to me was very touching.

Whilst he was still a judge and his wife had passed away, he used to drive his car himself, on the busy Delhi roads. He claimed that one day, he felt that his deceased wife Sharda was asking him not to drive on a particular day. He obeyed the departed soul's advice, only to later find that the car driven by his driver on that day, met with a minor accident. Justice Iyer was a firm believer in spiritual strength, and the influence of spirits in human life.

His flat was occupied by him, sans any family member, after his retirement. Both his sons, Ramesh and Paramesh, lived separately, away from him, with their respective families. In those days he was looked after by his loyal cook and a driver, in addition to his brilliant secretary and stenographer, Shri Nambiar who was a very honest and extremely hard-working person, devoted to his Master and his job. Often, I used to interact with him whenever I visited Justice Iyer. He showed sparks of intelligence which he had acquired during his long association with Justice Iyer. This fact will be apparent from a small incident.

Once, I asked him, "How is your health Mr. Nambiar?" He quipped, "O.K. I am in my neglected sixties, while Sir is in his protected eighties."

A few occasions when Justice Iyer was visiting Bombay are memorable. On one of these, as usual, I was informed that he would be landing at Santa Cruz airport, on a particular day. I drove my tiny Maruti 800 car myself, as I did not have a driver then. I had to park the car in a parking plaza from where I would have to walk for about ten minutes to the arrival lounge. By the time I reached the arrivals section of the Airport, I saw Justice Iyer standing with Mr. Nambiar, just outside the arrivals section. There were at least four white Ambassador cars, with red lights atop, waiting to pick him up, their front left doors open, in anticipation. Justice Iyer, for his part, was asking Nambiar where I was. In a couple of minutes, when I reached him, he asked me where my car was. I told him that my car was in the parking plaza, and it would take a few minutes for me to get it there. I later learnt that the beacon flashing Ambassador cars were sent by the Hon'ble Chief Justice of Bombay High Court, a couple of other High

Court Judges and the Collector of Bombay. Refusing to get into any of those cars, he insisted that I bring my car to drive him to the southern end of Bombay, which is about 20 kms. away from the Airport. He waited all the while till I brought my car to him. While I drove him to his destination, he sat next to me, discussing various issues all the way. The beaconed vehicles went back empty!

My association with him was during a period when we did not yet have mobile telephones. Our communication used to be personal, through telephone calls or by inland letters through post. I was fortunate enough to receive short inland letters that contained his brilliant writings. Even today, they are my proud possession.

In the eighties, I had organised a talk in Mumbai by this most sought-after jurist in the country. The subject, as suggested by him, was 'Personal Liberty and Judicial Guardianship'. The event was presided over by the then Chief Justice of Bombay High Court, His Lordship Mr. Justice Vijay Bhaskar Reddy. R.D. National College (my alma mater) was the venue. The hall was packed with sitting and ex-judges of all ranks, senior and junior advocates, and enthusiastic law students. The programme was a great success. The audience were thrilled by Justice Iyer's brilliant speech.

Justice Iyer agreed to be the patron of a group of activist lawyers in Bombay city urging them to form a team called 'Social Action Group of Advocates' (SAGA).

Shri Neemuchwala, Ms. Indira Jaisingh, Mr. Shrikant Bhatt, Mr. Anand Grover and myself, among others, were the members of SAGA headed by him. We used to have occasional meetings to discuss various problems, particularly connected with the bar and the bench, apart from other important social issues.

Post Babri Masjid incident in December 1992 there were communal riots which went on for a few weeks causing multiple deaths, destruction of public property and chaotic state of lawlessness prevailed for several days. Thereafter on 12th March, 1993 there were serial blasts which again resulted in mass killings and huge loss of public property.

Justice Iyer was deeply touched by all these happenings and he suggested that the government should take steps to identify the cause of the happenings and find out who were responsible for the mega crimes. He requested Justice S.M.Daud and Justice H. Suresh (both retired judges of Bombay High Court) to form a 'People's Tribunal' and start working by inviting common people to come forward and give evidence of what they knew of the riots. Both the Ld. Judges started collecting affidavits and recording statements of common people. There was overwhelming response from the public at large.

The media gave adequate space for this development which made the then Maharashtra government to set up an official Commission headed by a sitting judge of the High Court Mr. Justice Srikrishna. It was a one man Commission to probe into the Bombay riots. Justice Srikrishna Commission started its proceedings from one of the court rooms of Bombay High Court. Simultaneously People's Tribunal was also occupied in collecting evidence. Justice Srikrishna took the working of People's Tribunal by the two ex judges of the High Court as an act of contempt of his Commission. He thus issued contempt notices to the ex judges, Justice Daud and Justice H. Suresh.

This incident made a big news and it reached Justice Iyer's ears. He was annoyed and upset over the news. He called me and told me that he had written a confidential letter to Justice Srikrishna which was required to be handed over to him personally. He told me to do this job. I, then carried the sealed envelope containing his letter and went to the office of the Commission in Bombay High Court. I met the Secretary of the Commission and informed him that a confidential letter from Justice V.R.Krishna Iyer is to be delivered to Justice Srikrishna. I was promptly directed to meet Justice Srikrishna in his chamber. Thereafter I entered his chamber and told him that I was carrying a letter addressed to him by Justice Iyer . On this Justice Srikrishna was very excited. He told me that anything from Justice Iyer would be great. He took the envelope in his hands and opened it in front of me hurriedly. I had no occasion to read the contents of the letter. But I had the inkling that the contents were critical rather than complimentary. After having a glance at the contents of the letter Justice Srikrishna told me that the letter be handed over to his office secretary.

On the next day the news broke that Justice Srikrishna withdrew the contempt notices issued by him to the two justices.

Justice Krishna Iyer has the distinction of being known as the father of Public Interest Litigations (PILs). In fact, he had been a staunch supporter of personal liberty and bail. He propagated bail as a rule and jail an exception. 'Bail, and not jail' was his slogan.

In our country, almost all the advocates and judges are heard saying that whenever they come across the judgment of Justice V.R.Krishna Iyer, they need to refer to the Oxford English Dictionary to understand him.

1973-1980, the tenure of Justice V.R.Krishna Iyer, as a distinguished Supreme Court Judge, was perhaps the golden era of the apex court, in so far as the significance of personal liberty and bail jurisprudence is concerned. By his illustrious verdicts on personal liberty and bail he enlightened not just the Indian society but had global acknowledgement and impact. He is the giver of two important slogans, viz. (1) "bail and not jail" and (2) "right to bail accrues every day". Regrettably, the principles advocated by him are not strictly adhered to by the courts in India. Today bail has become an exception and jail a rule, resulting in overcrowded prisons in the country. The concept of the right of the accused to bail accrues every day is also wholly discarded, because bail applications are kept pending for weeks and months, in different courts, at all levels.

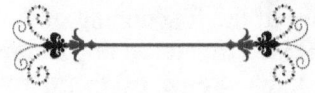

C

SIXTH JUSTICE V. R. KRISHNA IYER MEMORIAL LECTURE DELIVERED BY SHRI MAJEED MEMON AT KOCHI ON THE EVE OF HIS 105TH BIRTH ANNIVERSARY

HON'BLE justice Shri V Ramakumar, Chief Patron Justice V R K Iyer Legal Studies wing Calicut, Adv. M Asokan, Hon'ble Chairman, VRK Iyer Legal Studies wing,

Hon'ble members of the bar, ladies and gentlemen.

Good evening,

Happy Diwali to all of you.

It is my proud privilege to be delivering Justice V R Krishna Iyer Memorial lecture on the eve of his 105th Birth anniversary. I express my deep gratitude to Justice V R Krishna Iyer Legal Studies Wing of Calicut for having extended to me this honour.

Before me a few legal luminaries have delivered the Krishna Iyer Memorial lecture in the past six years, after his demise.

In the last seven decades of the functioning of the Supreme Court, about 200 judges, have contributed in interpreting statutes and the Constitution and evolving law in India. Some of them, rose to eminence to be remembered for their rich contribution and excellence in the discharge of their duties as judges. Justice Iyer ranks among the very few whose contribution in the making of the Indian Judiciary a formidable institution is remarkable, unmatchable and outstanding.

There is a lot of talk these days about cases relating to contempt of court and this reminds me of a very unique case.

"One day the people of this country will rise up and say that we don't want this magnificent red stone edifice on the Curzon Road because it is seen to be counter productive, and in turn, the High Courts. In this country, the Jesuses are getting crucified and the Barbases are very much upheld, thanks perhaps to the judiciary. Our whole judicial approach has a certain independence from all civilized behavior. In fact to speak very frankly the Indian judiciary is non est."

These are the words of none other than Justice V.R. Krishna Iyer at a symposium on "Approach to Judicial Reforms" organized in the premises of the High Court in Kerala as part of the Silver Jubilee celebrations of the Court in October - November 1981. Justice Krishna Iyer was invited as the main speaker and one of the Judges of the Kerala High Court Sri. G. Vishwanatha Iyer was in the chair.

One Sri. Vincent Panikulangara, was among the attendees in that symposium and he felt that the speech delivered by Sri. V. R. Krishna Iyer amounted to 'scandalisation of the authority of the Supreme Court and the High Courts' and therefore Sri. V. R. Krishna Iyer should be held guilty of criminal contempt and to that end he moved the Advocate General for sanction which was granted.

The petition came up for hearing before the Bench comprising of then Chief Justice of Kerala, Subramonian Poti and Justice K.S. Paripoornan who were faced with a unique problem.

The accused in the case, Sri V.R. Krishna Iyer was known to all the Judges. As a rule, no judge shall hear the case in which he is likely to be biased. This is a rule which can bear no exception. But faced with an unparalleled situation, as there was no other alternative, the case was posted before the Bench.

It was ironical that the one person who had done the most in the history of post-independence India to establish the rule of law and enhance the prestige and respect of the judicial system of India, stood accused of 'scandalising the Supreme Court and the High Courts' the very institutions he had nurtured with his sweat, blood and tears.

But what the Judges said in their judgement throws light on the great esteem and respect enjoyed by this great Judge and I quote the observations of the bench,

"An erudite Judge illumines the pages of law reports. He earns the respect and admiration of the members of the bar and the bench. The legal fraternity may remember him as his reputation survives to posterity. But rarely is such a judge widely known outside the world of law. Erudition coupled with a honest missionary zeal in the cause of social uplift gives a different image to a judge and makes him live not only the books of law but also in the hearts of men. Shri V.R. Krishna Iyer is known and respected by the public of this country. His tenure of office as a Judge of this Court, later as a member of the Law Commission and finally as a Judge of the Supreme Court has been marked by a distinction that singles him out from the rest of his colleagues. His decisions evince a new approach to Law and a new role for the Judge. While leaving a distinct mark of his personality in all that he did, Sri V.R. Krishna Iyer did challenge established traditional values and approaches and opened new vistas of thought and action to promote the social engineering process in the country.

His contribution as a Judge as a member of the Law Commission and as a powerful proponent of the cause of judicial reforms is well known. It is in this background that the statements made by him in his speech should be understood. By pointing out the weak spots in the judicial system and alerting the people to the need for a change lest the people as a whole reject the system, Justice Iyer was alerting his audience to bestow serious attention to the problem. The comments made by him are not of a person who is vituperative or one who wants to bring into disrepute the judicial system of this country but of one who was exhorting the people to bring about revolutionary change in the outlook concerning the problems of the judiciary."

After quoting extensively from Lord Denning and Edmund Davies, judges of the Court of Appeal in England and Professor Harold Laski and Justice Holmes, the Bench of the Kerala High Court concluded, " In the circumstances we find no reason to issue notice on this motion. We see no reason to call upon Sri V.R. Krishna Iyer to answer any charge of contempt. The petition is closed.

On law of contempt of Court, the observations of Justice V R Krishna Iyer needs to be noted here.

He wrote that unlike the executive or legislature, whose excesses beyond the constitution may be struck down by judiciary, the judiciary and judges may be corrected only by public criticism. The best answer to abuse of judges is not frequent or ferocious contempt-sentencing but fine performance". Justice Iyer was of the view that if the court **"delivers justice which is its professional, fundamental duty, criticism loses its sting".**

Shri Krishna Iyer was known as the conscience keeper of the justice system in India. I wonder what would be his reaction to the present abysmal state of the apex court when allegations are being hurled with high frequency at this once august institution, and on most occasions by responsible legal fraternity itself.

Justice V.R. Krishna Iyer was a blessed man. He was blessed with a long life, having lived for a complete 100 years. And he made the most of this blessing by ensuring that his entire conscious life was spent in the service of humanity and poor people.

Having graduated in law from Madras, he started practice in his father's chamber in 1938 at Thalassery, Malabar. A social activist, a member of the Legislative Assembly, a Minister in the communist government in Kerala in 1957, Judge of the High Court in 1968, member of the Law Commission from 1971 to 1973, and Judge of the Supreme Court of India from 1973 to 1980 when he retired. And till almost his dying day a strong advocate of the cause of justice in every forum, and an activist even participating in street protests. He maintained an open house and was accessible to all who sought his help or advice.

Dushyant Dave, the present president of Supreme Court Bar Association, in a full court reference, remembered Justice Iyer as *"one of the greatest sons of India"* and *"a legend, a phenomenon, a one-man army against injustices and upholder of all just causes and above all a great humanist".*

Like any righteous member of the Judiciary he was obsessed with the pursuit of Justice, but there was a difference - his concept of justice was blended with compassion, humanity. It was justice for all, the poor, the downtrodden included. In the words of an eminent writer, he made the Supreme Court of India, the Supreme Court for Indian people.

Armed with a prolific vocabulary and an inimitable felicity of expression in the English language, his judgements read like pieces of literature. As it is said, he did not write judgements, he composed poetry.

I cannot resist reading a few selected ones to give you a flair of the beauty of his language and the depth of his thought.

We in our experience, many times come across procedural deficiencies in administering justice and in that regard, Justice Iyer, guides us as to how, technicalities need to be ignored if it obstructs justice in following golden words.

"We must always remember that processual law is not to be a tyrant but a servant, not an obstruction but an aid to justice. It has been wisely observed that procedural prescriptions are the handmaid and not the mistress, a lubricant, not a resistant in the administration of justice.

Another example of his unconventional language is as follows:

Whenever fundamental rights are flouted or legislative protection ignored, to any prisoner's prejudice, this Court's writ will run, breaking through stone walls and iron bars, to right the wrong and restore the rule of law

For if courts 'cave in' when great rights are gouged within the sound-proof, sight-proof precincts of prison houses, where, often, dissenters and minorities are caged, Bastilles will be re-enacted. When law ends tyranny begins; and history whispers, iron has never been the answer to the rights of men

In one case he observed:

"Litigants are legal patients suffering from injustices seeking healing for their wounds. Would you tell a sufferer in hospital that because he disclosed a certain symptom very late therefore he would be discharged without treatment for the sin of delayed disclosure? Humanism, which, at bottom sustains justice, cannot refuse relief unless, by entertaining the plea, another may sustain injury."

He has been compared to Lord Denning of the UK, because of his eminence in jurisprudence, his compassionate approach, his far-reaching contribution to law, and easy flow of the English language. But I personally believe in the Indian context, he is unique, because of his multi-faceted personality and the fact that the good that he wrote and did has benefited millions of people and will continue to do so for years to come.

I could go on quoting from his judgements and writings, to highlight the zeal with which he espoused the cause of liberty, freedom, justice and human rights, the clarity of his vision, and his passion to provide a healing touch to the lives of the poor and the downtrodden. His pioneering work in setting up legal aid societies, the initiation of the Public Interest Litigation which was to become the ally of the little Indian, his innovative interpretation of statutes have all contributed to make the Indian Judiciary scale the great heights it has over the years. But all this information is available on the internet, to the seeker of knowledge, and the student of law and history of jurisprudence in India.

I would rather take this opportunity to highlight some personal and touching incidents from his life, which I have had the honour to share with him and to which people may have no access to.

I was fortunate enough to spend good time in his company during the past almost three decades till his death. During this time I came to know him closely. In his association, I gained considerable knowledge of criminal law and also the importance of human rights and human dignity. He was a father figure for me, till his demise in 2014.

His personal life had a great void. His beloved wife, Sarada passed away in 1974, a year after he became a SC Judge. The passage of time did not heal the wound and, he missed her immensely. His love for his wife can be gauged from what he has written in his autobiography, 'Wandering in Many Worlds',

"My wife Sarada and I had a happy span of conjugal, intellectual, aesthetic, ideological, philosophical, spiritual, and public-spirited commonality of interests and a hundred other common bonds"

He was obsessed with the idea of speaking to the soul of his beloved wife. He was trying to find any person or means through whom he could converse with the soul of Sarada. His intense search led him to a woman in Mumbai, who claimed that she had spiritual powers by which she could make a living person converse with any person who had left this world. He asked me to trace the woman and if possible take an appointment for him with her. I did exactly that and one day I had the privilege to accompany him to the private residence of that lady. Justice Iyer was anxious to hear the voice of his beloved wife and converse with her. I was skeptical but since he was so eager, we decided to pursue the course. In a private room, Justice Iyer was made to sit in front of a table in total darkness with a candle lighted in front of him. He was asked to chant some words and was given a pencil and a paper and the experiment commenced. For a few minutes, Justice Iyer was occupied and within minutes the experiment ended. When he came out, I asked him out of curiosity if he could speak to his beloved wife's soul, he reluctantly replied, "Not very sure and satisfied". For me this incident conveyed the intensity of the love he had for his wife and showed how desperately he missed her.

I have a few more personal experiences with the great jurist which I take this opportunity to share with you. After his retirement from Supreme Court, he did not take up any government assignment or professional briefs. He dedicated his time and life to public causes and travelled extensively to various parts of the country, at times at the expense of his failing health, attending functions, delivering lectures etc. He used to often visit Bombay and on each such visit, he would be good enough to inform me in advance so that I could be with him. The judges of the Bombay High Court ,including the Hon'ble CJ, would be very keen to spend some time with him, and despite his busy schedule, he would try to oblige every one. I have never heard him say 'no' to anybody, howsoever humble the person seeking his time was.

Let me narrate to you one such memorable visit when, he was returning to Cochin from Bombay airport. I was with him and we were seated in the VIP lounge of Santa Cruz airport, waiting for boarding announcement of his flight. Suddenly an airport official came and informed Justice Iyer that the current Chief Justice of India was around, and that he had learnt that Justice Iyer is here, so he had expressed his desire to meet Justice Iyer. Hearing this, out of respect for the CJI, Justice Iyer held my hand and got up. He said, "Majeed, let us go to meet the CJI". Upon this the official said, 'Your lordship, the instructions are to remain where you are, since the Hon'ble CJI is coming here to see you'. Justice Iyer told me that 'it is proper that we go to him rather than he come to us.' Within a few minutes, a crowd of 10-15 people, the CJI surrounded by security guards, protocol officers and airport officials was seen walking towards us. We stood to receive the Hon'ble CJI. It was a great scene. When the CJI was at a distance of about 2 metres from Justice Iyer we saw him suddenly fall prostrate at the feet of Justice Krishna Iyer, flat on the carpet. There was a bit of commotion and Justice Krishna Iyer bent down and lifted CJI by the shoulders to make him stand up. Every one was amazed. Justice Iyer said, 'Brother what are you doing?' Immediately, Justice Iyer introduced me to the CJI saying, "Meet Mr. Majeed, he is my friend and a lawyer in Mumbai." Upon this, the CJI turned to me and said these golden words which I quote verbatim,

"Mr. Majeed, do you know that this great jurist has laid down his office long ago. Years have rolled by, but not a single day passes when his name does not echo in the corridors of the Supreme Court."

Such was the compliment paid to him almost fourteen years after his laying down the office of Supreme Court Judge. I firmly believe this is applicable even today almost forty years after his retirement, and may ever continue.

I distinctly recall my experience while working on an international brief in London sometime in mid 90s. We were working on an internationally important extradition case under guidance of Queens Counsel, Mr. Clive Nicholls and his team. On one occasion while preparing the case, there was a conference attended by all eminent participants including prominent expert barristers, solicitors, juniors and chaired by Mr. Clive Nicholls, who was known as among worlds best counsel on extradition matters and who had among his clients, presidents and prime ministers of various countries. During discussions when my turn came and when I addressed the meeting, I read a small paragraph which alerted the chair. Mr. Nicholls in the chair was excited and asked me as to what I was reading. I informed him with pride, that I read the observations of Justice V R Krishna Iyer, an eminent Supreme Court Judge from my country. He was impressed to such an extent that he immediately asked one of his juniors to take the reference and get entire judgement for him.

Another memorable incident with Justice Iyer was when I was with him in Ernakulam. From his residence Satgamaya on M.G.Road to Marine Drive near Bharat Tourist Home, we used to go by car and then walk in that area every evening. While walking we would be joined by HC judges, Collector and other dignitaries whose residential complex is around. One day, Justice Iyer told me that he would like to introduce me to one of his dearest friends. I thought that as usual, he must be some judge or other important person. During our walk, we passed through Maharaja Law College, and a temple. Outside the temple entrance, there was an elderly beggar, sitting on the ground, a leper. Justice Iyer, took me and sat on the ground next to him. Spoke to him in Malayalam, and told me that here is that friend. I was emotionally touched and I could only acknowledge and applaud the extraordinary humane qualities of this great jurist.

Conclusion:

The best tribute one can pay to a great man is to continue and carry forward the good work he was doing and to create a system in which our justice system continues to benefit humanity in the future too. One should work towards inculcating his virtues not only in oneself and peers but also in the youth who should recognize and appreciate his value system and propagate it further.

In this context, the excellent work being done by inaugurating the Justice V R Krishna Iyer Legal Studies Wing, needs to be appreciated, encouraged and applauded.

Some people have suggested that the Bharat Ratna be awarded posthumously to Sri V.R. Krishna Iyer. Yes, surely for that would be one way of making him known to the future generations and ensuring his legacy lives perpetually.

Jai Hind.

Part 1

As Advocate

One

THE KILLER COP OF CISF

It was on 25 May 2003 that Ramnarayan Laltaprasad Namdeo, a Central Industrial Security Force (CISF) jawan (recruit, soldier) had gunned down his deputy commandant, at the Sahar International Airport, Mumbai. The jawan had also held six of his colleagues hostage, including four women, at gun-point, for six hours. The hostage drama ended after he dropped his weapons and surrendered. The deputy commandant, Shri A.R. Karanjikar had allegedly refused to grant leave to the jawan for taking his mother to Vaishnodevi temple, a very popular destination among devotees. This angered and infuriated the jawan and prompted him to shower bullets on the senior officer, while on duty. Namdeo was arrested immediately on his surrender and taken to the Sahar Airport police station. His inhuman act was an illustration of a revolt against the tyrannical behaviour of his superiors.

The police filed a charge-sheet against Namdeo, charging him under Sections 302 (murder), 307 (attempt to murder) and 342 (wrongful confinement) of the Indian Penal Code. As the advocate for Namdeo, I moved the Court of Sessions, for bail for the accused, in the month of July 2003. His father, Laltaprasad and mother, Umadevi, waited anxiously in room No. 17 of the Court of Sessions, at Mumbai, for a chance to address the judge. Though the hearing of the bail application was fixed at 11 am on that day, I did not pursue the bail application, as his parents wished to complain to the judge that the police had not recorded their statements in their language.

The presiding officer called Laltaprasad and Umadevi, one by one, to the witness box. Umadevi, who spoke first, said that her statement was recorded in Marathi and was not read over to her. Laltaprasad, who also worked for CISF, made the same complaint, and added that his department had punished him for his son's alleged misconduct, by transferring him to Bhopal, after the incident, and asking him to vacate his official quarters at Chembur, Mumbai.

After hearing both, the presiding Judge directed the Andheri Metropolitan Magistrate's Court to record their statements. Hearing on the bail application was adjourned to a future date, till the parents' statements were recorded by the Magistrate. At this stage, I was instructed to inform the Court that Namdeo's colleagues, whom he held hostage, wanted to speak, but were being terrorised, by the CISF administration. On this, the judge told the Investigating Officer that he should record statements of the CISF constables, not only those who were working under Karanjikar, but also those who work under other officers.

According to orders of the Sessions Court, the statements of both Laltaprasad and Umadevi were recorded by the Metropolitan Magistrate's 24th Court, at Andheri, Mumbai, on 6 July 2003. While recording her statement, Umadevi submitted that her son Ramnarayan Namdeo was very depressed prior to the unfortunate incident. He had confided in her the problems he was facing at his workplace. When she offered to speak to his superiors, Ramnarayan advised her not to do so as he feared she would be humiliated and insulted and this he would not be able to bear. Umadevi told the court that she wanted to plead before the superiors that her son was very keen to visit Vaishnodevi, along with her, but he had told her that his superiors were "stone hearted" and would not grant him leave.

Earlier, as Umadevi had threatened that she herself would end her life, I had told her that trying to commit suicide was an offence and that she should not compound the problems by taking such an extreme step. She should patiently wait, and justice would visit her.

When the bail application came up for hearing, in the Sessions Court, on 4 October 2003, I argued before the court that the act of the accused had not been premeditated, but impulsive. Besides, there was no motive behind the killing. I pleaded that in cases of similar acts, by other servicemen, the killing would be viewed as an act under extreme conditions. I pleaded for bail for the accused, on compassionate grounds. At that point, as the court's time was over, the bail application was adjourned to 6 October 2003.

On the appointed date, the prosecution opposed bail of the accused tooth and nail, stating that his act of killing a senior officer on duty amounted to cold blooded murder by misusing his official position and that he should not be set free. The prosecution argued that the accused poses a danger to society and his liberty might prompt him to take law in his hands again and commit similar acts of violence. The prosecution, therefore, prayed that the bail application of the accused be rejected.

As against this submission of the prosecution, I vehemently argued that it was not an ordinary case of murder, as the accused was frustrated because of his superior's attitude. As his reasoning stood eclipsed out of such frustration, he was taken over by the rash decision of shooting down his superior. The accused was a distressed public servant, who saw no end to his perpetual suffering and took the decision of gunning down his superior, to send a signal to society that subordinate employees in public service should not be taken for granted.

The presiding judge observed, "The police have already filed the charge sheet against the accused and the investigations are over. In the circumstances, there is no need to keep him in custody."

The Sessions Judge ordered the accused to be released on bail in the sum of Rupees ten thousand, with one surety of the like amount. He further directed the accused to attend the police station whenever required. Also, he was warned against tampering with witnesses and was asked not to leave Mumbai without permission of the court.

The judge turned down the plea of the prosecution and the CISF Counsel, for a stay of the bail order, saying it was unnecessary.

The bail granted to the accused created a flutter among the police and the CISF. Deputy Inspector General of CISF, Shri R.K. Mishra, said that it was a case within the CISF's fraternity, wherein both the victim and the culprit were part of it. The CISF and the prosecution soon decided to challenge the bail order in the High Court.

After he was released from Arthur Road prison Namdeo, told me that his superiors abused and harassed him. Asked if other jawans had similar grievances he told me that everybody faces the problem, but nobody wants to speak out. He declined to elaborate on the problems of others. He also refrained from commenting about what had prompted him to shoot his superior. However, he told me that he had earlier tried to commit suicide.

Namdeo's release from jail assumed significance because courts generally do not grant bail in a murder case, of rare nature, of the kind that Namdeo committed. The Sessions Judge refused to go into the merits of the case and upheld my contention that this was an unusual case. He rejected the prosecution's contention that bail should be denied to the accused as the case was "...rarest of rare case of cold-blooded murder". The judge had agreed with my contention that the case highlights how high-ranking public servants ill-treat their subordinates. The judge upheld my contention that instances of suicide and shootouts amongst the constabulary were growing because of professional stress.

I had appealed before the Sessions Judge to take a special view of the unequal battle between a humble and oppressed constable (jawan) and a powerful, mighty, and giant establishment. I further argued that Namdeo was overpowered by emotions and in a disturbed state of mind, took the extreme step of shooting his superior. Namdeo's insistence on addressing the media after the incident, testified that he had little trust in his superiors. I vociferously contended before the Sessions Judge that as long as Namdeo would be available for trial, he should be let off on bail.

The court agreed with my view that merely because the accused faced a charge of murder, bail should not be denied to him, and that granting bail would not be at variance with the very purpose of fair trial. The Judge further noted that, so far, there has been no complaint of witnesses being influenced. The court further specifically asked his parents, to stand surety for Namdeo, since he had surrendered at their behest.

The State was quick in moving the Bombay High Court, in getting the bail cancelled. Umadevi told me that officers from Sahar Airport police station visited their house at Chembur, around midnight, in the previous night, to serve them with a notice, regarding the "bail cancellation plea." "Is this the hour to come to anyone's home to serve notice?", she grumbled.

Namdeo's bail cancellation petition came up for hearing before the High Court on 13 November 2003. The prosecution argued that the Sessions Court erred in granting bail to the accused, presuming that Namdeo's was a case of single murder, but his intention was much more than just killing his superior. He not only fired seven rounds at the victim, but also fired four rounds in the air to scare others. The State further argued that the way Namdeo obtained the weapon to kill the officer suggests that it was very much a premeditated murder and that the Sessions Court failed to appreciate these facts. The High Court observed that Namdeo's crime was heinous, and continuation of his bail would encourage him to commit further such acts. His bail thus stood cancelled by the High Court.

After the bail was cancelled by the High Court, the parents of Namdeo came to me and informed me that he was in Delhi and was in the process of getting the order of the High Court set aside in the Supreme Court. However, amidst varying information, I learnt that Namdeo was absconding.

One fine morning, while I was in my office, Umadevi came to my office and told me that her son had committed suicide after writing a suicide note for his parents. In his letter, he had blamed the Maharashtra Government, the CISF and the police for his suicide. He accused them of constant harassment and of not keeping up the promises given to his family to let him off. There was no remorse for him for bumping off his superior and holding his colleagues hostage. Instead, he named RCF commandant Bhushan Devrani, CISF officer I.G.Kirpekar and two other officers whom, he says, he wanted to kill, but hoped that someone else would finish the job for him.

Excerpts from the suicide note read thus:

"The appeal was filed on the very next day, because it was not their father's money that they were spending but the State's money. Others accused of more heinous crimes have been set free, but because I am a constable, they have shown promptness in filing the appeal. The Government is a traitor and never keeps its word".

"I killed officer Arun Karanjikar for my rights. He was a very *kamina* (mean, cruel) person".

"I wanted to kill RCF commandant Bhushan Devrani, CISF officer I.G.Kirpekar and two other officers. But I am letting them off, because I do not want to show disrespect to the court, which gave me bail, because of my mother. I will only have one regret that I am letting the officers live because of whom I am taking this extreme step. May be someone else will finish the job for me".

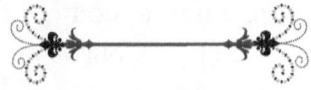

Namdeo's lawyer threatens to quit

Majeed Memon, Namdeo's lawyer

Wants him to surrender before next hearing

Prasad Patil
prasad@mid-day.com

A DAY after the Supreme Court served an ultimatum to absconding former CISF jawan Ramnarayan Namdeo, asking him to surrender to the police, his lawyer Majeed Memon threatened to withdraw from the case.

Advocate Memon yesterday said, "The next hearing in Namdeo's case in the sessions court is on January 19. I have made it clear to Namdeo's parents that I will withdraw from the case if Namdeo does not surrender before the next hearing."

Explaining his decision, Memon said Namdeo is damaging his case by evading arrest. "The sessions court was sympathetic towards him, which was the reason he got bail. In my opinion, he will lose the sympathy if he continues to hide," Memon said.

The Supreme Court on Monday granted two weeks time to Namdeo for surrendering. He allegedly shot dead deputy commandant A Karanjkar when the later refused to grant him leave.

Meanwhile, Namdeo's parents have decided to publish a notice in newspapers requesting the public to come forward and provide any information about their son's whereabouts. "The informants will be rewarded suitably," Memon said.

In a related development, the Sahar police have pasted copies of a sessions court order, which said Namdeo will be declared a proclaimed offender if he does not appear in the court on January 19, outside Namdeo's house and the CISF quarters' main gate at Chembur.

Advocate Ravindra Garia, who appeared for Namdeo in the Supreme Court, has informed advocate Memon that there are fair chances the case will get a patient hearing. "In such a situation, it becomes important that Namdeo surrenders and a surrender certificate is sent to us as soon as possible," Garia said.

According to Garia, the division bench of the SC hearing Namdeo's case has orally observed that if the accused does not surrender, even a meritorious case might be thrown out.

A Mumbai Sessions Court had granted bail to Namdeo. The state, however, challenged its order in the Bombay High Court, which cancelled his bail. Namdeo has challenged the high court order.

My superiors abused, harassed me: Namdeo

By Swati Deshpande and Aneesh Phadnis
Times News Network

Mumbai: Sacked Central Industrial Security Force (CISF) jawan Ramnarayan Namdeo, who was released on bail on Wednesday, said that other CISF jawans are being harassed by their superiors but are afraid to speak out.

Namdeo (23) is accused of killing his deputy commandant, A.R. Katranjkar, and of holding six colleagues hostage at the Sahar International airport on May 24.

Speaking to TNN at his lawyer Majeed Memon's office on Thursday, Namdeo alleged that his superiors abused and harassed him. Namdeo, who sported a red tikka on his forehead and was accompanied by his mother Uma Devi and a friend, appeared calm.

Before the incident he had confided to his parents about the difficult working conditions and "total lack of co-operation" of his bosses.

Asked if other constables had similar grievances, he replied, "Everybody faces the problems, but nobody wants to speak." He declined to elaborate. He refrained from commenting about what had prompted him to shoot his superior. But he said that he had earlier tried to commit suicide.

His release from jail may have eased the stress on his family, but

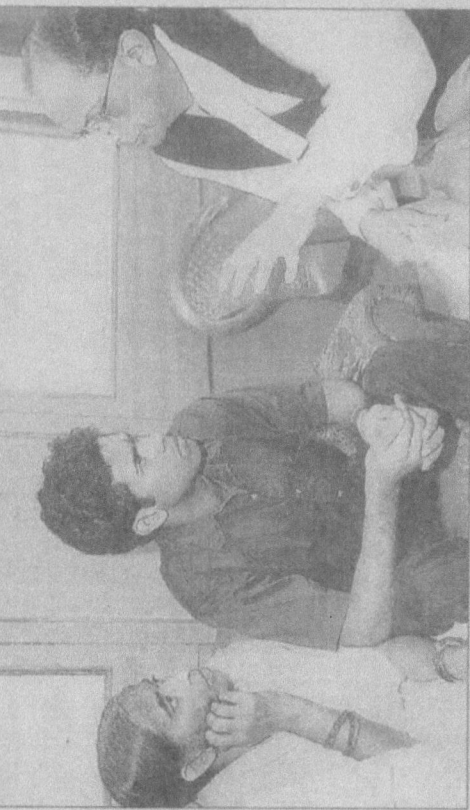

CISF jawan, Ramnarayan Namdeo, with his mother (left) and lawyer Majeed Memon.

only marginally. The state was quick to move the Bombay high court to have his bail cancelled. The matter is expected to come up on Friday.

The family also fears harassment from the police. Namdeo's mother said that officers of Sahar police station came to their home in RCF colony, Chembur, around midnight on Wednesday to serve them with a notice regarding the bail cancellation plea. "Is this the hour to come to anyone's home for serving notices?" she asked.

Namdeo's release on bail assumes significance because courts rarely grant bail in murder cases if a prima facie case is made out. But

sessions judge N.D. Deshpande refused to go into the merits of the case and upheld Mr Memon's contention that this case was an unusual one.

He rejected the prosecutor S.P. Desai and special CISF counsel Arun Gupta's position that bail should be denied because this was "a rarest of rare case of cold-blooded murder".

The judge appears to have agreed with Mr Memon that the case highlights how high-ranking public servants ill-treat their subordinates. He recorded Mr Majeed's submission that instances of suicides and shootouts among the constabulary were growing as a result of "professional stress".

The court would have to take a special view of the unequal battle between a resourceless oppressed constable and a giant establishment, he argued. Mr Memon also contended that Namdeo was overpowered by emotions and, in a disturbed state of mind, took the extreme step of shooting someone. He also said Namdeo's insistence on addressing the media after the incident testified that he had little trust in his superiors. He argued that as long as Namdeo would be available for trial, he should be let off on bail.

The judge felt that merely because Namdeo faced a charge of murder, bail should not be denied to him and that granting bail would not defeat the purpose of organising a fair trial, especially since the chargesheet had been filed. He noted that, so far, there had not been any complaints of witnesses being influenced. The judge specifically asked Namdeo's parents to stand in as his surety since he had surrendered at their request.

THE TIMES OF INDIA   SATURDAY 17TH JANUARY 2004

'I have asked Namdeo's parents to ensure he surrenders'

MAJEED MEMON
Advocate
On his decision to give up Ramnarayan Namdeo case

What prompted you to give up the case?

As an officer of the court, more than the lawyer of Central Industrial Security Force (CISF) Constable Ramnarayan Namdeo (the constable has been accused of killing his superior at the international airport), my duty is to ensure that no person who escapes from the law or shows disregard to the court is helped. If my client defies law contrary to my instructions, and I am unable to regulate his conduct, the least sense of professional ethics requires me to seek discharge from such legal matters.

Where is Namdeo? Have you urged him to surrender?

I have asked his parents to ensure that he surrenders in obedience to the apex court order. Failure will only involve the court's wrath as well as a loss of sympathy.

Do you accept his parents' claim that Namdeo has committed suicide?

He is a disappointed, broken boy who feels responsible for the plight of his parents. He is sensitive to the harassment of the CISF constabulary by superiors and apprehended a threat to his life. Given this, one can't rule out the possibility of him going underground to save himself.

Isn't this disappearing act unfair to the entire case, especially to the deceased commandant and his family?

We don't in the least justify the killing, but the circumstances preceding the incident can't be lost sight of. Namdeo's case is an illustration of an uncivilised revolt against inhuman behaviour of his superiors.

There have been several instances of people jumping bail.

In our criminal justice system, every person is entitled to be presumed innocent until proven guilty by a judicial verdict.

SHARMISTHA CHATTERJEE
sharmistha.chatterjee@timesgroup.com

> **'If I am unable to regulate my client's conduct, it requires me to seek discharge from such legal matters'**

In a Lighter Vein

Once an accused was desperately roaming in the vicinity of a Metropolitan Magistrate's court as he was informed by the police that the court had issued a warrant of arrest against him for nonattendance in his case on the previous date of hearing. He wanted to get his warrant cancelled but he had no money to pay the advocate's fees. In the situation, he consulted one of the court staff who told him to go to the typist and get an application for cancellation of warrant prepared and then present it personally before the court. The accused was satisfied on this legal advice of the court staff. Accordingly, he got the application prepared and presented it before the presiding officer soon thereafter. As the application was called out, the accused stood before the Magistrate with folded hands. The Magistrate questioned him as to where his advocate was. He replied that he had no advocate. However, the Magistrate insisted that he would present the application through an advocate. The accused was nervous and he went out of the court. After few minutes he came back to the court. His application was called out once more. He again stood before the Magistrate without an advocate. This time the Magistrate was a bit angry on him. He asked the accused as to why he came back without an advocate. To this the accused replied that he could not afford an advocate as he had no money to pay the advocate's fees. The Magistrate fired the accused and told him to pay rupees twenty to any lawyer in the court compound and come with him to the court. The accused disappointedly went out again. He entered the Bar Room of the advocates and there he met a reputed senior advocate. The accused described his plight to the senior advocate. The advocate was irritated to learn that the Magistrate insulted the advocates' fraternity in suggesting that any advocate is available for a paltry sum of rupees twenty to appear for an accused.

The senior advocate took the accused aside and instructed him to appear before the Magistrate once again without any advocate. The accused was scared but was encouraged to appear again without an advocate. The senior advocate further told the accused that in the event the Magistrate again insisted on getting an advocate for cancelling the warrant he would help him but he must tell the Magistrate " Sir I checked around the court for an advocate at rupees twenty, but I was told that there are no such twenty rupees advocates as all such advocates have become Magistrates".

With lot of persuasion, the accused again entered the court room. This time too the Magistrate curiously asked him where his advocate was. The accused replied to the Magistrate as he was instructed by the senior advocate. The Magistrate had to put his head down and quietly cancel the warrant.

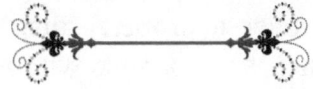

Two

THE GRAND TRAGEDY OF GRAND PARADI

Balkrishna Dalal and his wife Sonal were defended by me in a case where they were facing trial for suicide of Balkrishna's aged parents due to alleged torture, meted out to them by Balkrishna and his wife. Both the aged parents were retired college professors. They were allegedly tortured by their son and daughter-in-law over a property dispute. It appeared that the couple used to lock their aged parents without food or water, for days together. On several occasions, the elderly couple had complained to the Housing Society about the harassment by their son and his wife, but the Society could not do much to make the two accused desist from inhuman treatment since it was essentially a domestic dispute.

Neighbours at the posh residential building, Grand Paradi, bordering the Parsi Tower of Silence (where Parsis lay their dead) seemed to keep their distance from the Dalals. They preferred to avoid the family, ever since they came to know of the torture meted out to the aged parents. It was the constant torture by the Dalal couple, inflicted upon their septuagenarian parents, which led them to commit suicide, by leaping out through the window of their 8th floor flat. Soon after the suicide of the elderly couple, the Malabar Hill police registered a case against the younger couple, charging them for abetment to commit suicide.

The police recovered a suicide note from Vasudev, which read:

"I, Mr. V.H.Dalal, and Mrs. Tara Dalal, my wife hereby commit suicide because of the constant abuse and harassment by my son Balakrishna Dalal and his wife, Sonal Dalal. We are both old. They want us to die. This is the absolute truth. Mr. Ashok Kadakia (Chairman of the building's co-operative housing society) holds B.V.Dalal and Sonal Dalal in high esteem. Dying persons don't tell lies. I am leaving behind the legacy of Rs.50 crores. We are so old, disabled and feeble that we can't go out of our flat".

Based on this suicide note, the police arrested and charged Balkrishna and his wife Sonal for abetting suicide of the elderly couple. After the charge sheet was filed and the case was committed to the Sessions Court, the younger couple was facing trial in that court, on a day-to-day basis. I was conducting the case as the Defence Counsel. The Dalals, who never missed a single date of hearing in the trial, surprisingly, chose to put an end to their lives too, in mysterious circumstances, on 28 March 2005, shortly before the judgment was to be delivered in the case. Balkrishna, too, had a suicide note in his pocket. The note did not mention anything about the parents or their death and the pending case against them. The note simply and clearly said, "I, Mr. Balkrishna Dalal and my wife, Sonal Dalal and daughter Pooja Dalal, are committing suicide, as we are fed up with our lives and nobody shall be given blame for this".

The grisly suicide had spooked residents of Grand Paradi, not merely on account of the familial pact, but also because everything about the suicide was brimming with an eerie mystery.

A driver at Grand Paradi, who claimed to have witnessed Balkrishna's fatal leap, in the early morning, said that the diamond merchant leapt from the 8th floor balcony of his flat, only after ensuring that his wife and daughter were done away with, in a similar fashion. Soon after hearing a thud, the driver, who was cleaning a car, in the sprawling building compound, off Kemp's Corner, in Central Mumbai, saw Balkrishna peeping from his balcony. The driver followed the direction of the sound only to find Balkrishna's wife Sonal and daughter Pooja lying in a pool of blood. Before he could react, Balkrishna followed suit and fell onto the ground, with another thud. The senior Dalals' suicide had highlighted the plight of senior citizens in the city, who are at the mercy of their children. Balkrishna had claimed that his father was depressed, but according to witnesses in the court, Balkrishna was known to be very rude to his father. The police, too, found that the bedroom of the old couple was dirty, stinking, and had not been cleaned for several days. However, it was not clear why Pooja, their only daughter, who was just 12 years old at the time of the suicide of the elderly couple, too, jumped to her death. Was she forced to? It remains a mystery.

Ten days before their death, Balkrishna and Sonal had visited me in my office with sweets, to thank me for being their counsel, defending them in the court. However, I could find Balkrishna depressed, when I met him a couple of days thereafter, just before the incident.

A security guard who happened to be around at the time when they jumped to their death, told the police that Balkrishna and his family leapt to death at around 6.30 am, that fateful day. According to the security guard, he first heard the scream of the daughter, Pooja. Within minutes, there was a second scream, coming from Sonal, followed by that of Balkrishna.

The tragedy took place just a day before the judgment in their case, in the suicide of senior Dalals, was to be delivered in the Sessions Court. Balkrishna and Sonal were a stable couple. They were quite confident of winning their case and being acquitted honorably. I had a very strong case in my hand for an honorable acquittal of the accused. The evidence against the Dalals solely rested on a suicide note. Before the trial court, I cited Supreme Court rulings and emphatically argued that conviction could not be based only on a suicide note, much less on an imperfect one. Further, the two police officers, among the eight witnesses examined by the State prosecution, had differed in their evidence. The investigating officer said that the suicide note was found in a shirt pocket of Vasudev Dalal, while the Police Sub-Inspector said that it was in the vest pocket. Also, the suicide note written on a page pulled out of a note book lacked a date and signature on it. Besides, the body lay face down in a pool of blood, but the note produced in the court was not blood stained. Vasudev mentioned the legacy of Rs.50 crores, while the police investigation revealed that the Dalals were worth just about three crores.

The evidence brought before the court against Balkrishna and Sonal was riddled with lacunae. In the circumstances, a clean acquittal of the accused was the only remedy before the trial court. I attribute the mental stress that the family went through after Vasudev and Tara killed themselves, to the suicide of Balkrishna, his wife and only daughter.

They were fed up with being mentally assaulted by their relatives and the people in their building. Incidentally, there was no fear of conviction in their case.

Investigations further revealed that the Dalals had been contemplating suicide for quite some time, and had, accordingly, made preparations. They had drafted a Will four days before their death, in favour of one Dr. Vikram Maniar, who was the brother of Sonal. Their estate included all the self-acquired properties, consisting of shares, fixed deposits, bank balances and other assorted investments. The Will, along with an unsigned letter written by Sonal was sent by post to Maniar. But he received it after the incident. In the letter, he was asked to probate the Will (get it legally registered), within a month. About two days before the triple suicide, Balkrishna had left several important personal documents and jewelry with Dr. Maniar. He had told his brother-in-law that the valuables could be stolen from his own flat.

As the karta (head) of the Hindu undivided family, Balkrishna Dalal had bequeathed his estate to his brother-in-law, Dr. Vikram Maniar. The Will mentioned that in the event of the death of all the members of the family simultaneously, Maniar would inherit the estate. Ironically enough, Maniar was at the place of Dalals, discussing cricket, just a day before the incident.

After their death, Maniar informed me that they were, in fact, very skeptical about the court verdict. In a letter to Maniar, Sonal wrote, "Dear Viku, you will pardon us. We are going away. Do not cry much for me. Though we have hired the best of the best advocates, there is still no hope, and everything seems very dark. Nothing will make the three of us happier than you staying here (at the Grand Paradi flat). All cheques are ready for you, transfer them to your account. Keep the driver and use the car in style."

The case against the Dalals, for abetment to commit suicide of the senior Dalals, stood abated in the Sessions Court, upon their death.

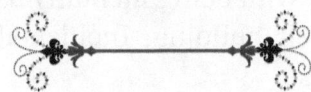

Wednesday • April 13, 2005 • Mid Day, Mumbai

Did Dalal's will hide suicide note?

Will states if all members of family die simultaneously, estate will go to brother-in-law

The Dalal family in a file photograph (left to right) Tara, Sonal, Pooja and Balkrishna and Vasudev Dalal

Sanjeev Devasia

THE three-member Dalal family who committed suicide on March 28 from their eighth floor flat at Kemps Corner, was contemplating suicide for quite some time and had accordingly made the preparations. According to Majeed Memon, the family's lawyer, Balkrishna Dalal (50) had left several important personal documents and jewellery with his brother-in-law, Dr Vikram Maniyar, around two to three days before the mass suicide of the three-member family. Dalal had told his brother that the valuables could be stolen from their flat.

Besides, Balkrishna Dalal has also bequeathed his estate as the Karta of the Hindu Undivided Family to his brother-in-law. The will also mentions, that in the event of the death of all members of the family simultaneously, Maniyar would inherit the estate. Sonal's will was also found.

The Dalals had also prepared a will on March 24, naming Maniyar as the inheritor of the estate. The estate includes all the self-acquired properties consisting of shares, fixed deposits, bank balances and other assorted investments worth Rs 5 crore approximately.

"The will along with an unsigned letter written by Sonal was sent by post to Maniyar, but he had received it after the incident, a week ago," said Memon. While Maniyar did not bring up the will during the 10-day mourning period, the letter asks him to execute the will within a month, added

> **THE WILL ALONG WITH AN UNSIGNED LETTER WRITTEN BY SONAL WAS SENT BY POST TO MANIYAR, BUT HE HAD RECEIVED IT AFTER THE INCIDENT, A WEEK AGO**
>
> *— Majeed Memon, the family's lawyer*

Memon.

The Dalals were named in a criminal case of abetment of suicide of their parents; Memon was the defence lawyer. Legal steps were being taken with regard to the fate of the estate, Memon said, adding that ironically Maniyar was at the Dalals' discussing cricket, just a day before the suicide. The case relating to the abetment of suicide was closed by Additional Sessions judge S J Shah as the accused were no longer alive, Memon said.

In a Lighter Vein

In the year 1996, the Government of Maharashtra designed a scheme, under which poor cobblers of the State could get a fillip to their trade. Under this scheme, it was notified that cobblers would get tax concessions and bank loans, at lower rates of interest. The giants in the leather industry and top-notch shoe companies in the city of Mumbai, made tons of money out of the scheme, allegedly through a huge financial scam. Fake co-operative societies, with imaginary cobbler members, were floated, and the Government was thus defrauded of huge sums. The scam was soon unearthed and was widely dubbed as the Shoe Scam Case. The money involved in the scam was later accounted to be worth 600 million USD.

The Special Investigation Team (SIT) swung into action without delay and booked almost all the reputed names in the shoe business in Mumbai. The proprietor of Dawood Shoes, owners of Metro Shoes, Milano Shoes and City Walk Shoes, among others were arrested and taken into custody. There was a hue and cry for the release of the arrested bigwigs.

MM was approached, to get some of them released, on bail. The State appointed an elderly counsel, advocate Namjoshi, as Special Prosecutor, for opposing their bail applications. A bunch of bail applications, for the release of the arrested persons, came up for hearing before the vacation judge, in the Bombay High Court.

While appearing in the court, advocate Namjoshi used to wear slippers, highly uncommon in Bombay courts. On the date of the hearing, MM met Shri Namjoshi in the corridor of the court. MM was surrounded by the family members of the accused. Shri Namjoshi told MM, "Your clients are giants in shoe manufacturing and even exporting their products. Look at my feet, I wear these humble chappals (leather slippers).

As a retort, MM jibed, "Mr. Namjoshi, considering the situation you are in, if you demand, the accused will agree to part with their own skin to make your shoes."

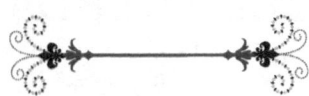

Three

THE TERRIBLE TUESDAY AND THE BITTER PIL

The torrential downpour on 26 July 2005, in the city of Mumbai continued to haunt the State Government, when the city's celebrity brigade united to file a Public Interest Litigation (PIL), seeking to fix the responsibility for the destruction of life and property. The PIL had named the State Government, Municipal Corporation of Greater Mumbai (MCGM), the city's Police Commissioner, Mahanagar Telephone Nigam Limited, Central and Western Railways and the Meteorological Department, as Respondents. The petitioners pleaded before the Bombay High Court to direct each of the respondents to file a detailed report about the action taken, to anticipate and control the impact of the heavy downpour. The 944 mm rain that hit the city on 26 July 2005 had resulted in a deluge of an unprecedented scale and caused havoc. The city of dreams had become a city of nightmares, that day.

According to the petitioners, the devastating impact of the heavy rain could have been minimised, had the authorities issued a timely warning, ensuring that the citizens stayed indoors and took precautions to protect their lives and properties. Searching reasons why the Meteorological department failed to forecast the heavy rains, the petitioners asked the State Government to provide the details of the equipment used for weather forecasting, and called for its upgradation to international standards, for more accurate weather forecasting, in future. They further asked for the drainage system in the city to be revamped.

The PIL was filed under the banner of JAAG India, which is part of Project Smita, an NGO (non-government organisation), established in memory of late Smita Patil (a brilliant actress, who died young), by film-maker Mahesh Bhatt, producer-director Ashok Pandit, theatre and advertising personality Alyque Padamsee and other film personalities.

The PIL asked the court to direct the respondents to furnish a list of people who died in the flood, and to ensure that the relatives of the deceased received compensation, without delay.

Appearing for the petitioners, at the admission stage of the PIL, I prayed to the court that the Government should implement the guidelines issued under a status report of 2004, of the Union Home Ministry, on disaster management in India. The PIL was filed to ensure that the Government is equipped to deal with such situations in future and see that a disaster management plan was put in place.

It was a natural calamity, but it could have been mitigated if the disaster management cell of MCGM was alert. Instead, the very same cell had become a 'disaster creation cell' on that day, due to its acts of omission and commission. The petitioners had also proposed to collect ten lakh signatures, protesting the Government inaction, and submit them to the Prime Minister.

Over five hundred people died in the city, on that day. Such a huge number of casualties could have been averted, if only the State Government had put in place a warning mechanism and taken steps to control the tragedy. As Counsel for the petitioners, I urged the court that not providing basic services is a violation of human rights. Encroachments on the Mithi river, destruction of mangroves and illegal quarrying, prima facie, appeared to be the root cause for such an unprecedented deluge.

My humble submission before the court was on future steps that needed to be taken by the State, as well as corrective measures, in case of recurrence of such an eventuality. I further insisted that disaster management be in place and the forecast office should lead, rather than mislead the people.

There was nothing political about the petition. Though, from certain quarters, an attempt was made to give it a political colour. The petition was apolitical and was motivated by nothing other than a right to call the elected leaders to account and protect Mumbaikars from being subjected to the kind of hardship and loss of life that they suffered on that 'Terrible Tuesday'.

The tone and tenor of the PIL clearly explained what prompted the petitioners to file such a PIL. It was with utmost despair that like-minded petitioners approached the court. That was the last resort of law-abiding people and the only civilised and legal way to express their anguish over the happenings in the city. The petition very clearly showed that the petitioners only sought to find out if the calamity could be averted, had there been proper administrative efforts and alertness, on the part of the Government.

The gravity of the situation was the result of lack of timely communication. *Mumbaikars* (inhabitants of Mumbai) apprehended that they could have another, similar, disaster knocking on their doors. The people of Mumbai are entitled to know what steps would be taken to avert a repeat of the tragedy. The petitioners wanted the experts from different fields to put their heads together, for an effective remedy, in the event of a repeat of 26 July. They were simply asking the Government to provide data to the court on certain vital questions. The petitioners demanded that the disbursement of the Central Relief Fund should be transparent and expedited, so that victims do not have harassment added to their hardship.

In a packed courtroom of the Bombay High Court, a Division Bench, consisting of Chief Justice Mr. Daleer Bhandari and Justice Mr. S.J. Vazifdar, on the date of hearing, 10 August 2005, directed the Maharashtra Government to act before it was too late.

"Don't wait till epidemics erupt like a volcano. Go on a war footing and take preventive measures". Thus ordered the Chief Justice.

The Chief Justice further suggested that if an epidemic did break out, the State should inform the public through the media and be prepared with sufficient medical supplies, doctors, and nurses. "We hope nothing like this happens. But equip yourself for such an emergency." He added that garbage dumping grounds, like the one at Gorai, which is 45 ft. high, are hazardous.

The Bench was not very happy with the Indian Meteorological Department. "Let me not comment. But shouldn't the Meteorological Department give an inkling of what was to happen?" asked the Chief Justice.

The Chief Justice further directed the MCGM to submit a list of those who died or were missing in the deluge, within three days.

I had submitted a list of 42 other NGOs who were deeply concerned about these issues. The court then directed the State to take their assistance, for rehabilitating the flood victims.

"The city was unprepared for the disaster. That was the reason for the loss of lives and properties. Unfortunate events like this should not recur," observed the Bench.

The Bench further observed that the Meteorological department would have to consider setting up sophisticated equipment for proper prediction of weather.

The Bench went to direct the State Government to file a detailed reply on the flood situation.

The State was ready with a list of 546 persons, who died in the deluge, including 79 killed in landslide. Appearing on behalf of the petitioners, I informed the court that the NGOs, which were ready to work in co-ordination with the Government, would like to verify the names and other details of the victims, only to ensure that aid reached the right people. The court then observed that by providing the petitioners with the list of people affected, the data could reach other organisations, which could possibly come up with certain schemes to help the affected people. On this, I informed the court that even celebrities could be asked to appeal to the people to donate generously to the affected families.

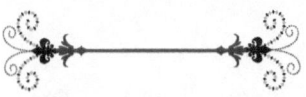

METRO

Celebs fight for public cause

HT Correspondent
Mumbai, August 3

A GROUP of television and Bollywood personalities today filed a public interest litigation (PIL) in the Bombay High Court asking the court to direct the Centre and state governments to list the steps that have been taken to provide relief to victims of the recent flood in the state.

The PIL was filed under the banner of Project Smile, an NGO established in the memory of late actor Smita Patil, by filmmaker Mahesh Bhatt, producer-director Ashok Pandit, theatre personality Alyque Padamsee and other film personalities including Raman Kumar, Vinta Nanda, Soni Razdan and Anu Ranjan.

Other respondents in the PIL are the Municipal Corporation of Greater Mumbai (MCGM), the commissioner of police, railway authorities and the India Meteorological Department.

The PIL also asks the court to direct the respondents to furnish a list of people who died due to the floods and to ensure that relatives of the deceased receive compensation without delay.

The NGO has requested that the meteorological department be asked to file an affidavit stating the equipment being used to forecast weather and has demanded that the equipment be upgraded so prediction are accurate

it asked that the drainage system in Mumbai be revamped.

Menon revealed that the PIL requested that the government implement the guidelines issued under a status report of 2004 of the Union Home Ministry on disaster management in India.

The petition will be heard before the division bench of Chief Justice Dalveer Bhandari and Justice S.J. Vazifdar in the next two days. Majeed

Menon, the advocate for the NGO, said the petition seeks to identify the cause behind the flood and the authorities responsible for it, an also the steps needed to prevent such an occurrence in the future.

The PIL was filed to ensure that the government was better equipped to deal with such situations in the future and to see that the disaster management plan was put in place, Menon said.

(Left-right) Alyque Padamsee, Mahesh Bhatt, Majeed Menon, Vinta Nanda and Nurjan Bajaj filed the PIL.

PIL demands

- Provide relief to victims
- Furnish a list of people who died
- Ensure relatives of deceased receive compensation without delay
- Revamp city's drainage system
- Upgrade Met equipment

Single window admissions for medical students

HT Correspondent
Mumbai, August 3

MEDICAL STUDENTS who have taken admission through the management quota in private medical and dental colleges will no longer have to go from one college to another, filling forms and checking if they have got admission in a particular institution.

The Supreme Court (SC) passed a judgement on July 27, which has approved a single window, centralised admission system for management quota seats in private institutes.

There are 13 private medical colleges and 16 private dental colleges in the state. The order was passed after a petition was filed by the Parents' Association of Medical Students in the apex court in May.

Surendra Khodekar, an office bearer of the Association, said, "According to the court ruling, the first and second round of admissions will be conducted in a centralised manner. In case any seats are still vacant, they will be filled by issuing advertisements in local newspapers.

The admission process for the management quota in private medical colleges is to be completed by September 27.

48

In a Lighter Vein

An important criminal trial was going on before a Special Court in Delhi. The courtroom was filled with advocates and litigants. Junior advocates carrying thick briefs and heavy law books, stood ready to assist their seniors. Enthusiastic law students and media-persons thronged the corridors. There was no space left and the courtroom was jam-packed. An important witness was in the box and the prosecutor was examining him, whilst the defence team, led by MM, was carefully watching the demeanour of the witness. The learned judge was seriously recording the evidence and an atmosphere of total solemnity prevailed. Incidentally, an elderly advocate seated next to MM on his right-hand side had his eyes shut and was dozing. The sharp eyes of the learned judge caught the dozing advocate in the act. But the learned judge refrained from offending the concerned advocate, by pulling him up. Instead, he looked at MM and gestured that the advocate, seated next to him, should be disciplined. Immediately, MM nudged the dozing advocate and whispered into his ears that the court had taken exception to his lapse. The elderly advocate soon pulled himself up and apologised to the court. The learned judge smiled and, before the episode could get over, MM rose from his seat and told the judge, "Sir, this incident reminds me of the famous words of Abraham Lincoln, and I quote, 'Work eight hours, sleep eight hours, but make sure that they are not the same hours.'

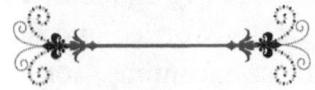

Four

A MOTOR ACCIDENT AND THE HISTORIC MIDNIGHT ORDER

A highly respectable and rich Gujarati businessman, who was a senior citizen at the relevant time, was once trapped and caught in a legal wrangle. The gentleman, Mr. Doshi, was from Ahmedabad in Gujarat. He was an ex-governor of the Giants' Club and owner of a few mills and factories, in the State of Gujarat. The gentleman was in Mumbai for a business trip.

On the fateful day, it so happened that he was driving on the Western Express Highway, in Bandra East. At a road signal in Kalanagar, when he halted his car near a red traffic light, a beggar came in contact with his shiny, silver Benz car and fell down due to the mild impact with the car. On seeing the rich man driving the vehicle, the over-smart beggar pretended that he was seriously hurt, though there were no visible external injuries. He perceived it as an opportunity to make quick money and so made a big issue of the incident. Within no time, several supporters of the beggar surrounded the car, and seeing them the victim beggar pretended to be groaning in acute pain. Mr. Doshi could not comprehend the gravity of the situation. Any clever person in his place would have simply offered a few hundred rupees to the victim and the story would have ended there and then. Innocent as he was, Mr. Doshi was greatly worried and did not know what to do in the given situation. In the meantime, some supporters of the beggar compelled Mr. Doshi to take the car to the nearest police station. Mr. Doshi complied and thus landed in Nirmal Nagar police station.

Since there was quite a commotion at the scene, created by the victim, who pretended to have sustained injuries, the police officer on duty was persuaded to register a case. Thus, a First Information Report (FIR) came to be recorded for the minor offences, under sections 279 & 337 IPC, which were both bailable offences. Mr. Doshi was told by the police officer that he need not worry and that it was a mere formality. He was assured that within minutes of execution of the bail bond, he would be allowed to go home. By this time, the sons of Mr. Doshi arrived and, after the paperwork was completed, Mr. Doshi was allowed to go home. Thereafter, the police did not inform him that he would have to face a criminal trial in court in future, and Mr. Doshi returned to Gujarat.

Many months later, the Nirmal Nagar Police filed the charge-sheet against the accused, in the Magistrate's court, at Bandra. According to the law prevailing the accused was to be served a summons for appearing before the court, on the appointed date. Years later, as the matter came up on the board of the concerned Magistrate for hearing the accused was not present, since he was not informed of the proceedings pending against him in the court. Thus, the negligence on the part of the police compounded the mess and the absence of the accused was marked in the court records. The court was upset at the repeated failure of Mr. Doshi to turn up, something that is mandatory and was, therefore, quick enough to issue a warrant against the accused. During the following two or three dates of hearing, which fell with an interval of about 2-3 months, the police did not execute the warrant, and this caused further annoyance to the court. In the situation, the court warned Nirmal Nagar police that if the accused is not produced on the next date, the court will be constrained to issue a non-bailable warrant against the Senior Inspector of Police, Nirmal Nagar police station.

Such a development in the court caused panic among the policemen in Nirmal Nagar police station and the jolt resulted in the policemen sifting through old papers, from the dusty heap at the police station. They managed to trace out the contact details of the accused, in Ahmedabad. The law-abiding Mr. Doshi was taken by surprise when he learnt that he was wanted in a criminal court in Mumbai, for a minor accident that had occurred years ago and regarding which the police had, at that time, misled him. He came down to Mumbai, post-haste, and got in touch with the Nirmal Nagar police. The police told him not to worry, but since there was a warrant against him, he had to simply appear before the concerned Magistrate in Bandra and apply for formal cancellation of the warrant, which was simple.

Accordingly, believing the police version, Mr. Doshi hired an advocate of average merit and presented himself before the Magistrate, with an application for cancellation of warrant. Neither he nor his advocate was aware of the grave situation reflected in the records of the court. It was about 4 pm on that day when his application was called out in court. The Magistrate opened the file and was aghast at the previous record of the long absence of the accused. The Magistrate looked at the face of the accused and told his advocate that the application for cancellation of warrant stood rejected. Consequent to this order, Mr. Doshi was taken into custody of the court and was pushed into a dingy dock, meant for people in custody who were involved in serious criminal cases.

This development in court was not anticipated. Mr. Doshi was nervous and perturbed. His son, who accompanied him to the court, was wondering how such an unanticipated tragedy could occur in his *Bapu's* (Gujarati for father) life and how could he be taken into custody? Even after all this, his advocate told him not to worry, as he would soon make an application for grant of fresh, enhanced bail, as the offences under sections 279 & 337 were bailable. Within minutes, in a rush, such an application was prepared which came up for hearing in the court. The Magistrate heard the advocate but promptly passed an order rejecting the same. By this time, the court hours were about to end and Mr. Doshi, along with a group of other people held for serious criminal offences, was put in a police van and whisked away to Arthur Road prison. This turn of events was very disturbing for the entire family of Mr. Doshi. There was a furore in the court. Mr. Doshi and his people were wondering how such a thing could happen? His son exclaimed "*Bapuji* (Dad) is taken to jail and he will stay behind bars for the night!"

The court rose. There was an uproar. Sympathizers of Mr. Doshi and even the court staff and other advocates were discussing what could be done next, in the given circumstances. Almost everybody opined that whatever was done at that late hour, its result would be known only the next morning. However, soon, some members of Mr. Doshi's family reached the vicinity of the court, and it appeared that they were advised by some locals to approach me to handle the case. This came as a surprise to me as those days I had just begun my practice and had yet to build a reputation for myself.

By 7.30 pm that day, Doshi's family reached my office. Luckily, I was in. I was told about the tragic happenings in the court earlier that day and with tears in their eyes Mr. Doshi's son and his wife told me, "If *Bapuji* remains in jail overnight, till the sun rises the next morning, there will be two cases of suicide in the family." They fervently pleaded with me, with folded hands, to find some way of bringing Mr. Doshi out of the prison the same night. I thought for a while and got myself acquainted with the entire background. The one over-riding thought that gripped me was, "what next?" It was obvious that no serious crime was involved. In fact, Mr. Doshi was a victim of a conspiracy by some urchins to knock out money from him, though he had committed no wrong, not even a breach of traffic rules. He was also a victim of miscommunication and negligence on the part of the police. I needed to explore all possible avenues to get Mr. Doshi out before midnight. As per rules, if a person has been ordered to be taken into custody by a Magistrate having jurisdiction, no application for his release can be made before the night Magistrate. However, as a special case, I contacted the designated night Magistrate and explained to him the details of the matter. The Magistrate, after hearing the facts of the case, told me that he had no power to overrule the orders of the regular Magistrate. However, such exceptional powers are vested in the Chief Metropolitan Magistrate (CMM) of the city. I was relieved a bit on hearing this and passed on the information to Mr. Doshi's son. He was ready to go to any extent to see that his father was released forthwith from the hellhole of a prison.

The CMM of the city, at that point of time, was a fine gentleman, called Shri Chandrasen Kotwal. There were no mobile phones in those days and very hesitantly the night Magistrate permitted me to use his telephone. He, however, told me that I should not tell the CMM that I was calling from his residence. I agreed. It was well past 9 pm by then. I told Mr. Doshi's son that time was running against us. Yet, I took the risk of making a call to the CMM. I explained the details of the matter in a few minutes and the CMM was quick to grasp the entire episode and understood that an innocent gentleman had landed himself in custody, due to circumstances beyond his control. My point that no summons had been issued to the accused on filing of a charge sheet against him, as mandatorily required and, as such, he was not aware of the pendency of the case against him, made an impact on the mind of the CMM. Thus, it was not a case of willful disobedience of the orders of the court. Within a couple of minutes, I was successful in persuading the CMM to agree to entertain my bail application, as an exceptional case. He was a little annoyed, though, perhaps because we called so late on the day; he told me to reach his place before 10 pm, or else, we would not be entertained. The distance between our place and the residence of CMM was about 15 km drive, which, even at that late hour, would take at least 20 minutes to cover.

We thanked the night Magistrate and rushed to CMM's abode. At 10 pm, on the dot, I anxiously pressed the doorbell of his house. Mr. Doshi's son was accompanying me, and we saw the CMM himself opening the door for us. We were made to sit in the front room. The CMM, Shri Kotwal, was in his night dress. He sat on a sofa opposite us. I started making my submissions, by narrating the background of the case. At one point in an extremely dramatic way, charged with emotion, I submitted that I would never have bothered the Hon'ble CMM at that late hour to deal with a bail application but for the extraordinary situation prevalent in the case on hand, that night. I also stressed the point that we were not dealing with a case of a crime committed by a criminal. If Mr. Doshi remained in prison overnight, an irreparable miscarriage of justice would result.

The CMM was moved by my submissions. As I concluded my submissions, he pulled out a sheet of paper from a shelf behind him and started writing the order. I was hopeful that he had decided to release Mr. Doshi. It was nearing 11.30 pm when he commenced. He went on writing till the page was filled. He then turned the paper overleaf and continued writing, till he had exhausted the second page too. We were anxious, as the clock was ticking, and time was running out. The CMM continued writing till he exhausted the second page as well. And he went on. He next pulled out another leaf and went on writing. It took 15-20 minutes for him to wind up his order. After he finished writing, he raised his head and looked at me. He uttered one sentence from his order, "I have held the accused be forthwith released on bail, in the sum of Rs. 5000/-, with one surety in the like amount." On this, I heaved a sigh of relief, and said, "Hail Justice."

However my anxiety continued, for I pointed out to the CMM that at that midnight hour, the procedure of furnishing surety could not practically be complied with and also there was no provision for depositing cash bail amount at that hour in prison premises. As a result, the whole purpose and the spirit of the order would be frustrated. The CMM considered my point. After thinking for a while, at the bottom of his order, he added, "I order release of the accused, Doshi, forthwith, on my personal security, without executing any bond, till 11 am tomorrow, when the accused is directed to appear before the concerned court and execute the required surety bail bond. The order must be complied with forthwith."

We were delighted at this development, and I thanked the CMM profusely. We left his home with the three-page handwritten order of the CMM. Our next stop was the Arthur Road Central prison. By then, it was well past midnight.

Precisely at 00.40 hours, we reached the main entrance of the prison and I was proudly flaunting the midnight order of the CMM. All around, there was a deserted look. Not a bird or beast was spotted or heard, except a solitary owl. There was total silence, in a city that is otherwise known for its hustle-bustle.

At the main gate of the prison, we found the guard dozing and he had to be woken up from his deep slumber. We asked him where the jailor was. The guard was loathe to answer us, at that odd hour. When I identified myself and told him that I was carrying an urgent court order, reluctantly, he told us that the jailor was upstairs, in his quarters and that the entrance is from outside. He also warned us that no one is permitted to disturb him at that odd hour, and if we were going to him, we were doing so at our own risk. He was not supposed to allow us to go upstairs, and we must not tell the jailor that he had let us approach him. We paid heed to all his stipulations and, with a sense of relief, reached the door of the quarters of the jailor. I lightly pressed the bell and waited for a few minutes. But there was no response. After some time, the door was slowly opened by a middle-aged, burly man, looking haggard and angry.

The furrows on his forehead revealed the annoyance at the intruders causing an unexpected interruption in his nightly bliss, away from the hardcore criminals of the prison. Standing at the door he asked us, "Who are you and what is the time?" Apologetically, I explained to him that I was an advocate who had to approach him at that odd, nightly hour, with an important court order for the forthwith release of an apparently innocent accused. I pacified him and requested him to excuse us for that late hour's visit. It was unavoidable; we had no option but to disturb him. Reluctantly, he let us in and made us sit comfortably. I handed over the order to him and he started reading the order most unwillingly. Since the order was a little too long for a quick reading, I told him to skip the details and read the last paragraph which was the operative part. On this, the jailor turned and read the last few lines on page 3.

On reading the lines, he was wonder struck. He looked at me, putting down the order on the little table in front of him. Soon he took off his spectacles and put them on the table too. Slowly, he approached a wash basin nearby, and sprinkled water onto his face, multiple times. He then wiped his face with a towel by the side of the wash basin. He came back to his seat and took the order again in his hand. He then read it again and again and again. After reading it multiple times the jailor raised his head and looked at me. Then he said, "In my twenty-eight years' career I have never come across such an order;

neither have I ever heard of such an order or complied with such a direction. I am shocked." Saying so, the jailor got up from his seat, put on his overcoat and took a long torch in his right hand, from an open shelf. With the pages containing the historic midnight order in his left hand he then asked us to follow him. We followed him up to the entrance gate of the prison. He then entered the jail premises. We followed, as directed. He asked us to follow him to the interior of the jail and took us right up to the cell where Mr. Doshi was lodged. He ascertained the prisoner's identity. The jailor then asked Mr. Doshi to come out of the cell and brought him to the main entrance of the prison, where the jailor's office was situated. It was well past 1.30 a.m. by this time.

The jailor again expressed his great shock and dismay over the order in his hands. He said, "In the history of this Arthur Road prison, or for that matter any other prison in the country, no under-trial accused has ever been allowed to walk out of the prison in the middle of the night, even without executing a bond." He complimented us and allowed us to take Mr. Doshi with us. The three of us then crossed the prison gate and went into the open. The jailor went his way. The father and the son hugged each other with a feeling of intense happiness and relief. They had no words to express their gratitude to me for this midnight miracle in their life. I took leave of the Doshis, with a sense of personal triumph.

Mr. Doshi's release from the prison, before sunrise, as desired by his family, made them jubilant. Mr. Doshi himself was overjoyed and said that it was a divine test for his son and the entire family and that he was glad they had passed the test successfully.

Next morning, at 11 o'clock sharp, it was my duty to produce Mr. Doshi before the concerned Magistrate in the 12th court at Bandra, Mumbai. He was to be presented before the same Magistrate for executing necessary bail bond who had ordered Mr. Doshi to be taken into custody the previous evening, after rejecting his bail application. When I made Mr. Doshi stand in front of the Magistrate and the detailed order of the CMM was placed before him, the Magistrate was furious. He could not believe that the CMM would pass such an order. However, he had no option but to permit Mr. Doshi to execute the required bond as ordered and the whole story ended happily in that fine morning.

Long thereafter, one day, CMM Shri Kotwal met me, after his retirement. During our casual talk, he reminded me of the above episode. He then told me that the Magistrate of the 12th court at Bandra had filed a complaint against him, in the High Court, for passing that midnight order and that an enquiry was held against him in the matter. However, since there was nothing improper in passing the order, the enquiry was dropped.

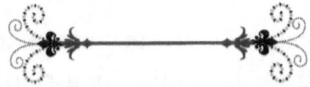

In a Lighter Vein

MM had the reputation of tearing the witness into pieces if the witness dared to stick to falsehood or exaggeration. In one such extremely important police 'encounter' trial, the trial judge concluded that it was not a case of a chance encounter but was a case of cold-blooded murder of the victim, by the police. When the trial was on, it generated a lot of public interest and media attention.

While the evidence was being recorded in the trial court, before the Principal Judge, in the Sessions Court, at Mumbai, the court used to be fully packed, with enthusiastic journalists, junior advocates, students of law and members of the public. MM was cross-examining a senior police officer, who was in the witness box. Every question that he put to the witness was being answered with a great amount of caution and fear, with pauses. The presiding officer was also curious about the gradual emergence of truth. At one point, the proceedings became a bit dull, and MM saw someone yawning. He felt that there was a need at that juncture to inject some light-heartedness or else the atmosphere would slip into boredom.

MM rose and submitted to the court that he just remembered the conversation between his son and himself, the previous evening, in which his school-going son asked him "Dad, why do you travel so often to London and other distant places for discussions and conferences, when we have the facility of video-conferencing with the help of which you can speak to your counterpart anywhere in the world from your office? He can also exchange his views with you, as though the two of you were sitting across the table, physically."

MM thought that what his son told him was worthy of consideration.

He next told the court that he was shocked when the boy added that he could even shake hands with his counterpart anywhere in the world. At this, the learned prosecutor rose from his seat and brilliantly retorted, "It is possible in the case of MM only as he has very, very long arms." The whole court burst into loud laughter.

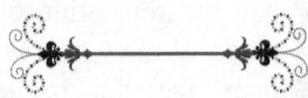

Five

THE PAEDOPHILE CASE

It was in September 2004 that my British client, Alano Wolf (name changed), was brought to Mumbai (the new name of Bombay) by a two-member police team, following extradition from New York.

He, along with another Briton, called D'Sa Rose (name changed), was wanted by the Bombay police, in the infamous Anchorage Abuse case. Wolf was accused by four street children, aged between 13 and 18 years of sexually abusing them, at Anchorage Shelters, set up in 1995-96 by D'Sa Rose. He was produced before a Metropolitan Magistrate in Esplanade Court, on 8 September 2004.

I was assigned the case for bail hearing, and trial. While I was arguing and pleading for bail for Alano Wolf, a group of street children from the Shelter Home in Colaba were watching the proceedings inside the court hall. As it was not an ordinary case, I was concerned for my client who appeared to be a respectable man from the U.K. I was afraid that he would be subjected to a high-profile media trial. I argued before the Magistrate that the treatment meted out to the extradited client in custody should be in accordance with the international guidelines set by the United Nations. I also cited 11 guidelines, set by the Supreme Court in the famous D.K. Basu vs Union of India case which pertains to the rights of the accused. The accused was, nevertheless, remanded to a week of police custody, to enable the police to pursue the investigation into the case.

Soon thereafter, some inmates from the Anchorage gathered outside the court room, ready to give statements to the media, to throw light on the Briton's efforts to improve their life in the Shelter Home. One child said, "Since Father D'Sa has left, money has dried up for the Shelter, and I had to drop out of my school."

The British Government slept over the plea by the Government of India, for extradition of Alano Wolf, for over two years until he was nabbed by the United States police, at the JFK airport, in July 2003. His custodians in the city, the Colaba Police, were in a catch-22 situation. This was for the first time that a foreign national had been brought to the Bombay police custody, from a third country (the U.S.A.), through the extradition process. For that matter the treatment meted out to the accused was being closely monitored by the United States, the United Kingdom, as well as Interpol which facilitated the extradition process.

An interesting aspect of this case is that my client was very much at his Hampstead house and the British authorities were quite aware of the pending Interpol warrant against him. Further, the co-accused in the case, D'Sa Rose, was frequently shuttling between London and Dar-es-Salaam, (Tanzania), during this period, despite the warrant against him. Since I had vehemently urged that the treatment to be meted out to my extradited client in custody should be as per the international guidelines, the court had asked the Colaba police to keep him in a separate cell in the police station or shift him to a crime branch lock-up.

In July 2005, co-accused D'Sa Rose came down to Mumbai from London and surrendered to the police, for the same offence. The 61-year-old Rose had established three Anchorage homes in South Mumbai and Murud, for street children, in the year 1995-96. His friend, Alano Wolf regularly visited the shelters. It was in the year 2001 that following the complaints of four children, the Mumbai police registered a case against the duo, in November 2001. The two then fled India. While Alano Wolf was arrested from New York, following the red corner alert by the Interpol, Rose escaped to Tanzania, where he set up another Anchorage shelter, in Dar-es-Salaam. In February

2002, after Rose refused to return to India, stating that he would not get a fair trial here, a red corner notice was issued against him.

In 2004, students from the Jesuit school in Dar-es-Salaam raised concerns that children in Anchorage shelter in Dar-es-Salam were being sexually and physically abused. The Tanzanian Government then deported Rose to the U.K. According to police sources, Rose who was deported from Tanzania to the U.K. on 1 June, managed to disappear from the Heathrow Airport. His escape was facilitated by a few British policemen, who subsequently claimed that he had given them a slip, while being escorted to the washroom. It was difficult for anyone to believe that a deportee could escape from police custody in Heathrow airport, where the security is foolproof. Interpol suspected foul play and apprised senior officers of London police about the developments.

The policemen, who had apparently helped Rose to escape from the Airport, came to know of the Interpol meeting with senior officers. Those cops then traced Rose to his hideout in London and threatened to arrest him if he continued to live in London. He was, however, given the choice of leaving the country and surrendering before the Indian police. The Mumbai police claimed that the surrender was a result of four years of their persistent efforts to seek the extradition of the fugitive.

I was engaged to represent the accused in the Sessions Court, at Mumbai. I convinced the presiding officer that it was better for the accused to surrender to the Law, rather than the police, so that he would get justice. The court, therefore, directed the Colaba police to bring the accused before the court on the very same day. Amidst legal wrangling, the accused was ordered to be remanded to police custody for eight days. Rose was almost unfazed by the allegation and the legal battle in India.

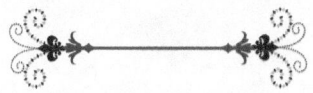

In a Lighter Vein

Once, MM was seated in a Magistrate's Court when a rookie advocate was addressing the Magistrate. His language was poor, and it was difficult to understand what he was seeking to convey to the court in broken English.

To add to his agony, the advocates present in the court found that the response from the judicial officer was no better. His English, too, was pathetically poor. It was a great display of ignorance of language from both the Bench and the Bar. As the submission went on for a few minutes, MM was getting restless and irritated.

Another junior advocate, seated near him asked him what case was going on in the court. MM unhesitatingly answered, "A murder case."

The surprised advocate then asked him whether murder cases could be tried in a Magistrate's court. MM was quick enough, with a sarcastic reply, "Yes, of course, watch and listen for yourself. The English language is being murdered right before this Magistrate."

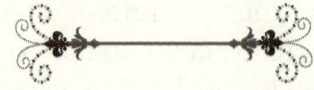

Six

ANUPAM KHER VS SURJEET

Desaffronise Our Institutions, was the headline of an article in the Communist Party-Marxist (CPM)'s journal, 'People's Democracy,' in its issue dated 10 October 2004.

The article listed nine individuals, who were part of the Government run institutions, as 'RSS (Rashtriya Swayamsevak Sangh) Men Still in Key Positions'. Under each name, Harkishan Singh Surjeet, the CPM ideologue, revealed his or her RSS/BJP (Bharatiya Janta Party) affiliation. To name a few, L.M. Singhvi (BJP Member of Parliament), Tarun Vijay (Editor, RSS mouthpiece, 'Panchjanya'), M.V. Kamath (Columnist for the RSS publication 'Organiser'), and Sonal Mansingh (BJP Campaigner). However, only in the case of Anupam Kher, did Surjeet not explain the link to the saffron brigade. The CPM ideologue merely mentioned, 'Anupam Kher continues to Head the Film Censor Board.'

Two days after the news item was published, Anupam Kher was asked to resign from the post. This had irked Anupam Kher to such an extent that he decided to put up a fight against the Central Government. He said, "The witch-hunt harks back to America's McCarthyism period. Now my credibility is at stake and aspersions have been cast upon my character. I have been made a scapegoat for the impotency of a government that leans on others' shoulders to run its affairs. I am a secular person in life. This is not the way to deal with citizens, forget whether they are prominent or not."

Another prominent CPM leader, when asked what led his party's patriarch to term Kher an RSS man said, "We were extremely peeved that the film on the Gujarat riots was held up by the Censor Board". To this, Kher had retorted. "If I hadn't personally intervened, the film would never have been cleared for ten years". According to the Left parties though, that decision of Kher to clear the film 'Final Solution' without any cut was perceived as "too little, too late".

Hence, in a peculiar situation, while the name of Sharmila Tagore was announced as the new Chairman of the Central Board of Film Certification, Kher decided not to step down from the post. A question arose: Are there two Censor Board Chiefs, concurrently? Kher had a quick reply to this question as well. "I am the only CBFC Chairman". According to him Ms. Tagore had not contacted him before accepting the assignment.

On 19 October 2004, Kher approached me with a request to take up his cause and file a defamation case against Harkishan Singh Surjeet, General Secretary of Communist Party of India (Marxist) for describing him as a RSS man. I accepted his brief and filed a defamation case against Harkishan Singh Surjeet, in the concerned Esplanade Court in Mumbai. The case was filed under sections 499 and 500 of Indian Penal Code. Kher in his petition had alleged that Surjeet in his article, in the Party journal, labelled him as a Rashtriya Swayamsevak Sangh man working to suit the Sangh's ideology. He was further described as one of the RSS men still in a key position, operating from behind the scenes.

I told the court that Surjeet had mentioned Kher's name, without providing any details of his link with the RSS. As an artiste he had never been associated with any political group or party and to link him with any such group was nothing but a blot on his career. He pleaded in his complaint before the Magistrate that Surjeet had written an article in the CPM Journal 'People's Democracy', in which he had alleged that there were certain persons who were staunch pro-RSS communal elements, occupying high positions in public institutions, continuing from the previous National Democratic Alliance (NDA) government at the Centre. He alleged, in his complaint that the impugned article, titled 'Desaffronise Our Institutions', suggested the forthwith removal of such persons from key posts, including Kher who was described as a RSS man and blamed for initiating a saffronising process in the Central Board of Film Certification (CBFC).

Talking to the media about the alleged article, after filing the case, Kher said "It has hurt my secular credentials. When my relatives were thrown out of Kashmir, I never expressed my anger in an undemocratic way. I have been defamed when they call me a RSS member."

There were two aspects to Kher's case. On the one hand he was protecting himself from wild and irresponsible allegations of being communal. On the other, he was seeking to sustain the dignity and autonomy of the office of the Chairman of the Censor Board. Kher was not upset over his removal from the post, but at being labelled as a RSS man. He was an artiste, engaged in the field of art and entertainment, and did not belong to any party or ideology.

As his counsel in the court, I submitted that the allegations made by Surjeet were false and imaginary. It had caused him great mental agony and undeserved embarrassment. The charges levelled against him by the accused were with the vicious intention of harming his reputation. He was not in any way, directly or indirectly, associated with any pro RSS communal elements and he had nothing to do with the alleged communal line of RSS. The words and expressions attributed to him were clearly with a view to defaming him and damaging his esteem in the eyes of the people. Kher had struggled for years to make a career in films and had acquired a reputation and status, not just in India, but also in the world. He had always stood firmly for secularism, patriotism, peace, and harmony among the people of India, irrespective of caste, creed, or religion.

When I stood up and argued, the court was convinced that a case is made out against the accused, and issue of summons was ordered. Upon service of summons to the elderly communist leader there was a lot of noise in the media. Surjeet however, did not personally appear before the court on the appointed day. The court was constrained to issue warrant of arrest against him. This further aggravated the situation against the accused and his party. Surjeet was indeed a very feeble and sick person who was unable to travel to the court for personal attendance. He, therefore, chose to engage Senior Advocate Shri Ram Jethmalani who appeared in the court and tendered unconditional apology to the complainant on behalf of his client. The remarks made by the accused against the complainant were withdrawn with expression of regret. The case thus ended up there.

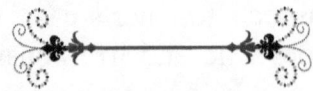

The Free Press Journal ■ Mumbai ■ Wednesday October 20, 2004

Anupam files defamation complaint against Surjeet

BY A STAFF REPORTER

Actor and former Censor Board chairman Anupam Kher yesterday filed a criminal complaint of defamation against CPI (M) general secretary Harkishan Singh Surjeet for alleging that he (Kher) had contributed to saffronisation process of the Board as an RSS functionary.

Kher, who was unceremoniously removed as Central Board of Film Certification chairman on October 13, filed the complaint in the court of magistrate C. B.

Anupam Kher with his lawyer Majid Memon outside the magistrate's court.

Havelikar who adjourned the matter to November 17 for its verification. The actor told reporters outside the court that he was not upset over his removal from the post of CBFC chief but over his unceremonious removal after being labelled as an RSS functionary.

Kher said this had hurt him the most and added that he was an artist engaged in the field of art and entertainment and did not belong to any party or ideology. Therefore, to link him with any political organisation was nothing but a blot on his career, he said. Kher said in the complaint that Surjeet had written an article in CPM journal 'People's Democracy' in which he had alleged that there were certain persons who were staunch pro-RSS communal elements ocupying high positions in public institutions appointed by the previous NDA government at the centre. The actor alleged in the complaint that the impugned article titled 'Desaffronise Our Institutions' suggested forthwith removal of such persons from key posts including Kher who was described as an RSS man and blamed for initiating saffronising process in CBFC.

Kher submitted that the allegations made by Surjeet were false and imaginary, and had caused him mental agony and undeserved embarrassment. Kher said the charges made by the accused were intending to harm his reputation.

Kher denied that he was in any way, directly or indirectly, associated with pro-RSS communal elements or that he had anything to do with the alleged communal line of RSS.

"I wish to reiterate that I have no links whatsoever with any other political party or ideology either. The words and expressions attributed to me are clearly to defame me and damage my esteem in the eyes of the people," Kher said.

The actor said in the complaint that he had sent a legal notice to Surjeet through his lawyer Majeed Memon on October 14 calling upon him to withdraw his allegations. As the accused did not respond, he had no other option but to file a defamation case, Kher contended. The former Censor Board chief said he had struggled for years to make a career in films and had acquired reputation and status not just in India but also in the world. "I have always stood firmly for secularism, patriotism, peace and harmony among the people of India irrespective of caste, creed and religion." The actor was accompanied by his lawyer Majeed Memon. He cited six witnesses, including film-makers Mahesh Bhat, Yash Chopra, Vijay Kher and Ashok Pandit. ■

The Times of India, Mumbai   **Wednesday, March 16, 2005**

Bailable warrant against Surjeet

TIMES NEWS NETWORK

A Kher

Mumbai: Standing in the witness box, actor Anupam Kher heaved a sigh of relief when metropolitan magistrate M H Belose read out a bailable warrant against Harkishan Singh Surjeet, general secretary of Communist Party of India (Marxist), for not appearing in the court despite a summons on Tuesday.

The court has asked Surjeet to provide a surety of Rs 10,000 in lieu of the warrant issued against him and asked him to appear in person on April 25. In the afternoon, just before the proceedings were to begin, an exasperated Kher was seen pacing up and down the courtroom after learning that Surjeet had decided to play truant again. "This is not done. No one is above law, I'll fight this case to the finish," said Kher. This is the second time Surjeet failed to appear in the court despite a summons.

Kher had dragged Surjeet to the court for allegedly defaming him in articles by describing him as an "RSS agent" and alleging that he (Kher) had saffronised the Censor Board in his capacity as its chairman.

The proceedings began with the defence lawyer submitting an application for exemption of appearance on medical grounds. The lawyer argued that his 90-year-old client, who was suffering from a host of geriatric ailments, had a fall recently which resulted in a head, shoulder and back injury. Submitting a medical certificate issued by Metro Hospitals and Heart Institute, Noida, the lawyer said that Surjeet has been advised not to travel for at least four weeks.

Countering the claims, Kher's advocate Majid Memon said that Surjeet was seen practically every day on television attending public and political party functions. "In fact he even went to Pakistan recently," said Memon, adding that the senior leader was being disrespectful to the court.

In a Lighter Vein

A case of rioting that resulted in the death of a young boy, in a clash between two groups in a football ground, was being tried by a Sessions Judge. This was yet another case where an incompetent prosecutor was given the responsibility of proving the charges of rioting and murder against the accused. MM was the leading defence counsel in the trial.

In brief, the case of the prosecution was that whilst playing football the youngsters on both sides clashed with one another, and a sudden riot took place. Within minutes their friends arrived with stones, lathis (thick canes) and tube lights to inflict injury on the rivals. In the melee, one of the young boys sustained fatal injuries, while a few others, on both sides, were seriously injured. The game of football was admittedly being played at dusk, after sunset, and there was insufficient light. In the circumstance, the defence questioned the veracity of identification of the accused. In the evidence, MM had taken enough precaution to see that the evidence about insufficient light was satisfactorily brought on record.

At the end of the trial both the prosecution and the defence, were required to summarise their submissions regarding the evidence on record. As a rule, the prosecution must advance arguments first and the defence would reply thereafter. The learned trial judge, by that time, has heard all the evidence to appreciate the arguments put forth by both sides. In his characteristic style, MM took the learned judge through the evidence and laid emphasis on the plea of mistaken identity of the accused. Taking much pain to establish this point, MM drew the attention of the learned judge to such portions of the evidence that indicated that there wasn't sufficient light on the spot of the incident at the relevant time. As such, he argued that there was a high probability that the witness was not able to see the faces of the assailants involved in the assault. When it came to the crucial question of confirming the identity of the accused, MM argued that the benefit of doubt had to be extended to his clients, who were in the dock. The learned judge meticulously made notes on the points raised by him.

Then, it was the turn of the prosecutor to put forth his arguments. However, the submission of the prosecutor was no match to that of the defence. The prosecutor was not able to make any convincing arguments; nor was he able to counter the plea of the defence. He cut a sorry figure in the court, while sweating and turning the pages of evidence in his hands in a haphazard manner. On a query by the learned judge on the condition of visibility in the ground at the time of incident the prosecutor started shouting, "Sir, there was sufficient light, I would point out here and now." The learned judge looked at the prosecutor with sympathy as he knew that there was no evidence of the sufficiency of light on the spot. He mischievously said, "Mr. Prosecutor, please enlighten the court from the evidence, whether there was sufficient light."

Again, turning the pages of evidence, the prosecutor was thrilled with joy. He exclaimed "Sir, I got it." The learned judge asked him to show where he got it in the evidence. On this, showing the deposition of a certain witness in a particular paragraph, the prosecutor drew the attention of the learned judge to it. Turning to the relevant portion, the learned judge asked the prosecutor to read aloud where it was mentioned that there was sufficient light. The prosecutor then argued, "Your Honour, the accused were holding stones, lathis and tube-lights." At the mention of 'tube-lights' there was loud laughter all over.

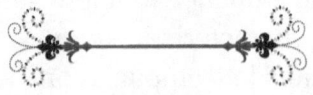

Seven

A FIANCEE'S BRUTAL MURDER

Pragnesh Desai was a Gujarati businessman, living in New Jersey. In the course of his business dealings, as a partner in Bukhara Grill Restaurant, Manhattan, he happened to meet a New Jersey model, Leona Swiderski. Young Leona fell in love with forty-year-old Pragnesh, who was married and had a family, in Manhattan. Throughout the affair, Pragnesh smartly concealed the fact of his married status from Leona.

After a couple of months of steady love affair, Desai proposed to Leona. Reposing full faith in her Indian lover, Leona readily agreed to the marriage. From then on, Pragnesh discussed with Leona their marriage, and their future life together. He assured her a very high lifestyle both in New Jersey as well as in India, after their marriage. Leona had no reason to disbelieve or suspect her ardent lover.

Having gained her full confidence, Pragnesh started discussing the style of marriage which they should adopt to solemnize and affirm their sizzling love affair. He proposed a lavish local marriage in New Jersey, or a traditional Indian style marriage, with pomp and glory in India. The choice was hers. Leona was thrilled at the prospect of the marriage in India. It was then that things started moving fast for hawk-eyed Pragnesh Desai.

Pragnesh and Leona planned their marriage in a five-star hotel, in India, in February 2003. Just before leaving for India from the U.S., Desai bought two insurance policies, each of USD five hundred thousand, in the name of Leona, of which he was the sole beneficiary.

On 8 February 2003, early in the morning Pragnesh and Leona landed at Mumbai's Chhatrapati Shivaji International airport. They had travelled from New York on an Air India flight. Asking Leona to relax in the restroom as she was tired after a long journey, Pragnesh disappeared. Unsuspecting, Leona went to the restroom, having no reason not to obey her-soon-to-be husband and long-time lover. In the meantime, Pragnesh travelled to south Mumbai's Taj Mahal hotel and booked a suite for himself.

However, he did not fail to approach the Sahar International Airport Police Station and lodge a missing person complaint stating that Leona had gone missing while he was in the restroom. The police recorded a complaint and Pragnesh went back to the hotel suite in south Mumbai.

On 9 February 2003, a group of farm hands were working in a field, along Mumbai-Ahmedabad highway, in the jurisdiction of Kashi Mira Road police station, in Thane District, about 30 kilometers north of Mumbai. It was by sheer chance that they came across the body of a white woman. The shocked farmers immediately informed the local police station about their discovery and the Kashi Mira Road police swung into action. An autopsy of the body revealed that the woman was strangled to death.

Soon after the preliminary investigation was over, Kashi Mira Road police arrested Pragnesh. After sustained interrogation, he broke down and admitted to the horrendous crime he had committed.

Asking his fiancée to wait in the restroom of the airport, Pragnesh had arranged for a friend's car to transport Leona, purportedly to Gujarat, to 'make arrangements for their marriage'. Leona occupied the back seat of the car along with Pragnesh on one side and his friend on the other side. The plan worked well, just as he had worked out.

Pragnesh and his friend Vipul had hired two killers, Altaf and Farook Patel. This was revealed by the main prosecution witness,

Rashmibhai Patel, to the police during investigation. He said that Altaf and Farook met them at Kashi Mira Road. While Pragnesh and his friend came out of the car on seeing the hired killers, Leona sat in the car. After a short and hushed conversation with Pragnesh, the killers got into the car and overpowered Leona. The frail female could not do much and surrendered to the strong masculine muscles that strangled her within no time.

Their next destination was a proper dumping ground for the dead white woman and that's how they reached the borders of the farmland. After dumping the body, Pragnesh returned to his suite in the Taj Mahal hotel. Everything was going his way, till he was arrested by the police for the murder of Leona.

After the investigation was over, the Kashi Mira Road Police filed a charge sheet before the concerned Magistrate, in Thane Court, against four accused, viz. 1) Pragnesh Desai 2) Vipul 3) Farook Patel and 4) Altaf Patel. After the charge sheet was filed, the Magistrate committed the case for trial before the Court of Sessions, at Thane.

I was engaged to defend Pragnesh. On the face of it, the police had done a shoddy investigation into the whole case, which fact was pointed out to the trial court. The prime prosecution witness, Rashmibhai Patel, turned hostile at the time of the trial. "Desai and Vipul hired Altaf and Farook Patel to kill Leona," he had told the police during investigation. But he did not stick to this statement in court.

The trial before the Sessions Court was concluded within a month and on 26 September 2003, sadly all the accused were acquitted for want of evidence against them.

"News of acquittal is like repeating February 8 all over again, the day I got a call that Leona had been murdered, " said Madeline Swiderski, Leona's mother, on a call from the U.S. She added, "I cannot understand how he has been acquitted. He took my daughter away from me, but he is not going to get away with this. I don't know what is going on there. I am getting bits and pieces of news from here and there. But I am going to see that this man is brought to justice ".

Her attorney, Amato Galasso, said, "Desai's motive was money. Just before leaving the U.S. for India, he bought two insurance policies of which he was the sole beneficiary."

After his acquittal in the case, Desai was arrested again on 9 October, so he could be deported to America, since a warrant had been issued against him, through Interpol, for illegal money transfer to allegedly pay for the killing. The action was based on an arrest warrant issued against him on 5 May 2004, by a court in New York. One day later, the U.S. Consulate in Mumbai revoked his passport.

I contacted the Consulate and put to them that Desai be given the right to be defended through an attorney of his choice there.

"He has been cleared of all the allegations against him here. It cannot be said that he is absconding or evading the district court in New Jersey. He is anxious to clear his name of false accusations against him, in the U.S. Courts," the Consulate was told.

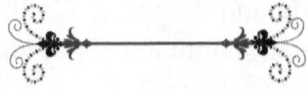

US News

Desai acquitted of fiancée's murder in Mumbai

SYED FIRDAUS ASHRAF and TANMAYA KUMAR NANDA
in Mumbai and New York

News that a Mumbai court acquitted Pragnesh Desai in the murder of Leona Swiderski has shocked the victim's family in New Jersey.

"I cannot understand how he has been acquitted," Leona's mother Madeline Swiderski told *India Abroad*.

"To me, something funny went on there. He's out the door just like that," she said.

"They took my daughter away from me but he's not going to get away with this."

Swiderski said extradition papers for Desai have been prepared.

September 26, a sessions court in Thane, north of Mumbai, acquitted Desai, an India-born New York restaurateur, of the charge of murdering fiancée Leona Swiderski, a New Jersey model.

The acquittal came after Rashmibhai Patel, a key witness, turned hostile.

February 8, Desai, a partner in the Bukhara Grill restaurant in Manhattan, filed a complaint at Mumbai's Chhatrapati Shivaji International Airport police station stating Swiderski had gone missing while he was in the restroom. He said they had landed in Mumbai from New York on an Air-India flight.

Police found Swiderski's body the next day by the side of the Mumbai-Ahmedabad highway, 30 kilometers north of Mumbai. An autopsy found she had been strangled (*India Abroad*, February 28).

After investigations, the Thane police charged Desai with murder. The prosecution claimed Desai broke down during investigation and admitted to the crime.

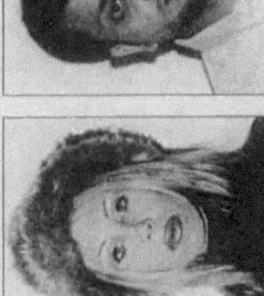

■ Leona Swiderski and Pragnesh Desai

The prime witness for the prosecution's case was Rashmibhai Patel, a brother-in-law of Desai's close friend Vipul Patel.

During investigations, Rashmibhai Patel allegedly told the police Desai and Vipul "hired Altaf and Farooq Patel to kill Swiderski."

In court, Rashmibhai Patel turned hostile, and said he had no information linking Desai or Patel with the crime.

"News of his acquittal is like repeating February 8 all over again, the day I got a call that Leona had been murdered," her mother told *India Abroad*.

"I don't know what's going on there. I'm getting bits and pieces of news from here and there. But I'm going to see that this man is brought to justice."

Amato Galasso, civil attorney for Madeline Swiderski, alleged Desai's motive was money. "Just before leaving the US for India, Desai bought two insurance policies of $500,000 each in Swiderski's name, in which he was the sole beneficiary," Galasso said. "For that, I believe he was guilty."

Galasso said there was nothing he could do, given that he was a civil attorney. "But something is definitely fishy."

"The authorities in India weren't cooperative initially. It took us five months to get a copy of the death certificate and the autopsy report. The cop failed to show up in court. And finally Desai is acquitted. It's just too coincidental. Even now, the information we are getting is very sketchy and is mostly from the Internet."

"We had strong circumstantial evidence but unfortunately Rashmibhai turned hostile," said Ramrao Pawar, Superintendent of Police (Thane Rural), who headed the investigation.

"We arrested Desai again October 9 so he could be deported to America, as a warrant had been issued against him through Interpol for illegal money transfer," Pawar told *India Abroad*. Desai was granted bail that day but ordered to present himself in court when required.

A day later, the US consulate in Mumbai revoked Desai's passport.

The action was based on an arrest warrant issued against Desai May 5 by a court in Newark, District of New Jersey, on charges of illegally transferring money to India to allegedly pay for the killing.

"We have informed the consulate and asked that he be given the right to legal counsel there," Desai's lawyer Majeed Memon said.

"He has been cleared of all allegations against him. It cannot be said he is absconding or evading the district court in New Jersey. He is anxious to clear his name vis-à-vis false accusations against him in the US courts."

city

HC to rule on NRI's extradition today

He has been accused of murdering his girlfriend

Shibu Thomas
shibu@mid-day.com

NRI murder accused Pragnesh Desai wants to be extradited to the US. The Maharashtra government is, however, not willing to play ball. The government wants the lower court's order clearing Desai of charges of murdering his girlfriend Leona Swiderski overturned. The deadline for Desai's extradition expires today, and the Bombay High Court will decide today whether the NRI will be finally extradited.

Additional public prosecutor Aruna Kamat said, "If Desai is extradited to the US, he may not return to face the murder charges."

Desai, who was born in Vadodara and is a US citizen was charged with killing his fiancee, Leona Swiderski, for financial gains when she arrived in Mumbai on February 8, 2003. Desai along with his friend Vipul Patel and two hired killers allegedly strangulated Swiderski to death and dumped her body near Versova village on the Mumbai-Ahmedabad national highway. In September 2003, a sessions court acquitted Desai and Patel of all charges.

Last month Federal Bureau of Investigation officials had visited Mumbai to seek Desai's extradition. In the US, Desai is facing charges of fraud and possibly a murder charge. Desai had taken two life insurance policies worth $1 million in Swiderski's name, naming himself as the beneficiary.

Desai's counsel Majeed Memon insists his client wants to return to the US. "Desai wants to be extradited to the US and face all the charges against him," Memon said. "He is sure of his innocence and wants to clear his name."

The metropolitan magistrate of the Patiala House court in Delhi, had ordered Desai's extradition in January 2004 under the Indo-US extradition treaty.

The Extradition Act, 1962, specifies that an accused has to be extradited within two months, with the deadline expiring on Friday. The high court is likely to pass orders in the matter today, after a similar petition is heard in the Delhi High Court.

> **DESAI WANTS TO BE EXTRADITED TO THE US AND FACE ALL CHARGES AGAINST HIM**
>
> — *Pragnesh Desai's counsel Majeed Memon*

Leona Swiderski was murdered in February 2003

Cases against Pragnesh Desai

In India

Desai was born in Vadodara and is settled in New Jersey, USA. He married one Trupti and has two children. He had a love affair with US-based model Leona Swiderski, following which he divorced Trupti.

Faced with increasing debt on account of his flashy lifestyle, Desai invited Swiderski to India. He allegedly paid his friend Vipul Patel and two others Rs 30 lakh to murder Swiderski.

On February 8, 2003, Swiderski and Desai arrived at the Chhatrapati Shivaji International Airport. On their way to Vadodara, Desai and the three others allegedly strangled Swiderski and dumped her body near Versova village on the Mumbai-Ahmedabad highway. Thane police arrested Desai and Patel for Swiderski's murder, but the duo were acquitted in September last year.

In the US

Desai is facing fraud-related charges in the US District Court for the District in New Jersey. Desai suffered huge financial setbacks and had run up a huge credit card debt.

He had taken out two life insurance policies – New York Life Insurance policy and Banner Life Insurance policy – each worth $500,000 in Swiderski's name. In both policies, Desai has named himself as the beneficiary. Under US laws, Desai faces an imprisonment of over 20 years.

In a Lighter Vein

In a highly sensitive and important bail application, MM was asked to do his best to secure bail for an important person, who was charged with many serious offences and was incarcerated in Arthur Road Jail. A good amount of preparation was needed, both on facts and law, to persuade the learned Special judge, before whom the matter was listed for hearing. It was not an easy task to obtain bail for the accused, as he was charged with serious charges and there was strong opposition from the State. The final hearing in the matter was fixed on a working day, post lunch and, as usual, the court was packed with people connected with the case as well as junior advocates, law students, anxious court staff and media-persons. They were all patiently awaiting the final hearing of the matter.

MM apprised the court of the importance of restoration of personal liberty to his client, in the given situation. The vehemence with which he stressed his points was remarkable. It had a magical effect on everyone in the courtroom.

Finally, as MM finished his arguments, the prosecutor took over. He took his time and pointed out various grounds for denying bail to the accused. After the prosecutor's argument was concluded, the court turned to MM, for rebuttal. MM rose again, to argue with great vim, vigor and vitality, coupled with sheer professionalism. This had a mesmerising effect on the presiding officer, which was palpable.

As soon as MM stopped his submissions, the learned judge rang the calling bell to summon his stenographer. He then started dictating to the stenographer who emerged from the cabin with a notepad in his hand.

"For reasons to be separately recorded, the petitioner is ordered to be released on bail, in the sum of rupees one lakh, with one surety in the like amount, with following conditions."

Soon after the verdict, the learned judge rose from his seat, as his official time was over and went back to his chamber. Suddenly there was noisy jubilation in the court. Securing bail in that case was an impossible task and this had surprised all. As MM walked out with his team of assisting advocates carrying voluminous books, there were congratulations all around. The TV reporters chased him as usual for bytes.

A relative of the client who was in custody stopped him on the way and anxiously asked him if the accused could be released the same evening. MM replied that it was late on the day and as the formalities of preparing the order will take more time it was unlikely that the Arthur Road prison would release the prisoner that day. MM then asked one of his juniors to help him get the writ of bail, without delay, the next morning.

In the following morning, the junior went to the stenographer of the learned judge. A request was made to him to type out the order and keep it ready for signature by the learned judge, so that without loss of time, the order could be taken to prison for release of the accused. The stenographer agreed to oblige and accordingly he typed out the order and placed it on the table of the judge for his signature. At about 10.20 a.m. the learned judge arrived and went into his chamber. After ten minutes the stenographer called the junior advocate of MM, who was waiting for the order. The steno slowly whispered in his ears that he had to ask him something very confidential. The junior advocate was surprised and told the stenographer that he could unhesitatingly ask him whatever it was. The stenographer asked him anxiously "Does MM know hypnotism?"

At this strange question from a stenographer the junior advocate was astonished, and he queried as to why such a question was asked by him about his senior counsel. The stenographer replied.

"Yesterday, in front of everybody my boss dictated the release order of the petitioner and accordingly I prepared the order for his signature. This morning, after reading the order, he was asking me, have I really passed the release order of the petitioner, in fact?"

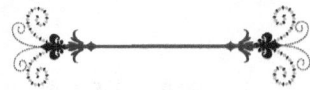

Eight

SHOOTOUT AT MAHIM

It was on 4 March 1999, at around 10 pm, that Milind Vaidya, ex-Mayor of Mumbai, and *Shiv Sena* Corporator from Mahim, was sitting on a bench, by the side of Mori Road, in Mahim, near a *Shiv Sena Shakha* (branch), with a group of his friends. They were engaged in their usual, daily banter. Soon, there was a rain of bullets on them, from a Maruti 800 car, in which three of Vaidya's associates, including his bodyguard, were killed on the spot and six others were critically injured. Vaidya himself was critically injured but survived. In fact, the target of the assailants was none other than Vaidya himself.

The prosecution case was that the attack on Vaidya was master minded by gangster Chhota Shakeel. Police were quick enough to nab the shooters, Zuber Kasam Shaikh, Fazal Sheikh and Azizuddin Shaikh. Abdul Hassan Mistry was the driver during the initial survey mission. Mohammed Farooq, Gafoor Chipa Rangari and Mansoor Hassan Haji Pankar had stolen the Maruti 800 car used in the operation and arranged for the weapons. All the accused were duly arrested and were made to face charges.

On 4 March, at around 10 pm, Zuber, Fazal and Azizuddin had surveyed the area, where Vaidya and his group were sitting at the relevant time, in the Maruti 800 car, which was stolen earlier by their above-named associates, for the intended killing. The car was driven by Abdul Hassan Mistry.

After the survey, the foursome took a turn and went towards Khilnani School, Mahim. There, Abdul Hasan Mistry got down, and after exchanging mobile phones, he walked away. Now Fazal Mohammed Shaikh got into the driver's seat. The car took a round of Navjeevan Society, Mahim, and then returned to Mori Road. Soon, they came back to the *Shiv Sena Shakha* and opened indiscriminate fire at Vaidya. Azizuddin Shaikh used an AK 56 assault rifle. Zuber Shaikh used a 9 mm pistol and Fazal Shaikh used a .30 Mouser Pistol. The job done, they sped away taking a right turn on Panjwani Road where they fired a few rounds in the air, at the Navjeevan Society gate. Their intention was to scare away the bystanders before escaping.

On arrest, the accused were charged with the stringent special law, called Maharashtra Control of Organised Crime Act (MCOCA). The trial was conducted before the special court for MCOCA, in the Mumbai Sessions Court. Each of the accused had appointed his separate advocate. After an exhaustive hearing in the court which went on for months, the trial judge convicted three accused with death sentence, and others with life imprisonment and other varying sentences. Zuber Shaikh, Fazal Shaikh and Azizuddin Shaikh were the ones sentenced to death under the stringent Act.

Relatives of the accused rushed to me with a request to take up their case in appeal against the sentence. After initial hesitation, I agreed to accept their brief as I saw an opportunity to get them relief from capital punishment. This was the first death sentence awarded under the Maharashtra Control of Organised Crime Act since it came into force.

The Milind Vaidya attack case was one of the fastest murder trials in the city and the verdict from the special Court was out in September 2000. The city police had touted this case as the first case under MCOCA, which they had cracked. A former Deputy Commissioner of Police had bagged the prestigious Deepak Jog Award for Best Detection in this case. For the officer, the death sentence awarded to the three accused was a major achievement for himself as also the Mumbai Police's Crime Branch. Incidentally, he was also conferred with the President's Police Medal, in August 2002, for meritorious service. His superior officers, who had recommended his name for the medal, considered the Vaidya case to be one of his main achievements.

The High Court was jointly hearing the State's reference on confirmation of death sentence, awarded to the trio, and the individual appeals filed by the convicts against their conviction. Earlier the judges, who comprised of the Division Bench, had even visited the scene of offence for a first-hand account of the crime committed by the convicts. The learned Judges were led by the counsel of the respective parties.

When the appeals of Fazal Shaikh and Zuber Shaikh, my clients, came up for hearing, I took the judges through the evidence recorded in the trial Court highlighting the loopholes in it. I vehemently attacked the identification parades conducted for the accused pointing out that these were defective. I submitted to the Court that Zuber Shaikh was a squint-eyed person, but when the identification parade was held for him, the dummies were all normal eyed and not a single squint-eyed person was included. This had reduced the test to a mockery. I further argued that the trial Judge had erred in accepting a confessional statement. As against my submissions, the prosecution stated that they had a watertight case against the three appellants.

After hearing my detailed arguments in support of the appellants, much to the surprise of everyone, the High Court was pleased to acquit both my clients. It was thus a case of one extreme to the other. The trial court had awarded the highest possible punishment to the appellants, and the appellate court pronounced them 'not guilty'. The High Court thus reversed the finding of the trial court, in totality, and ordered the acquittal of the appellants.

It was a landmark judgment. Generally, in a case where death sentence is awarded to the appellant and if the High Court feels that the appellant doesn't deserve the harshest punishment, the High Court will set aside the verdict and impose life sentence. Acquittal of an appellant in a death sentence is seldom heard of. Here both the appellants were found 'not guilty' and were surprisingly acquitted.

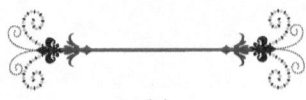

city

Vaidya shooting case goes on location

MIDDAY FRIDAY 26TH SEPTEMBER, 2003

Prosecution and defence take judges to scene of crime

Shibu Thomas
shibu@mid-day.com

FOUR years after former Mumbai mayor Milind Vaidya and nine others were shot, justices J A Patel and A S Augiar, yesterday visited Mori Road at Mahim, the scene of the crime. The high court judges, who had expressed a desire to see the site first hand, were led there by public prosecutors Rohini Salian and Aruna Kamat and defence lawyer Majeed Memon.

The court is hearing a reference by the Maharashtra government to confirm the death sentences awarded to three accused, Mohammed Zuber Qasam Sheikh, Fazal Mohammed Sheikh and Azizuddinn Zahiruddin Sheikh.

Salian led the judges to the shakha and pointed out the bullet marks. As the prosecution and defence vied for the judges' attention, justice J A Patel remarked, "We can put up seats here on the road and allow you to continue your argument."

Both sides have wrapped up their arguments and the judges are likely to announce the date of the verdict on September 29.

The incident

Around 10 pm on March 4, 1999, alleged Chhota Shakeel gangsters opened fire near a Shiv Sena shakha at Mori Road, Mahim. Their target was former city mayor and Sena corporator Milind Vaidya, who was injured in the shoot out. Three of his associates were killed, while six others were injured.

Public prosecutor Rohini Salian, justices A S Augiar, J A Patel and defence lawyer Majeed Memon visit the site at Mori Road, Mahim, yesterday ● MILIND THAKUR

The accused

Mohammed Zuber Qasam Sheikh, Fazal Mohammed Sheikh and Azizuddinn Zahiruddin Sheikh were the ones who opened fire on Vaidya. Abdul Hasan Mistry was the driver during the initial survey mission. Mohammed Farooq Gafoor Chipa Rangari and Mansoor Hasan Haji Pankar stole the Maruti 800 used and also arranged for the weapons. All six have been convicted.

The punishment

Azizuddin, Zuber and Fazal were awarded the death penalty. Abdul Mistry was sentenced to life in prison, while Rangari and Pankar were awarded 10 years rigorous imprisonment.

Sequence of events

- Azizuddin, Zuber and Fazal surveyed the area in a Maruti 800 driven by Abdul Mistry.

- Mistry got down near Khimani school and I J Dress Road. Mobile phones were exchanged and Mistry walked away. Fazal got into the driver's seat.

- The car made a round of Nav Jeevan society and returned to Mori Road.

- At the Shiv Sena shakha, they opened indiscriminate fire. Azizuddin used an AK-56 assault rifle, Zuber a 9mm pistol and Fazal a .30 Mauser pistol.

- They sped away and took a right on Panjwani Road, where they fired a few shots in the air at the Nav Jeevan gate to scare away bystanders, before escaping.

Lawyers speak

THE judges wanted to acquaint themselves with the area, to appreciate the evidence put forward by the prosecution. You cannot get an idea of the actual incident as it happened just by looking at a map.
Rohini Salian
Public prosecutor

WE have pointed out various flaws in the prosecution's theory. The judges will now get a chance our arguments into context. They will be able to decide whether the witnesses would actually have been able to see the incident from where they were standing.
Majeed Memon
Defence counsel

Justice J.A. Patil (second from left) and Justice A.S. Aguiar (third from left) visit the spot in Mahim where former Mumbai mayor Milind Vaidya was shot at in May 1999. At extreme left is defence counsel Majid Memon and on the extreme right is public prosecutor Rohini Salian.

In a Lighter Vein

A criminal trial for offences of cheating and misappropriation was being conducted at a Magistrate's Court, in Mumbai. MM and his team were appearing on behalf of the accused, an elderly person. He appeared to be a popular person with a large following. On every hearing date, he would be accompanied by a crowd of thirty to forty people who would fill the courtroom; the judicial officer and his staff noted this every time. It became a prestigious matter, and as such, MM and his team took great pains to do their best for the client.

After the recording of evidence was concluded, the case was argued by MM very effectively and the matter was listed for judgment on the following date.

On the day of judgment, there was a festival-like atmosphere and the supporters of the accused turned up in large numbers. Interestingly, among them was a strangely attired 'saintly' person. He was a man with a long grey beard and a turban on his head. Before the court commenced its proceedings, the person was made to sit in the court hall exactly opposite the chair of the Magistrate to enable him to look at the Magistrate straight in the eye. At eleven o'clock sharp, as soon as the Magistrate took his seat, the saintly person started staring at the Magistrate and softly chanting some verses. He would, at intervals, blow out air in the direction of the Magistrate, with his eyes shut. This drama went on for a few minutes and, fortunately, his activities went unnoticed by the court. However, the admirers of the accused who had thronged the court were all very particular about the happening inside the court.

As scheduled, when the case was called out, the accused came forward and stood in front of the Magistrate. After the judgment and order were dictated by the Magistrate, the judicial clerk loudly read out the final verdict, which said that the accused was found 'not guilty' and hence acquitted of all the charges. Soon, there was a noisy jubilation inside the courtroom. At this point of time, the police swung into action, and they had a tough time driving out the crowd from the court room. MM and his team of juniors came out and stood in the corridor of the court on one side, while the accused and his admirers chased the saintly person, who had emerged 'victorious', in their eyes. To the shock and surprise of the legal team, they were told that the acquittal of the accused was the result of the *'karishma'* (miracle/spell) cast upon the Magistrate by the saintly person, and not due to the hard work and efforts of the defence team. I rest my case.

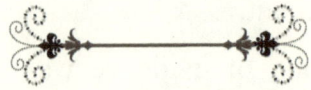

Nine

A MESSY MISSING MYSTERY

On 2 December 2002, there was a blast in a BEST (Bombay Electric Supply and Transport) bus, at Ghatkopar, in which two people died and scores were injured. Police investigation into the unfortunate incident revealed that there was a conspiracy hatched by a couple of suspects.

Khwaja Yunus, a 27-year-old Chemical Engineer, working in Dubai had come on leave to his hometown, Parbhani. Sleuths from the Mumbai Crime Branch picked him up in December 2002, in connection with the blast. He, along with some other suspects, was booked under the stringent Prevention of Terrorism Act (POTA).

On 7 January 2003, Assistant Sub Inspector Sachin Vaze filed an FIR, stating that Yunus had escaped from a police jeep in Ahmednagar, while he was being transported there, for investigation. When the other accused, Dr. Abdul Mateen, Zaheer Ahmed, and Mohammed Muzamil Ahmed, were produced before the special POTA Court, they were remanded into judicial custody.

In one of those cool January mornings, while I was in my office, a frail, sad man visited me. He told me that his name was Saeed Khwaja Ayub, from Parbhani. Shedding tears, he narrated the story of the arrest of his only son, Yunus, by the Crime Branch officers, and then the shocking news of his young son's disappearance from their custody. On hearing the facts of the case, I feared that his son had died in police custody.

The story of the police, about the escape drama, had curious twists and turns, as was published in the media, as well as reported to the special court. The tale had the elements of a Bollywood blockbuster. Read on.

The prosecution story was that on 7th January 2003, Yunus was being transported to Ahmednagar, in a police jeep, with both his hands cuffed and tied up to a rod on the ceiling of the jeep. Four, well-built police officers were guarding him during the trip. On their way, the jeep met with an accident, on Pune-Aurangabad highway. All the four officers were injured, and they became 'unconscious'. Yunus grabbed the opportunity and escaped!

The question remained, as to how four well-built armed policemen got injured and all of them became unconscious, but a half-starving, thin, young boy could remain unhurt, and escape? All the while, his hands were cuffed and tied to a rod atop. To this day, the question still looms large, unanswered, even after two decades.

On the remand date, the distraught father, Saeed Khwaja Ayub was put in the witness box by the special judge and asked to say whatever he wanted to. He, however, broke down as soon as he started talking about his missing son. "Suddenly, one day, the police came home and picked up my son. My son weighs just 40- 45 kg, and is barely 4 ft. and 9 inches tall," he cried.

Appearing for the father, Saeed Khwaja Ayub in the special court, I told the court that my client suspects that his son is dead, and he might have died in custody. I then prayed to the court that there must be a judicial probe into the alleged escape of the suspect from police custody.

I argued that the whole police version of the incident seemed improbable. It was not possible that four policemen escorting Yunus became unconscious, whereas Yunus managed to escape. The prosecution strongly opposed my prayer and informed the court that a departmental enquiry is being conducted into the incident and the four policemen have been suspended. After hearing the prosecution, the special court, however agreed with me. The court observed, "Since the accused was in police custody, under orders passed by this court, the police had an obligation to produce him before the court, for the next remand."

The court further ordered that the four policemen accompanying Yunus at the time of his escape also be produced before the Court, on the next remand date. A probe was ordered to examine if Yunus had indeed escaped from police custody and if so, under what circumstances. I relied upon the press clippings to show alleged police lapses, as I could smell malicious intentions of the police, who might present a concocted story about his alleged escape. However, I made it clear that I was not making specific allegations against the police, though it was difficult to digest the police story. The prosecutor filed a report of the accident and said an enquiry was on and the police had alerted the CBI and Interpol, to apprehend Yunus.

On 22 January 2003, the special court ordered a preliminary judicial enquiry to discover the whereabouts of the absconding accused and to investigate the facts and circumstances leading to his alleged escape from custody. The court asked all the four police officers, who had escorted Yunus, as well as his father, Saeed Khwaja Ayub, to be present before the court on 27 January to record evidence in the judicial enquiry. It was a day of high drama in the special court. The court ordered a judicial enquiry with a view to bring out what were the real facts.

"If my son is guilty, let the court hang him. But let the police produce him at least in court. He is my only son. The police seized our bank accounts and my daughter's wedding had to be put on hold because of that," Ayub broke down in the court. The court also issued directions to the DCP of Aurangabad to furnish all information to the DCP, Crime Branch, Mumbai, regarding raids conducted by the police. In a raid on a software firm, called Pragma, in Aurangabad, police had recovered four computers, thirty compact discs, twenty floppy discs, three hard discs and two printers, etc.

As the judicial enquiry started, Saeed Khwaja Ayub stepped into the witness box and narrated everything about his son. His son, Yunus, had graduated in Instrumentation Engineering, from Parbhani, in the year 1997. But he did not get a job for nearly three years. Ayub, therefore, set up a Subscriber Trunk Dialling (STD) booth, in his name, in Parbhani, so his son could have some income. Police had alleged that the booth was used by the accused to communicate with each other. He further told the court that, in March 2001, Yunus got a job in Dubai and from there, he sent his family Rs.20,000/- every month. He was supposed to return to work on 15 January 2003 and had booked his return ticket for 13 January.

Ayub told the Court that on 25 December, police, from Parbhani and Mumbai, reached their house and told him that Yunus had met with an accident. They asked him to call Yunus on his mobile. He asked his daughter to call Yunus. His daughter then called Yunus. Yunus told them that he was returning home. When he returned, Karanje police arrested him, and the Mumbai police took him to Mumbai. Ayub emphasised, "... if Yunus had to run away, he would have done so when we called up and talked to him, on his mobile."

The police theory of all the four police officers fainting at the time of the vehicle accident and the escape of Yunus at that time, took a U turn, when one of the officers, who was escorting Yunus, was cross-examined in the judicial enquiry. He stated that he had jumped out of the Gypsy Jeep before it met with an accident and only one of the officers had fallen unconscious. Due to the accident, the rod to which Yunus' cuffs were attached, had come loose. After the accident, when they called out for Yunus, there was no answer, he said.

Answering the questions fielded by me on behalf of Saeed Khwaja Ayub, the officer said that the driver of the Gypsy lost control when a truck was approaching it, from the front side and another Tempo car was trying to overtake it. There was a milestone in front of a tree, and the vehicle rammed into it. It went down the slope and overturned. Answering my questions, the officer continued, "I did not find any object or instrument that Yunus could have used as a weapon. Moreover, the rod, to which Yunus' cuffs were attached, was neither cut nor broken."

In an answer to my question, the officer revealed that the police jeep did not have a wireless system attached to it and he did not have a walkie-talkie either. When I asked him about his mobile phone, he told me that he had forgotten his mobile at home and the other policemen too, did not carry any. "It did not strike me that a mobile phone would have been useful while we were going to Aurangabad," he added.

I further urged the court that apart from the policemen, three other accused in the case be allowed to depose before the court. My prayer was strongly opposed by the prosecution. I then told the court that the opposition of the prosecution reflected the fear of the police that the facts they were trying to conceal might come out in the open. I told the court that there was no reason for the prosecution to oppose my prayer for examination of the three co-accused, who were last seen with Yunus, before his trip to Ahmednagar, in the Gypsy.

My prayer for examination of the co-accused was granted by the Court, over-ruling the strong opposition of the prosecution. Thus, the co-accused, Dr. Mohammed Abdul Mateen, was in the witness box, on the next day of hearing of the judicial probe. When he stepped into the witness box, Dr. Mateen told the judge that just before the start of the proceedings, a crime branch constable had threatened him against tendering evidence. He said the policeman told him *"Chhootna hai ya pareshaan hokey phansna hai?"* (Do you want to get released or be harassed and get entrapped).

The prosecutor's prayer, to have the deposition made in camera was rejected by the court, outright. He was examined in a packed courtroom. Dr. Mateen's was an eyewitness account of the terrible happening in the lock-up that involved Yunus. He told the court that he had seen the police beating and kicking Yunus mercilessly, a day before the alleged escape from police custody. He further told the court that Yunus had vomited blood due to the beating he had received and so he could not have escaped, as the police claimed. Dr. Mateen, an MD in forensic medicine and toxicology and a former lecturer at the J.J. Medical College, Mumbai, said he had been picked up from his Aurangabad residence on 23 December, in connection with the Ghatkopar blast. He said, all through the police were beating him while escorting him to Mumbai. He further said that the police used belts and sticks to beat him and he was unable to eat or walk.

In response to my questions, Dr. Mateen said that on 6 January, another co-accused, Zaheer, Yunus, and he, had been taken to the Ghatkopar Crime Intelligence Unit, from Powai. Yunus was stripped to his underwear and had his hands tied behind his back. The officers repeatedly questioned Yunus about his role in the blast. When Yunus said that he had no role at all, the officers kicked him. At that point of time, Mateen saw Yunus vomiting blood. He was then taken to a room and beaten up. Alleging that they were severely beaten-up while in custody, Mateen claimed, "In the evening of 6 January, I was returned to Powai, but I don't know about Yunus." His entire deposition was marked with extensive allegations of physical torture.

Dr. Mateen claimed that on 6 January, while they were in Ghatkopar, the police asked him to sit in a passage, while Yunus was taken to a room. After some time, he heard Yunus shouting and the cries came from the room in which he was taken. Mateen further told the court that on 10 January, another Senior Inspector came to meet him and asked him whether he knew what happened to Yunus. When he said that he did not know anything, the officer told him that Yunus had escaped from custody. To a question put up by me, Mateen answered, "I do not believe that Yunus could have run away. He had many injuries and would not have been able to escape."

Speaking about the torture meted out to himself and the other co-accused, Mateen replied that between 27 December and 3 February, he was interrogated and beaten up daily. He also said that when he was brought from Aurangabad, the police beat him as if he was an animal. On being asked why he had not informed the court of this fact earlier, Mateen said that the police had threatened him. He said for the first time he saw the other accused, Yunus, Zaheer and Muzammil, when they were produced in court on 3 January. They were thereafter taken into custody by the Powai Crime Branch.

In his deposition before the judicial probe, co-accused Zaheer

Shaikh, too, stated that he heard screams from the room in which Yunus was taken for interrogation. Afterwards, policemen were heard saying that Yunus had vomited blood. As soon as he stepped into the witness box, Zaheer told the judge that he would speak out only if the court granted him and his family protection, since the police had threatened him not to depose. Like Mateen, Zaheer too, deposed before the court that he was violently thrashed by the police, during interrogation and was made to hang from the ceiling, with both his hands tied.

During cross examination by the prosecution, both Mateen and Zaheer denied that they had concocted their stories to malign the police.

After the deposition of the witnesses was over, the matter was kept for argument. Arguing my case, I pointed out to the court certain vital points in favour of accusation of custodial death. The police sought custody of the accused till 26 January but did not interrogate them after 6 January. Police custody was sought with a view to buying more time to hush up the matter. I further put before the Court that lock-up entries were fabricated. The entry on 3 January showed that the accused were in Ghatkopar lock-up from 3.30 to 5.30 pm. However, they could not have been in the lock-up as they were produced in court on that day for extension of remand.

It was alleged by the co-accused that Yunus was beaten up in the lock-up, on 6 January. However, in the lock-up records submitted by the police to the court, the entry for 6 January was missing.

Another twist in the ghastly saga came to the fore when an accused in a case under the Maharashtra Control of Organised Crime Act, Imran Mehdi, from Arthur Road jail, informed me that Mateen and Zaheer had been threatened in jail and they were fearing that they would be killed in custody. According to Mehdi, the jail authorities would fudge records and fake circumstances, to make it appear that the two were killed in a botched escape bid. He also said that the Crime Branch officers had asked authorities to tie a handkerchief on the duo's necks to distinguish them as terrorists.

When I put forth these probabilities to the court, the Judge said that the government's credibility was at stake. He further added that Yunus' disappearance is shrouded in mystery. The judge directed the Chief Secretary of State to conduct a detailed enquiry and submit the report to the court.

I re-affirmed my stand before the judge, "Yunus' disappearance is nothing but a custodial death, a death that the police are now trying to disguise as a fabricated escape bid."

The prosecution had defended the police version and said that Yunus must have been helped by God. They argued that the two co-accused had concocted their allegations about police brutality.

"Fifty-one days have passed. The State is duty bound to produce Yunus, dead or alive. Since Yunus was in police custody, by orders passed by this court, the police had an obligation to produce him before this court," the judge observed, after hearing both the prosecution and the defence.

Concluding a month-long judicial enquiry into the disappearance of Khwaja Yunus, the court passed an order, directing the State to pay compensation of Rs.5,000/- every month to the family of Khwaja Yunus, till he was traced. The court added that if it was discovered that Yunus had escaped on his own, the family would have to reimburse the State.

"The family of Yunus and the general public are entitled to know his whereabouts," the court observed stating that it was the State's duty to ensure that the accused in police custody would not do a 'vanishing trick'. The court added that the State must not leave any stone unturned, to trace the accused. The court further observed that a high-level enquiry be undertaken, to check whether the rules and regulations and standing orders have been followed or not.

The court also commented that if an accused is booked under any serious acts, like POTA or MCOCA, like in this particular case, the police should have taken extra care, while moving him from one city to another. The investigating officer must travel with the accused, more security must be provided, and proper means of communication should also be provided.

Observing that the right to life was most fundamental and no one could be deprived of it, except by law, the court said that the father of Yunus could file an appropriate writ in the High Court. The manner of disappearance of Yunus could be considered as a human rights violation.

For me, it was a victory of truth. I then decided to move a habeas corpus petition, asking the State to produce Yunus, dead or alive.

No amount of legal wrangling could help the family of Yunus. Even after the passage of two long decades the question still looms large. Where is Khwaja Yunus? Dead? Alive?

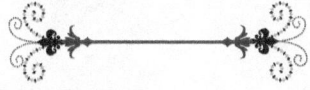

Wednesday • March 9, 2005 • Mid Day, Mumbai

In your face!

State CID shows Yunus's pictures to arrested cops to get them to confess

Vinod Kumar Menon
vinodm@mid-day.com

THE state Criminal Investigation Department (CID) probing the alleged death of Ghatkopar blast accused Sayyed Khwaja Yunus made yet another unsuccessful attempt to get the arrested crime branch officials to confess yesterday.

Yesterday afternoon, the arrested officials were grilled for four hours at the state CID office, Konkan Bhavan, Navi Mumbai, by four officers of the rank of deputy superintendent of police, who had come from Pune for the purpose. Throughout the questioning, the CID officials pointed to a photograph of Yunus and kept questioning the arrested officers, but it 'surprisingly' did not have the expected results.

The state CID, however, refuses to give up. Confirming that photographs of Yunus were shown to the officers, Sudesh Padvi, superintendent of police, state CID, said they would also be pasting Yunus's photographs on the walls of the detection room. The purpose? The arrested officers may just 'feel' like opening up on seeing the dead man's photo.

Conceding that it wouldn't be easy to get them to confess, Padvi said, "The arrested officials are not hardcore criminals or terrorists, but are officers with good credentials. They have done some great detection work and are well-versed with detection procedures. So it will not be easy to make them confess. We are now looking at other methods of questioning."

Ridiculing the CID's attempts to get the accused to confess, advocate Majeed Memon appearing for the blast accused, said, "How can you expect a person in custody to speak the truth against the policemen in whose custody he himself is? It is, however, heartening to find that the state CID has, albeit belatedly, admitted that the escape story was concocted and that Yunus died in custody."

Senior crime branch officers and encounter specialists have already condemned the arrest of Praful Bhosale and his three men. Public prosecutor Rohini Salian shared the same opinion. She pointed out that in Abdul Mateen's inquiry recorded before the court on oath on February 18, 2003, he stated that four police officers had assaulted Yunus, but did not name anyone. "Interestingly, two years later, he recollects the names of every police officer. This needs to be cross-examined during the trial," Salian asserted.

Meanwhile, the state CID will be producing the arrested officials before the metropolitan magistrate court, Vikhroli, this afternoon.

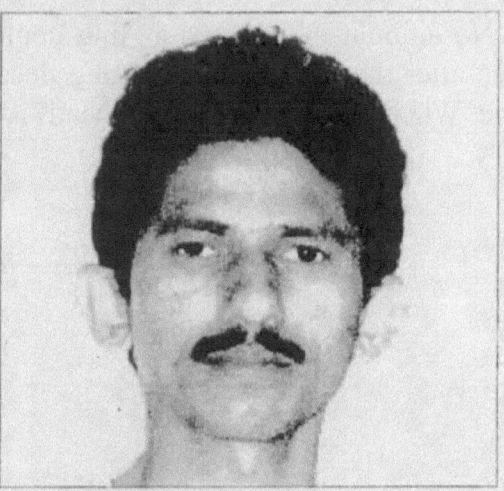

Khwaja Yunus's photographs will also be put up on the walls of the detection room to make the arrested officers 'feel' like opening up on seeing the dead man's photo

" THOSE ARRESTED ARE OFFICERS WITH GOOD CREDENTIALS. THEY ARE WELL VERSED WITH DETECTION PROCEDURES. SO IT WILL NOT BE EASY TO MAKE THEM CONFESS. WE ARE NOW LOOKING AT OTHER METHODS OF QUESTIONING

— *Sudesh Padvi, superintendent of police, state CID*

FOUR POLICE OFFICIALS SENT TO CUSTODY

By OUR CORRESPONDENT

Mumbai, March 6: The special holiday metropolitan magistrate court, Bhoiwada has remanded four crime branch officials including senior inspector of Ghatkopar unit-VII to police custody till March 9, in connection with the alleged custodial death of Khwaja Yunus, an accused in the Ghatkopar bomb blast case.

The state crime investigation department or CID, on Saturday, arrested senior inspector Praful Bhosale, assistant inspector Hemant Desai, assistant inspector Rajaram Vanmane and sub-inspector Ashok Khot under Section 301 and 201 of the Indian Penal Code, for murder and causing disappearance of evidence, respectively. Bhosale has over 70 encounters to his credit.

The city police commissioner A.N. Roy said, "The arrested officers will be suspended from the police department following their arrest by the state CID."

The state CID, in their remand-sheet application, mentioned that Yunus did not flee from police custody but he was instead killed there.

The state CID urged that they need the custody of the four officers, to find out the involvement of other officers and the whereabouts of Yunus' body, which is untraceable so far. Yunus was allegedly beaten to death at the Ghatkopar crime intelligence unit office where Bhosale was the senior inspector.

However, the counsel for all four officers, Vaibhav Bobade alleged that the arrest of the officers is unconstitutional and violation of the state government's notification.

The notification clearly mentions that before arresting a serving officer the investigation agencies have to take permission from the state government and concerned superior of the department.

Mr Bobade said that the state CID only informed the police control room about the arrest.

They were not granted permission from the competent authority to do so.

The metropolitan magistrate P.D. Jadhav quashed the plea and granted the police custody.

Meanwhile the court has granted permission for home food for the arrested officers and permission to meet their advocate in the custody.

The state CID has also questioned assistant police commissioner Ambadas Pote and senior inspector Arun Borude in the same matter but they have not been arrested.

The CID is probing the custodial death of Yunus after the Bombay high court directed it to treat the statement of another blast accused Abdul Mateen as a first information report.

Mateen in his statement alleged that Yunus was badly beaten up in custody by crime branch officials in which he named assistant police inspector Sachin Vaze and other police officials.

Vaze was arrested and released on bail after 57 days.

The police version was that Yunus managed to escape from police custody after the jeep carrying him along with a police party to Parbhani, overturned at Parner in Ahmednagar district on January 7, 2003.

OUTRAGE OVER KHWAJA YUNUS CASE

Mahesh Bhatt, director and producer

'I think it is high time for civil society to wake up and express its outrage strongly. I ask the chief minister of Maharashtra to recognise the urgency of the situation and give a compensation of Rs 1 crore to Yunus' mother. It is under the Congress-Nationalist Congress Party government of chief minister Vilasrao Deshmukh and the then deputy chief minister Chhagan Bhujbal that Yunus disappeared.'

'It is not just a case of custodial death, it is a case of destroying evidence and misleading the court. In the case of Yunus, not only a young qualified engineer from the Muslim community was brutally tortured and done to death, but his body was destroyed by burning the same as it appears at this juncture.'

Majeed Memon, Khwaja Yunus' defence lawyer

THE ASIAN AGE MUMBAI 7 MARCH 2005 15

The Times of India, Mumbai
** Monday, March 7, 2005 5

Yunus' mother wants Rs 1Cr

Mumbai: Khwaja Yunus's mother has demanded a compensation of Rs 1 crore from the state government, defence lawyer Majeed Memon said in a statement on Sunday.

Yunus was a 27-year-old engineering graduate when he was accused of being involved in the Ghatkopar blast. He is alleged to have died in police custody in January 2003.

Memon said the Yunus case establishes that more than one policeman from the crime branch related false accounts under oath of the accused escaping from custody. "The state should spare no effort to ensure that the erring cops are punished adequately," he added.

In a Lighter Vein

A good-looking young lady was on the witness stand before a very sharp and intelligent judge of the Sessions Court, in Mumbai. She was so conscious about her looks that, off and on, she opened her bag and looked into the small mirror that she had in the bag. Her body language suggested that she was extremely concerned about her looks.

The judge also took note of this fact. During the proceedings, as part of the procedure, the Judge asked the lady, "What is your age, madam?" She smiled but evaded the answer. The judge repeated the question. This time again, she did not answer. In a bid to conceal her age, she started looking here and there. This annoyed the judge. The judge then raised his voice and reprimanded the lady in the witness box, saying, "Answer the question I have asked you, without loss of any further time, because time is running against you."

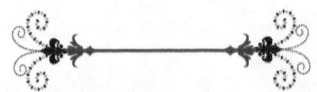

Ten

THE MURKY RAPE OF A SWEDISH NATIONAL

The morning papers of the third week of February 2003 used to be abuzz with the news of the rape of a Swedish National. 29-year-old Marina Britto (name changed) was a friend of 17-year-old Hamid Shaikh (name changed), who lived in Bandra, Mumbai. Hamid was alleged to have raped Marina on 15 February, in her room in Bandra, where she lived as a paying guest.

Hamid Shaikh was arrested in the rape case on 26 February and was produced before the Juvenile Court on the next day. His family came to me and requested that I must appear for him in court for his bail.

As Hamid was produced before the court to my shock and surprise, Marina came forth and told me that she had no complaint against Hamid, and that he should be released on bail forthwith. In an affidavit filed by her in the court, she had denied all the charges levelled against Hamid.

In the affidavit she not only confirmed her friendship with Hamid, but also maintained that he visited her with her consent. She further stated in her affidavit that Firoz Sama, her former boyfriend and the one who accompanied her when she filed her complaint on 16 February, had pressurised and threatened her to lodge the complaint against Hamid.

Marina told me that Rizwan, son of an alleged gold smuggler had accompanied Firoz Sama when the complaint was lodged at Khar police station. She also alleged that Firoz had good connections with the police and that is how the rape case was registered.

After Hamid was released on bail, Marina started staying with Hamid's family. Marina was aggrieved on various counts. She told me that she had been through a lot and was not in the right frame of mind because of the series of tragic events. Her reason for living in Hamid Shaikh's house was that Firoz Sama had threatened her and she could not live alone.

Surprisingly, Hamid's family seemed supportive of her and was willing to give testimony about her relationship with him. Marina was a regular visitor to my office, hoping in great anxiety, that the case against Hamid would be dismissed at the earliest. She told me that there was no rape at all. Firoz Sama was behind the whole matter, something that she learnt only later. She said she knew Firoz since 1999 when she first visited Mumbai and was "very friendly with him till recently."

She said that she had lodged the original complaint of rape against Hamid Shaikh under pressure from him, but changed her mind when she saw Hamid, her friend, being beaten up and harassed by the police, based on her complaint. She thus decided to withdraw her complaint but was not allowed to do so by Firoz who threatened her with dire consequences if she did any such thing. She subsequently approached the police, to register a complaint against Firoz. However, much against the version of Marina, the version of the police was that her complaint of rape was registered after due verification and after repeatedly questioning the complainant.

In a fresh twist to her story, she reportedly stated to the press that she was going to sue the police for what she called their misconduct and misdemeanor. "They did not even want to write my complaint. They were misbehaving with me," she told the press.

Marina was planning to sue the police on various counts. Firstly, the police recorded her statement in Marathi. Secondly, they did not give her a copy of her statement. Thirdly, she was made to wait at the police station for 15 long hours. Fourthly, they took her to a hospital, where a male doctor examined her. "I would never allow a male doctor to examine me," she fumed.

After the charge sheet was filed by the police, before the Juvenile Court, Marina said in the court "I will now sue the police for subjecting me to emotional and mental rape." She told the court that she would withdraw her complaint. In fact, Marina was aghast after witnessing the inhuman treatment meted out to the teenager. She pleaded with the police to release him since she had no complaint against him. "He is innocent" she said.

Marina submitted an affidavit in court, in which she said, "I am friendly with one Hamid Shaikh of Bandra. On 15 February 2002, early in the morning Hamid visited me and we spent time with each other, with my consent. He used to visit me frequently and I enjoyed his company." She further stated that she had severed her relationship with Firoz Sama since she discovered that Firoz was married, and his parents did not approve of her. In the affidavit, she further stated that Hamid Shaikh was brought to the police station and was brutally beaten up. Her protests fell on deaf ears, and she was shoved into a police van and was taken to Nagpada hospital, for a medical examination. In the hospital, there was no female doctor. Against her wish, she was asked to sign a paper and a male doctor asked her to undress for examination. She felt humiliated.

"I hate India, its people and the police," the Swedish woman declared, in front of the media. The media and the police were now in jitters, since by retracting her original rape allegations, she now accused the police of inhuman and near barbaric treatment. She claimed that the torture inflicted upon her seemed to have disturbed her mentally. Before an impromptu media briefing, she vowed to sue the police for the "grave injustice". She further said, "I will not leave the country until I am given justice."

She wanted the police to return her passport to her. The seizure of her passport had grounded her movement completely, ever since the FIR was lodged.

I advised Marina to move the State Human Rights Commission, against the alleged ill treatment meted out to her, a foreign national, a guest of the country. I felt that the matter ought to be investigated properly else it would bring disrepute to the entire country. Unless justice was done to her, it would set a bad precedent and scare foreign nationals away from visiting India.

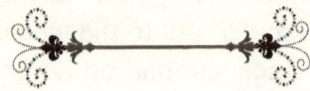

In a Lighter Vein

In an old matter before a Sessions Court Judge, an advocate defending the accused, pleaded for an adjournment. It was a High Court expedited matter; the Judge was not inclined to adjourn the case due to pressure from the appellate higher court. However, the court, reluctantly, agreed for a short adjournment.

The court fixed the next date of the hearing for 16 February of that year. The defence counsel protested and pleaded that 16 February may not be given, for personal reasons. Upon this, the court curiously asked the counsel what his personal difficulty was.

The counsel then hesitantly said "Sir please give me any other date after 16 February, as that is the day when I am getting married." The judge smiled and said, "All the more reason, I must fix the actual hearing on that day to compel your presence before me. If possible, I must also order the presence of the priest performing your marriage in my court, to save you from life imprisonment."

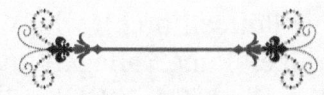

Eleven

CRUSADER ANNA HAZARE V/S ABDUL KARIM TELGI

The beginning of the decade of 2000 was pulsating with the infamous stamp paper scam that swept over the city of Mumbai. Abdul Karim Telgi, the kingpin behind the scam, had swindled more than Rs.21,000 crores, by transacting in bogus stamp papers. He had tactfully influenced high officials in the State Home Department and the Police Department, to look the other way, by liberally paying them off. High ranking officials in both the Departments turned out to be on his payroll.

The scam was unearthed in Pune, when the local police found fake stamp papers in a car. The seizure was only the tip of the iceberg; later, more raids and seizures followed, in Bhiwandi and Mumbai, and gradually through the length and breadth of the country. The case turned controversial after Mr Shamsuddin Mushrif, Deputy Inspector General (State Reserve Police Force), who was, then, the Additional Commissioner of Police, Pune, alleged that some junior officers were demanding bribes from Telgi. Following these allegations, the Government appointed a Special Investigation Team, headed by Shri Subodh Jaiswal.

Maharashtra-based renowned social worker, Anna Hazare, an anti-corruption activist, was not going to let this matter slip through. He came over to my office and discussed in detail the stamp paper scam; we decided to approach the High Court through a writ petition praying for a probe into the scam.

Under his banner, I prepared a writ petition, praying for a judicial review of the Special Investigation Team's (SIT) report, pertaining to the scam.

The petition followed the clean chit given by the State Government to the police officials, indicted by the Jaiswal Committee report that probed the alleged anomalies in the earlier investigation into the multi-crore scam. My main contention in the writ petition was that, though the SIT's report was endorsed by the Additional Director General, Shri G.P. Bali, it was subsequently rejected by the State Government. Shri G.P. Bali had supported the Jaiswal report and had come down heavily on the "shoddy investigation".

The Bali report had also taken to task Mr. R. S. Sharma, the then City Commissioner, Pune, for the delay in charging Telgi and other accused under the stringent Maharashtra Control of Organised Crime Act. Mr. Sharma had come under fire on several counts. The telephone calls intercepted by the Karnataka police between accused Telgi and Assistant Commissioner of Police (ACP), Mulani, mentioned the payment of Rs.15 lakhs as a bribe for dropping the names of some of the accused. The act on the part of the Government, of giving a clean chit to the officers indicted by the Jaiswal Committee report, had raised question marks over the functioning of the police.

The prayers in the writ petition invoked that the SIT's report should be examined by the court and that the respondents, that included the State of Maharashtra, Deputy Chief Minister Chhagan Bhujbal and 11 others, should be dealt with a heavy hand. The petition further prayed that the guilty should be punished adequately, under the Indian Penal Code and the Prevention of Corruption Act. It also prayed for making public the Jaiswal-Bali reports, that indicted police officers, including Commissioner R.S. Sharma.

Taking a dig at the laxity on the part of the State Government to act against police officers, including R. S. Sharma, later promoted as Commissioner, Mumbai city, Hazare mounted a scathing attack on Chhagan Bhujbal. He claimed that no action was taken against the ACP, who was alleged to have taken a bribe of Rs. 15 lakhs from Abdul Karim Telgi. The petition stated that if law-keepers become lawbreakers, society would be doomed. It further said that the stamp paper scam had the potential to derail the country's economy.

The Public Interest Litigation (PIL) urged that all records of the investigation, including the recorded telephone conversation between prime accused Abdul Karim Telgi and ACP Mulani, which was in possession of the Karnataka police, be produced in court. The petition was filed against several respondents, including Chhagan Bhujbal, the Additional Chief Secretary, Government of Maharashtra, Ashok Basak, Police Commissioner R. S. Sharma, ACP Mulani, Director General of Police (DGP), Subhash Malhotra, the Additional Police Commissioner, S.M Mushrif and other investigating officers.

During the hearing of the PIL, the Advocate General made a statement before the court that the State wanted to probe the culpability of all those involved in the scam, including high ranking police officers. The court was further informed that the State would also investigate cases where a charge sheet has already been filed and act against defaulting officers. It was obvious that, but for the court's intervention and monitoring, the State would not have taken any action in actively pursuing the probe. I prayed to the court that it continued monitoring the scam probe. The Advocate General agreed with me and said that investigation reports would be submitted to the court.

I further prayed to the court that the State needed to take stern action against senior police officers responsible for lapses in the probe, to ensure that the police stopped conniving with gangsters. I submitted before the court that any acts of omission or commission, by senior police officers in this case, could be tantamount to abetment of underworld activities under the Maharashtra Control of Organized Crime Act. On this, the Advocate General submitted that the State was willing to appoint an Additional Director General of Police to supervise the investigation under the SIT. However, the court was reluctant since the appointee and the police Commissioner would be of equivalent ranks. The Advocate General then suggested the names of former Chief Secretaries, D.M. Sukhtankar and B.G. Deshmukh to supervise the probe.

On 3 September 2003, during hearing of the PIL, the Advocate

General made the revolutionary revelation to the court that action had been taken against 27 cops in the scam. Reportedly, it was the first time that action was taken against so many police officers in a single case. Two senior officers viz., Assistant Commissioner M.C. Mulani and Inspector P. R. Deshmukh were already suspended for their alleged complicity in the case. The PIL had urged for application of stringent provisions of Maharashtra Control of Organised Crime Act against police officers accused of inept investigation in various fake stamp paper scam cases, from 1995.

Opposing an appeal for a Central Bureau of Investigation (CBI) enquiry, the Advocate General proposed a series of measures in investigating the case. He said, "The SIT should be headed by an Additional Director General of Police. Both Deputy Inspector General of Police S.B. Jaiswal and Additional Commissioner Sanjay Barve, should be part of the team. The terms of reference for the SIT should be expanded to look into all cases against Telgi, and 35 other cases of fake stamp papers. The SIT would investigate the culpability of any police officer, however high his rank be," said the Advocate General.

A report by Sanjay Barve, Additional Commissioner of Police, Economic Offences Wing, filed in the High Court, said that, as against 15 cases of fake stamp papers estimated earlier, there were 51 cases, dating back to as early as 1991. Barve's report also brought to light how Telgi and others exploited loopholes in the system to forge and sell fake stamp papers to the tune of over Rs.21,000/- crores. Shri Barve further asked the State government to enquire into some public and private sector institutions including, Ashok Leyland and Telco Dealers Leasing and Finance Company Ltd, which might have dealt with Telgi in purchasing or selling of stamp papers.

I questioned why Barve's report does not mention the role of R.S. Sharma. S.B. Jaiswal had highlighted the allegedly slow investigation into Sharma's role. "All the while, the State Government and police tried to protect the accused police officers. It was only when the court pulled their ears, they started digging the gravel and discovering the mess," I submitted before the court. The fact was that Barve was appointed to conduct the investigation by Sharma himself. Action was instituted against lower-level officers, while top officers had been let off. I, therefore, prayed to the court that all officers, including Sharma, who were under a cloud of suspicion, should be transferred to lesser important positions, so that they may not influence the investigation.

There was no system of branding or cancelling used stamps. Also, there was no control mechanism for granting licenses to vendors, thus providing unscrupulous vendors with an opportunity to indulge in the sale of unauthorised adhesive stamps. Receipts, issued by Central Stamp Office, for the sale of stamps were without proper security features. Furthermore, stamps printed by the Indian Security Press, at Nashik, don't carry markings of the State, nor do they carry batch numbers.

After hearing both the sides, on 4 September 2003, the court appointed Shri S.S.Puri, retired Director General of the Anti-Corruption Bureau, to supervise the Special Investigation Team. The Division Bench directed Puri to look into the alleged lapses on the part of the police, in the investigation. He was asked to submit a status report on the probe in four weeks. Puri emerged as the consensus candidate to head the SIT, after a string of names were suggested and shot down by both sides, including that of former police Commissioner, Julio Ribeiro.

On 16 October 2003, the court directed S.S.Puri to probe the culpability, if any, of Mumbai Police Commissioner R.S.Sharma, in the scam, as Mr. R.S.Sharma was retiring on November 30th. Mr. Sharma was indicted for dereliction of duty, while he was Police Commissioner of Pune, during the initial investigation against Telgi in the scam.

Additional Police Commissioner S.M.Mushrif had made certain allegations against Mr. Sharma and others, which were probed by Mr. Jaiswal. Mr. Mushrif alleged that Sr. Police Officers, including Mr. Sharma, and Telgi's wife and daughter, were named as 'wanted' accused, initially, but their names were later dropped. He had also alleged that certain evidence was suppressed and misused.

In his report Mr. Jaiswal, had blamed Mr. Sharma and other senior police officers for mishandling the case and asked the State Government to take appropriate action against them. However, in the

State's Action Taken Report, Chhagan Bhujbal gave Mr. Sharma a clean chit.

When I put forth a prayer to the court that, as Mr. Sharma was retiring the following month, the allegations raised by Mushrif against Sharma be probed soon, the division bench directed Mr. Puri to submit the report on Mr. Sharma by November 12. He was also directed to submit his report, on the culpability of other high ranking Police Officers and public servants, on that day.

The bench further directed the Karnataka government's special investigation agency to furnish the transcripts of the alleged telephone conversation between the main accused, Telgi and ACP M.C Mulani. Mr. Mulani had allegedly spoken to Telgi while he was lodged in Karnataka prison. The conversation had revealed that Telgi had paid a bribe of Rs.15 lakhs to Mulani to prevent the arrest of his wife and daughter, in relation to the scam. The Advocate General made a statement before the court that the SIT headed by Mr. Puri, had made breakthroughs into the scam probe and that the statements of 184 persons had been recorded so far, to trace the culpability of those involved in the scam.

In his affidavit, filed before the court in October 2003, Shri S.M Mushrif, who was the additional commissioner of Police, Pune had come out with patent flaws on the part of R.S. Sharma, in the Telgi case. Excerpts from the affidavit:

"On 13 June 2002, R.S.Sharma, the then Commissioner of Police, Pune, verbally directed S.M.Mushrif to supervise the investigation. S. M. Mushrif then suggested that it being a very important case, an investigation team, on the lines of Special Task Force of the Karnataka police, headed by a senior officer, be formed. But Sharma dismissed this suggestion, saying that the investigation would, for all practical purposes, be carried out under his own guidance. Mushrif then directed Inspector Prakash Deshmukh to arrest the wife and daughter of Telgi. Prakash Deshmukh informed Mushrif that the officers had returned from Mumbai without arresting the two women, as the women could not be traced. Mushrif suspected Deshmukh and as time passed, he again reminded Deshmukh to arrest the women. But Deshmukh curtly replied, "What have they got to do with this case? There is no evidence against them and, though Telgi's Indica car is in his daughter's name, she is a minor and hence there is no question of arresting her." On Deshmukh's reply, R.S.Sharma told Mushrif that the price for evading the arrest of the wife of a multimillionaire accused could be very high. He, therefore, asked Mushrif to investigate the matter Then, there was the turnaround. After about three days, Mushrif called on the CP and informed him that he could not get any concrete information so far about the search of the flat. On this, R.S.Sharma told Mushrif that there was no point in making further enquiries, as they did not have any definite information and that if they continued probing, the officers would think that their seniors had no faith in them, which in turn, would result in their morale going down. Mushrif was surprised at this statement of the CP but could not react.

On 21 July 2002, head constable Lele informed Mushrif that all the computer records seized at various places had been given to her team, for decoding P. I. Deshmukh had also given her some CD's, floppies, and other computer records, without disclosing their source. When Mushrif asked him where he got the additional computer records from, he could not give a satisfactory answer. He, therefore, suspected that the computer records had been decoded by some private agency, and only the unimportant ones were handed over to the team. Mushrif then gave Deshmukh a memo and sent a copy to the CP, with the hope that he would pull up Deshmukh. But, on the contrary, the CP advised Mushrif not to issue such memos in writing and to withdraw the one which was given to Deshmukh."

The rise of Mulani was sudden and unexpected. As Telgi was in the custody of Bangalore police at that point in time, and efforts were being made to get him into the custody of the Pune police, CP. R.S. Sharma visited Bangalore twice. Each time, he took ACP Mulani with him. Though Mushrif was the supervisory officer of the case, the CP did not ask him to accompany him even once.

From the first week of August 2002, CP. R.S.Sharma started holding separate meetings with ACP Mulani and PI Deshmukh. Mushrif realised that CP himself was guiding the investigation, and that certain important facts of the investigation were being concealed from him.

When he learnt that ACP Mulani was involved in a corruption case, under the Prevention of Corruption Act, while he was a PI in Mumbai, a few years ago, Mushrif informed the CP about this fact and suggested that he should not be associated with this case. But the CP did not agree with him.

On 26 August 2002, Deshmukh reported to Mushrif that Shirin Manzil, where Telgi's wife and daughter were staying, had been searched on 24 August and some fake stamps, stamp papers and computer records had been seized. In fact, the information about the flat was obtained about two and a half months earlier and it had been searched at that time. Mushrif found this suspicious. On 28 August, he sent a letter to the Director General of Police, stating that he was going on leave, as he did not want to be associated with the case anymore, for reasons mentioned in the letter. On this, the CP called him on the phone and convinced him that henceforth, he would not give any direction to the investigating officers, without his knowledge.

From 9 September to 14 September 2002, Mushrif went to his office, but nobody updated him about the details of the case. Before he went on leave on 15 September on account of his daughter's marriage, he called the CP and brought to his notice a letter received on 3 September 2002 from the Director General of Police against Mulani. This letter contained serious allegations of corruption and connection with criminals. But the CP observed, "We should not give any importance to such allegations."

On 3 November 2003, the court directed the Karnataka Government to handover the Telgi tapes by 10 November to the Government of Maharashtra. The Karnataka Government had made every conceivable excuse, from lack of adequate infrastructure and manpower to protecting the privacy of Telgi with a view to prevent the Telgi tapes from being handed over to the Maharashtra Government. The State's procrastination led even the court to comment, "The more reluctant you are to hand over the tapes, the stronger is the suspicion that you are trying to hide something."

The 56 tapes of recorded telephonic conversations between Telgi and 52 other persons ran into 100 hours. The counsel for the Karnataka

Government said that his government was not able to hand over the transcript in English. The reason he cited was that the conversation was in Kannada, Hindi, Marathi, Telugu, Urdu and English. It would take over 350 days to translate and transcribe, since it takes three to five days to transcribe one hour of conversation. The counsel for the Karnataka Government pleaded that some of the conversations had taken place between Telgi and his relatives. Putting such tapes into the public domain would encroach on Telgi's privacy and, therefore, they would submit only relevant portions of the transcripts. The court, however, turned down this plea of the Counsel.

I pleaded before the court that the Karnataka government was trying to shield some powerful persons, including ministers, top politicians, and police officers. The Government had not complied with the orders for over two months, spanning six hearings on the matter. The plea for another extension and the suggestion about producing selected recordings on the tapes before the court, I submitted, gave rise to suspicion that the Government is trying to shield powerful persons involved in the scam. They were perhaps scared that their government would fall, due to the disclosures. I further pointed out to the court that the taped conversations were about a year old and questioned Karnataka's silence on the dates. "We are afraid that unless the tapes are produced immediately, they would even be tampered with," I pleaded.

The Advocate General of Maharashtra submitted that Karnataka had enough time to comply with the court's orders and hence the tapes must be handed over to the SIT to bring about transparency in the probe. As directed earlier by the Division Bench, S.S.Puri's report 'Involvement of R.S.Sharma' was filed in the court on 12 November 2003. The report suggested that the Commissioner was not able to convince the Special Investigation Team of his innocence in the scam. Sharma was grilled by the SIT over two days, during which he was asked more than 300 questions; the SIT was apparently not satisfied with his replies.

Amidst high drama in the Court, Sharma's Counsel V. R. Manohar, raised the issue that the SIT had leaked the information about his interrogation to the press. Holding up a copy of Mid-Day, a Mumbai-based tabloid newspaper, I submitted that the newspaper report showed that it was Sharma himself who had leaked the information to the press and not the SIT. The contents of the report were not disclosed or discussed in the open court on that day, as it contained the names of some of the people who SIT wanted to interrogate to ascertain Sharma's culpability in the case. The allegations against R.S.Sharma, which led to S.S.Puri's enquiry against him, were varying in nature.

On 3 September 2002, the Home Secretary of Karnataka informed the Home Secretary of Maharashtra that Mulani spoke to Telgi on telephone and demanded huge sums from him. The Karnataka police had recorded the conversation and, as a result, Mulani was ordered to be transferred from Pune to Sangli (a small town), with immediate effect. Mulani challenged the transfer order before the Maharashtra Administrative Tribunal (MAT). On 6 September 2002, a team was formed to investigate the stamp paper scam. Sharma included Mulani in the team investigating the scam.

On 18 September 2002, Sharma sent Mulani alone to Bangalore, to expedite Telgi's transfer from Karnataka police custody to Pune police. This was even though Sharma was informed of the communication received from Karnataka Government, regarding Mulani's corruption.

The Government had decided to felicitate some of the officers for the investigation in the scam. Though Mulani's name was not on the list, Sharma recommended his name, adding it in handwriting.

Telgi's wife, daughter and brothers were shown as accused. But they were not arrested. On 31 October, Additional Home Secretary, Ashok Basak, had called for a meeting. Among others, Sharma and P.I. Deshmukh attended the meeting. At the meeting, P.I.Deshmukh took out a document to justify the inclusion of Telgi's kin in the charge sheet. To a question whether that document was mentioned in the panchnama (a practice of recording the statements of those who might be aware of the crime, often at the scene of the crime, or verifying evidence) and the case diary, Deshmukh replied in the negative. However, Sharma defended him, saying that it was inadvertently left out.

Application of Maharashtra Control of Organised Crime Act

against the accused was deliberately delayed by Sharma. Sharma's counsel, Shri V.R.Manohar, vehemently argued in the court, to prove his client's innocence. Shri Manohar argued that before 18 October 2002, Sharma was not aware of Mulani's tainted character. He further submitted that the SIT leaked information of Sharma's interrogation to the press with a view to maligning the Commissioner. Above all, Shri Manohar's argument was on the assumption that Puri's report was based on the report of Jaiswal and that Jaiswal was biased against Sharma.

Countering the arguments of V.R.Manohar, I submitted to the court that there were instances on record, which suggested that Sharma was aware of Mulani's malpractice, even before 4 September.

The State Advocate General, too, countered the arguments of V.R.Manohar, by submitting that Mr. Puri has not included a single statement from Jaiswal's report. He submitted that Puri had interrogated Sharma and had gone into every aspect before preparing the report. With this, the fate of Sharma was almost sealed.

I then pointed out to the court that the city police chief was actively involved in corrupt practices and there was enough material against him. I further brought to the notice of the division bench that incidentally, the police chief was due to attain superannuation (retirement) in the month of November 2003, and the ambit of law must reach him before that.

R.S.Sharma was Commissioner of Police, Pune, before he was appointed Commissioner of Police, Mumbai, on 1 January 2003. Allegedly, he was so posted upon supersession of a few other officers. A disciplinary proceeding was initiated against him, on this count. However, without taking any further action against him on this issue, he was allowed to superannuate on 30 November 2003, on humanitarian grounds.

Immediately after his superannuation, Shri Sharma was summoned by SIT officials, for questioning. Interrogation of Shri Sharma for few hours by the officials drove the investigating agency to arrest him on the very next day, after his superannuation. When he was arrested on 1 December 2003, there was lot of noise and buzz, because, in the history of Mumbai, a Commissioner of Police, sitting or retired, was never ever arrested in any criminal case.

On the grounds of his alleged involvement in the stamp paper scam, after his arrest on 1 December 2003, he was produced before the concerned court, in Pune, on 2 December 2003, in remand. He was charged for offences under sections 3(2) read with section 24 of the Maharashtra Control of Organised Crime Act, (MCOCA.) The police sought his custody in remand for 15 days. However, he was remanded to police custody till 9 December 2003 and thereafter, to judicial custody. His application for bail was rejected by the Special Court, Pune, by an order dated 19 January 2004, whereupon he filed an application for grant of bail, before the High Court, where too it was rejected.

As a result, Shri Sharma was forced to approach the Supreme Court for bail. Ultimately, he was granted bail by the Hon'ble Supreme Court on 4 January 2005. By then, he had been in incarceration for more than a year.

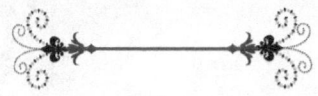

Social activist Anna Hazare and his counsel Adv Majeed Memon share a light conversation after coming out of the Mumbai High Court on Thursday. Anil Bhartiya

संपादकीय — 16 नवंबर 2003

'तेलगी स्टैंप महाघोटाले को लेकर जनहित याचिका दायर करनेवाले समाजसेवी डा. अन्ना हजारे मुंबई हाईकोर्ट के बाहर अपने वकील मजीद मेमन के साथ.

AFTERNOON THURSDAY 16TH OCTOBER 2003

HC QUESTIONS SHARMA'S ROLE IN STAMPS SCAM

SIT asked to submit report on Mumbai Police Commissioner before he retires next month

BY A STAFF REPORTER

In a significant development, the Mumbai High Court yesterday asked the Special Investigation Team (SIT) to submit its report on the involvement of Police Commissioner R. S. Sharma in the multi-crore fake stamp paper scam.

Chief Justice C. K. Thakkar asked former director general of police, Mr. S. S. Puri, who is currently heading the probe, to file the report by November 12, to make the court aware of the allegations levelled by former additional commissioner, Mr. S. M. Musharif, against Mr. Sharma when he was Police Commissioner of Pune.

Lawyer Majid Memon, who is representing the bunch of Public Interest Litigations (PILs) filed by anti-corruption crusader Anna Hazare on the alleged lopsided investigation, told the court that it was necessary for the SIT to file its report on Mr. Sharma's alleged involvement before he retires. Mr. Sharma is retiring on November 30.

To this the court agreed and asked the SIT chief to wind up the subjective investigation by November 12. Mr. Memon also recalled an earlier order of the High Court to Mr. Puri to submit the status report on the probe on September 4.

Mr. Sharma was in New Delhi yesterday where he is attending a conference of the police chiefs all over the country and was unavailable for comment. ■

MIDDAY THURSDAY 13TH NOVEMBER 2003

Court all but seals Sharma's fate

S S PURI's report "Involvement of R S Sharma" implies that Police Commissioner R S Sharma was not able to convince the Special Investigation Team (SIT) of his innocence in the multi-crore fake stamp paper scam.

Sharma had been grilled by the SIT over two days during which he was asked 300 questions, some of which were published by Mid Day (November 10). But the SIT was apparently not satisfied with his replies to some of the allegations against him.

In court yesterday, one of the points V R Manohar, who argued for Sharma, raised was that the SIT had leaked information about Sharma's interrogation to the press. But, holding up a copy of Mid Day, Majeed Memon, said that newspaper reports showed that it was Sharma and not SIT who had leaked the information.

Though the contents of the classified report presented in court yesterday were not disclosed, some remarks during the hearings made it clear that the Mumbai CP is fishing in troubled waters.

One of the reasons why the report was not made public is that it contains the names of some persons whom SIT wants to investigate in order to further ascertain Sharma's criminal culpability in the case.

The court will decide on November 27 whether to reveal some portion of the report. However, the CM will have to take

VIJAY D'COSTA

Advocate Majeed Memon displaying a copy of Mid Day, November 10, during a court hearing yesterday

2002.
● On September 6, 2002, a team was formed to investigate the scam and Sharma was its head. Meanwhile, Mulami had challenged his transfer before MAT. Sharma included him in the team investigating the scam.

recommended his name in handwriting;
● Telgi's wife, daughter and brother were shown as accused in the case, but they were not arrested. The then additional commissioner, S M Mushrif of Pune, had complained to additional home

R S Sharma" is the report on the alleged involvement of Sharma in the multi-crore fake stamp paper case. The report is classified, however, the state advocate general said that it details nine instances of alleged acts of commission and omission by Sharma in the scam

The Mid Day front-page story on November 10 that had details of Sharma's interrogation by the SIT. Advocate Majeed Memon demanded to know how the press got access to the confidential report

SIT wants to grill eight police officers

PURI in his report has informed the high court that SIT wants to interrogate eight police officer in connection with this scam. Sources indicated that it involves some top names. Puri has also informed the court that it will

speaks to the noted social activist about his relentless crusade against corruption

'The CM has to take action now'

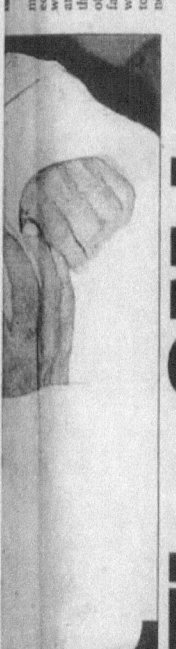

Anna Hazare with his lawyer Majid Memon at High Court yesterday.

Are you happy with the progress in the stamp paper investigation?
I am satisfied with the way things have turned up till now. The Special Investigation Team (SIT) has done a commendable job and its members have worked with responsibility and integrity in conducting the investigation.

Now that the court has directed the investigation team to submit its fact finding to the chief minister, do you think he will take appropriate action against police commissioner Ranjit Sharma if the report indicts him?
I don't see there is any escape for the CM. He has to take action if Mr. Sharma's involvement is established. At least to uphold the law and expectations of the people. Moreover, if he fails to act, we can always fall back on the court to seek justice.

You approached the court because you did not have faith in the government. How did you feel when court sent the SIT report for CM's deliberation?
The table has turned this time. However, the court will ensure that action is taken.

What made you file this petition?
The basic reason was to rid corruption preva-

lent in the society today.
Certainly yes. The scam was exposed much before and had the government conduced an enquiry soon afterwards, this mess would not have happened. When allegations and counter allegations were made against the police officials involved in the investigation of the scam, the government sat tight and failed to look into the matter. There were enough grounds for the government to act against the errant officers, which it never did.

You follow the Gandhian philosophy that held morality above all. Do you see a gross degeneration of values in the bureaucracy these days?
Yes, values like morality, ethics are fast becoming a thing of the past. They are on the wane. It can be gauged from the fact that even after these officers find themselves implicated on repeated occasions, they have the gumption to claim innocence. It is a dangerous trend and the security of the society is being threatened. Something should be done to put a stop to this.

The CM had said that he could not take action against Deputy Chief Minister Chaggan Bhujbal due to the compulsions of a 'coalition government'. Your comment...
Then why is there a government in the first place? If the CM says that he is bound by compulsions, then what right does he have to run the government?

What will be your next move?
As of now, my hands are bound as I have limited resources. A sustained fight against corruption also requires money. And at present I am penniless. I sleep in a temple in a village. It is my sympathisers and supporters, including lawyers, who have pitched in their assistance to further my cause. ■

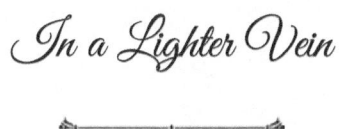

In a Lighter Vein

Whenever fresh judges are appointed in the High Court, there are always discussions at the Bar, regarding the new entrants in the judiciary. Sometimes, serving judicial officers in the lower courts are promoted to the High Court, and at other times, members from the Bar are directly elevated to the High Court Bench. On one such occasion, some members of the Bar were elevated to the Bench, resulting in the usual discussions and comments by members of the Bar.

Some senior members of the Bar were talking about one such elevated member of the Bar, 'Mr. X'. One of the senior members opined, "Mr. X, has a roaring practice. By accepting the position of a judge, he will be a big loser." Another member commented, "Mr. X' does not seem to be a man of impeccable integrity."

On this, MM rose to say, "In my considered opinion, 'Mr. X' is the second best person for this position."

This created a flutter in the group. MM was asked to elaborate, who, then, in his view, would be his choice as the 'first best person'? Pat came the answer, "Anybody Else!"

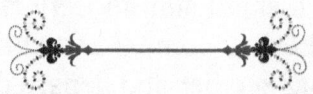

Twelve

THE HORRIFIC END OF AN INFANT AND HIS GRANNY

18 November 2003 was a fine day, as regular as ever, for the household of Mrs. Leticia Mendez, a, 54-year-old God-fearing housewife, living in her flat at Lopez Manor, I. C. Colony, Borivali, Mumbai. The other members in the household were her only daughter, Glenda and her one-year-old son Dylan. Leticia was a large-hearted housewife, who was ever ready to share her knowledge in cookery with anyone who approached her with a small fee. She was especially interested in teaching the preparation of chocolates to any interested person.

On 18 November 2003, five college going boys approached Leticia, with a request to teach them to make chocolates. Leticia readily agreed. They registered their names in the students' register that she maintained. They were 1) Ashish Waravale, 20 years 2) Clint Fernandez, 19 years 3) Karan Khanna, 17 years, 4) Clinton Fernandez, 16 years and 5) Wilfred D'Souza, 19 years. All of them were students, from Elphinstone College and St. Andrews College, Mumbai. They paid a small sum to Leticia, as advance payment of fees. Leticia asked them to come the next day and start learning the process. The boys thanked her and departed.

The next day, 19 November 2003, the boys reached the house of Leticia, at the appointed time. She was ready with her recipé. The boys rang the doorbell. As soon as Leticia answered the doorbell, to her horror, the boys turned into assailants. All of them pounced upon her with bare hands and closed her mouth. Two of them went to the kitchen and brought the knives that were available there. They then assaulted Leticia cruelly with the knives till she breathed her last.

Hearing the cries of Leticia, her 27-year-old daughter, Glenda, whose husband was working abroad, came running to the door. It was then Glenda's turn. The boys pounced upon the young woman and stabbed her too, till they thought she was dead; her body was thrown under a cot.

That was when chubby, cute, one-year-old little Dylan crawled into the room where the massacre was going on. The sight of the angelic little child did not evoke any sympathy in the five devil incarnates. On the contrary, they mercilessly caught hold of him and strangulated him to death, with a telephone cord. They hung his little body on the ceiling fan with the help of the same telephone cord. Then, they switched on the fan. All five of them burst into loud laughter at the sight of the infant's body rotating above their heads. They were enjoying their murderous spree.

Next, it was time for them to loot. One by one they removed the gold ornaments from the bodies of the women. They then did a search of the cupboard that was in the bedroom and collected more jewelry and Rs.74,000/- in cash. They felt delighted; it was enough for them to celebrate the birthday of one of them, Karan Khanna who was turning 18 after two days. For them this booty was enough for the time being and so they left the house.

Sometime after they had left, Glenda regained consciousness. Drenched in blood, she slowly pieced together what had happened a little while before. Unable to bear the ghastly sight of her darling son's body oscillating on a ceiling fan and her mother's lifeless body lying on the floor, she screamed at the top of her voice and hearing her screams, some of the neighbors came running. On seeing the ransacked house, the neighbors understood what had happened in the house. They immediately informed the local police. The police then swung into action. Glenda was removed to the hospital, along with the other bodies. Later, her First Information Report was recorded for offences of robbery, murder, and attempt to murder, etc. The sensational double murder had sent shock waves among the city dwellers, especially the Catholic community and the parishioners in Borivali.

All the accused were arrested within a couple of days, by the names and description given to the police by Glenda. In an identification parade held later by the police she identified all the assailants. Two of the assailants, Karan Khanna, and Clinton Fernandez were minors. Others were produced in the Metropolitan Magistrates Court, at Borivali, from time to time, till the charge sheet was ready. The minors were produced before the Juvenile Court. After the investigation was over, police filed the charge sheet in the Metropolitan Magistrate's Court at Borivali and the Court committed the case to the Court of Sessions, for trial.

It was then that the parents of Ashish Waravale and Clint Fernandez approached me, with a request to defend their sons. By looking at the enormity of the cruelty involved in the offence committed by the youngsters, I could not assure them that their sons would be spared by the court, even if I were to try out all the legal means at my disposal. However, they persisted in my accepting their brief and so I relented.

In the trial, there were a couple of other advocates too to lend me a helping hand. I appeared for Ashish and Clint. Wilfred D'Souza had a separate advocate. Throughout my legal career, which spanned more than 25 years till then, I had not come across such a mindless, multiple murder, as the one that was on hand. I had to take extreme caution to see that the accused at least escaped capital punishment. The case was famous and known as 'Borivali Double Murder Case'.

The prosecution case was that all the accused were considering various possibilities, ways and means to acquire adequate sum for a lavish celebration of their dear friend's 18th birthday. That was the time Wilfred D'Souza suggested the name of Leticia Mendez in the locality. He assured them that there were no adult male members in the family and that household was the most vulnerable, for their intended robbery. Wilfred D'Souza was personally known to Mrs. Leticia Mendez as he was her neighbour. He, therefore, chose not to be present at the time of their act. His suggestion was acceptable to all his friends, and they decided to go ahead with the plan. They, thus, hatched a conspiracy to rob and loot Leticia Mendez at her house. It was in this context that they visited her house on 18 November 2003, under the guise of learning chocolate- making. Blissfully unaware of the boys' evil motives, Leticia welcomed them to her house.

Glenda was the star witness in the case. She was the badly wounded victim and the author of the First Information Report too. She identified the accused in the court and recounted the happenings on the ill-fated day verbatim. The trial court had no reason to disbelieve her. I tried my level best to create a cloud of doubt in the mind of the Court. With this in view, my cross examination of Glenda continued for many days. I realised that I had a difficult task on hand and was well-prepared for any eventuality. The other main witness was a cousin of one of the accused, a teenager studying at National College. He testified to overhearing the conspiracy being hatched by Wilfred D'Souza.

One by one, the prosecutor examined his witnesses, and they were cross examined by the defence advocates till the trial came to an end, in the court. All the witnesses had supported the prosecution, much to the satisfaction of the prosecutor and to the discomfort of the defence. During the trial, it was found that my clients Ashish Waravale and Clint Fernandez, along with the minors, were the actual murderers and Wilfred D'Souza was only a conspirator. He was not even present at the scene of offence, as he was appearing for an exam in the college at the relevant time. But he was the brain behind the conspiracy. I did not leave any stone unturned in my effort to save my clients.

Then came the day for recording of the statements of the accused, under Section 313, of the Criminal Procedure Code. All the accused vehemently denied the charges against them and pleaded innocence.

On the day of judgment, the presiding judge took his seat at sharp 11 a.m. in the court, in all preparation to deliver the judgment and pronounce the operative order. I was keen to hear the verdict too. The judge read out the operative order thus:

"Accused No.1, Ashish Waravale, and accused No. 2 Clint Fernandez will be hanged by neck, till dead. Accused No. 3, Wilfred D'Souza will undergo five years' rigorous imprisonment and will pay a fine of Rs.5000/-.

The parents of the accused, present in the court, were numbed. However, the reaction of the accused was a chuckle. They could laugh even at that point in time, having no sense of any remorse for the ruthless act they had committed. Together they laughed as they did after committing the horrendous crime.

When I told the judge that in my legal career spanning around 25 years then, this was the first case to sustain a death sentence the judge said that it was the first case for him too, to award a death sentence. He further told me that he would have spared capital punishment to the accused, had they been a little less cruel to the innocent child, at least.

After the copy of the judgment was ready, the parents of the accused came to me again, with a request to prefer an appeal against the verdict of the trial judge. I agreed to do so, and an appeal was prepared and filed in the High Court.

On 9 August 2006 the appeal against conviction came up for hearing before the Division Bench of the Bombay High Court. Citing various judgments in favour of the convicts, I argued for setting aside the death sentence awarded to them by the trial judge and for commuting it to life sentence. I conveyed to the court that while awarding the extreme sentence, the court must take into consideration not just the crime, but the criminals too. In the appeal before the court, both the convicts were first time offenders and had a clean record, till they committed the offence in question. They were young boys, appellant Ashish Waravale being of 20 years and Clint Fernandez being of 19 years. They can be reformed in future, as they have a long span of life ahead of them. Their young age suggests that there is scope to reform them. Also, they had not gone to the house of the victims with a premeditated motive to murder anyone. Both the appellants came from respectable, middle-class families.

I further argued that the death sentence was not warranted, as both the convicts were not hard-core criminals. I pointed out to the court that even the prosecution case was that of a conspiracy, only to rob the household. Further, it was pertinent to note that none of the accused carried any weapon. This was so as they had no premeditation to commit murder. The only weapon which they used was obtained from the kitchen of the victims. I further argued that the two juveniles were the actual participants in the offence, who played a crucial role in the murder.

My next point of argument was that since they were five in number, jointly committing the crime at the same time, it was difficult to say who delivered the fatal blow. To sustain a death sentence, the prosecution must categorically prove by whose blow the victims died and, in the present case, this vital aspect is missing, I submitted.

As against my arguments for commutation of death sentence to life imprisonment, the public prosecutor urged the court to confirm the double death sentence, saying that the brutal murders committed by the appellants have no parallel and would qualify for the definition of 'rarest of rare'. The prosecutor submitted that the prosecution had mainly relied upon the evidence of the prime witness, Glenda who identified the accused and recounted the incident without flaws. He further argued for enhancement of Wilfred D"Souza's sentence to life imprisonment.

After hearing both sides, the Division Bench noted several points against the appellants.

"The appellants conspired together to rob Leticia Mendez as they knew that she had cash and jewelry in her house.

On 18 November 2003, they went to her house on the pretext of learning how to make chocolates. On the next day, they attacked Leticia Mendez with a knife. They then attacked the prime witness, Glenda, with an intention to kill, so that there wouldn't be any witness. Glenda survived the attack.

They also killed her one-year-old son, by strangulating him with a telephone cord and hung him from the ceiling fan, without any remorse, in the most barbaric manner.

They made off with Rs.74,000/- cash and jewelry, most of which was recovered at the instance of the appellants. The appellants indulged in extreme brutality. Their act was diabolic, cruel, and gruesome.

The fact that they come from middle class respectable and educated families, and have no criminal antecedents, is not at all a mitigating circumstance.

There was no remorse or repentance on the part of the appellants, at any point in time. Their age alone does not give them any right to clemency, or sympathy, from the Court."

Thus ruled the Hon'ble High Court.

My appeal for clemency on account of the young age of the appellants was thus not considered by the Court, due to the enormity of the cruelty involved in their acts. The appeal thus stood dismissed. However, the Court granted eight weeks' time to enable the appellants to move the Supreme Court.

Years rolled by and Justice Mr. S.A.Bobde, before whom I argued the appeal, was elevated to the Supreme Court of India. After a couple of years, he became the Chief Justice of the Apex Court. He was elevated as the 47th CJI, in November 2019. I was elected as a Member of Parliament (Rajya Sabha, Upper House) in the year 2014, from Maharashtra. Since he belonged to the State of Maharashtra and rose from Bombay High Court, I felt it appropriate to greet and congratulate him on assuming the highest judicial office of the country.

Thus, while I was in New Delhi, attending to my Parliamentary duties, I sought an appointment with the CJI, through his secretary, with the help of my Personal Assistant. I was given time during the lunch recess in the chamber of his Lordship, on a working day of the Supreme Court. I reached his chamber, accompanied by a couple of my junior advocates. As a custom, I carried a bouquet and a shawl for the CJI. I waited in the waiting room for a few minutes. Some more people were also waiting to meet the CJI. In no time, we were allowed to enter the chamber. I thought that since the lunch interval was brief, the CJI would only spare a couple of minutes for the formal greetings.

However, to my surprise, he received me very warmly. When I offered the bouquet and the shawl to him, he rose from his chair. He came closer to me and started talking animatedly. He reminded me that I had argued before him in an appeal against death sentence of some youngsters for dual murder, including the merciless killing of an infant child, by strangulation with a telephone cord.

That was the point of time when I was pleasantly surprised to recollect that the CJI was referring to this very same case, while I did not distinctly remember that I had argued the appeal before him, when he was a judge at the Bombay High Court. He then showered lavish praises on me, recalling how brilliantly I had addressed the court in such a difficult case. I was humbled to hear it, but greatly surprised to find that his memory was so sharp. He spent a good fifteen minutes talking about the case, unconcerned about the paucity of time. I could only thank him for the compliments and wish him good luck for his tenure as CJI.

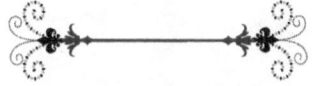

In a Lighter Vein

A senior advocate was arguing a matter before a High Court Judge in a dramatic manner, throwing his hands up into the air and shaking his body. It was an animated display of histrionic talents. The court patiently watched and listened to him for some time. Finally, the court lost its cool and in a fit of anger, the judge asked the advocate, "…why are you acting in this manner?" Promptly, the advocate replied, "My Lord may please look at my *vakalatnama* (the document showing that he has been appointed by a party as his advocate) and read the contents carefully. It expressly says that I have been appointed 'to act, appear and plead'. Acting is part of my brief, and I am thus sincerely discharging my duty to my client, my Lord"! The judge could only chuckle.

Thirteen

THE CONTROVERSIAL IPS OFFICER AND THE COURT-ROOM DRAMA

Additional Commissioner of Police, Shri A.K.Jain was the first Indian Police Service (IPS) Officer to be arrested in Maharashtra. The controversial officer was accused of accepting a bribe of Rs.2.10 lakh, through his Chartered Accountant, P.C Lodha, from Inspector Sanjiv Kokil, of the Byculla Police Station. The Anti-Corruption Bureau trapped and subsequently arrested Lodha, for accepting the bribe from Kokil, on behalf of Jain, on 26 May 2000. The bribe was allegedly paid to stop suspension of Kokil, for non-closure of Sairaj Bar, in Byculla, after the stipulated hours, on 21 May 2000.

As he learnt about his imminent arrest in the last week of June 2000, Shri A.K.Jain met me in my office, with a request to obtain anticipatory bail for him. My office staff got into action on an emergency basis to draft and prepare the petition.

On Wednesday, 28 June 2000, I moved the Hon'ble High Court, for bail, in anticipation of arrest of Shri Jain before his Lordship, Justice Vishnu Sahai. Despite my detailed argument about the merits of the case of Jain, the court was not inclined to give relief to the applicant, primarily, as he was a high-ranking police officer. My main argument was that there was no need for custodial interrogation of the applicant as there was no chance of his absconding or there was any likelihood of his non-co-operation with the investigating officers. I submitted before the court that a conspiracy was hatched against Jain by his seniors. I argued that he had always made himself available for interrogation and, in view of that fact, custodial interrogation was not warranted. I further submitted before the court that custodial interrogation would destroy the applicant's 18 years of unblemished service in the police force.

As against my submissions, the State prosecutor submitted that the applicant's 18 years of 'unblemished' service included an enquiry he was facing from the year 1994, for having assets disproportionate to his known sources of income. She told the court that Jain had five houses in various parts of the country and when he was promoted as Additional Commissioner, his office was furnished by Karishma Restaurant and Bar. I objected to this submission of the prosecutor as the case in court had no concern with such things. On this, the prosecutor made further submissions on the conduct of the applicant. She said that Jain was dodging the police since he was made an accused in the case on 3 June 2000. He went on leave and gave his office certain numbers, saying that he would be in Pune. But he could not be contacted on those numbers. However, when his calls to his home in Mumbai were traced, they were found to be from Delhi and Uttar Pradesh.

Following a day long argument for and against the bail of the applicant, Justice Sahai was not inclined to grant any relief to Jain. In his order, the Judge said, "Anticipatory bail is granted in exceptional circumstances and this court bears in mind the gravity of the offence, the nature of the offence and the position which the person is occupying. The circumstance that the applicant is an Additional Commissioner of Police does not go in his favour. On the contrary, it goes against him. People like him are supposed to lead from the front to set examples for others. It will send a wrong signal to everyone if he is granted anticipatory bail."

On a plea made by me, on behalf of Jain, that he be permitted to surrender on the next day, before the Anti-Corruption Bureau, the judge said, "Same treatment should be given to Jain as any common man would get from the police and courts." However, the judge asked the State Prosecutor to ensure that Jain is treated with dignity.

As soon as the order was passed, strangely enough, Jain was led by the investigating officer, Madhukar Kohe, out of the court premises through the judges' entrance and was arrested.

On 29 June 2000, Jain was produced before the Metropolitan Magistrate's Court, on remand. I appeared for the accused before the Magistrate at the Esplanade Court and vehemently argued on the merits of his case, for bail. I submitted that Jain was a victim of vendetta. On this, the court asked me to reveal the identity of Jain's adversary. I had to, therefore, reveal the name of the former Bombay City Police Commissioner, Mr. R. H. Mendonca, who was then heading the ACB. I informed the court that Mr. Mendonca was against Jain's appointment as Additional Commissioner of Police (Central Mumbai) in February that year. I told the Court that there was a letter in which Mr. Mendonca expressed his displeasure over Jain's appointment.

I further vehemently submitted before the Court that Inspector Kokil was aware that Jain had no powers to suspend officers of his rank and that such powers were vested only with the Commissioner. Hence, there was no question of Jain demanding any bribe from him. I submitted that since Jain had already acted against Kokil on 22 May, there was no question of demanding a bribe from him to stop his suspension on the next day.

As against my submission for bail of the accused, the State prosecutor, Mr. Shrikant Bhatt, argued vehemently that custody of the accused was necessary since he had made serious attempts to destroy some pieces of evidence against him. He further alleged that Jain had conspired with certain officials from the cellular (mobile) phone company, Orange, to destroy the recording of his conversation with Lodha on 26 May.

The prosecutor submitted that according to the post trap panchnama, Lodha called up Jain on his mobile on 26 May to confirm that Kokil had given him two lakh Rupees and that he would pay the remaining amount within a week's time. The ACB was interrogating a few officials from Orange and the possibility of their arrest for conspiring with Jain could not be ruled out. He further argued that Jain had tampered with documents in his office on 29 May. "There is evidence to suggest that he had asked for a matchbox from a peon to burn the paper from the report carrying his remarks on Kokil," argued the prosecutor.

After a day-long argument, by both the prosecution and the defence, the bail application of Jain was rejected by the court, as the court felt that custodial interrogation of Jain was necessary, in the circumstances mentioned by the prosecutor. He was later remanded to police custody for a couple of days more.

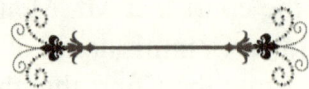

Nav Shakti 29/6/2000 मुंबई, गुरुवार, दिनांक २९ जू

निलंबित अतिरिक्त पोलिस आयुक्त ए. के. जैन यांचा बुधवारी मुंबई उच्च न्यायालयाने जामीन अर्ज फेटाळल्यानंतर त्यांना लाचलुचपतविरोधी खात्याच्या अधिकाऱ्यांनी अटक केली. तत्पूर्वी जैन यांचे घेतलेले छायाचित्र. (छाया : संजित सेन)

In a Lighter Vein

The court hall in the High Court, Mumbai, was packed with litigants and advocates. The listed cases for the day were being called out one by one. When one such matter was called out, the litigant was not present and hence the counsel's name was called out. Soon, a young female advocate emerged from the crowd and prayed to the Court to keep the matter back as the counsel was likely to enter the courtroom very soon. The judge asked the female advocate where the counsel was. The female advocate answered, "My Lord, he is undressing." The court was aghast! What the confused junior advocate was trying to say was that the counsel was putting on his gown and dressing up in the corridor in preparation to enter the courtroom. What a major slip of the tongue!

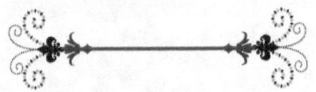

Fourteen

SUNIL DUTT V/S SANJAY NIRUPAM

On 24 June 2005, *Shiv Sena* M.P. (Rajya Sabha) Sanjay Nirupam, got the taste of being arrested, when he was taken into custody by a Metropolitan Magistrate's Court before being freed on executing a personal bond of Rs. 5,000/-. Nirupam's arrest was in response to a defamation case filed by the then Union Sports Minister and popular actor, Sunil Dutt. Both politicians were arch rivals as the two had fought a Lok Sabha election from the Mumbai North-West constituency. Dutt won the seat for Congress and Nirupam lost it on a *Shiv Sena* ticket. Soon after his release on bail Nirupam applied for exemption from future appearance. As the advocate for Sunil Dutt, the court asked me to file my say in the matter. The case was then adjourned to 23 August 2005.

On 10 May 2004, Dutt filed a complaint against Nirupam, before the Metropolitan Magistrate's Court, at Bandra, Mumbai, for making false allegations against him during the Lok Sabha poll campaign, in 2004. Nirupam had alleged that Dutt attended Parliament only on three occasions during his five-year term as a Parliamentarian in the erstwhile Parliament. Dutt said in the complaint that the claim of Nirupam was false, and he had made this false statement in public, knowing fully well that he was making an irresponsible statement. To substantiate his contention that Nirupam's statement was false and irresponsible, Dutt produced a certificate from the Lok Sabha Secretary to show that he had attended Parliament on 99 occasions during his five-year term and not on three occasions only as contended by Nirupam.

During the pendency of the proceedings, Nirupam joined the Congress party leaving the *Shiv Sena*. Though the Congress High Command approved Nirupam's entry into the party, the septuagenarian Parliamentarian Dutt was not ready to accept him. In a letter addressed to me, Dutt requested me to continue representing him in court, when the case came up for hearing on 23 August, as he was not able to be present personally; Dutt demanded a public apology from Nirupam for the irresponsible defamatory statement made against him.

After joining Congress, Nirupam wanted to meet Dutt personally and sort out the differences between them. However, before this could happen Dutt passed away. Thereafter, Nirupam sent feelers to the family of Dutt. His daughters, Priya, and Namrata, did not relent, saying that their father had said that he would not compromise under any circumstances. The sisters filed a petition in the court praying that they be made complainants in place of their deceased father. While their petition was pending, I managed to work on a mutual settlement between the parties as Mr. Dutt was no more. My efforts proved fruitful, and the case came to an amicable end.

Sunil Dutt sues Sanjay Nirupam for defamation

Cong leader defends Parliamentary attendance record

EXPRESS NEWS SERVICE
MAY 10

VETERAN actor and Congress candidate from Mumbai's North-West Parliamentary constituency, Sunil Dutt, filed a defamation suit against rival Shiv Sena MP, Sanjay Nirupam on Monday, for making allegations about Dutt's attendance record in Parliament.

At the Bandra Metropolitan Magistrate's Court this afternoon, Dutt attacked Nirupam's claim, made during the election campaign, that Dutt had attended Parliament only three times in the last five years.

Dutt, accompanied by his lawyer Majeed Memon, said he had proof of attending Parliament 99 times, despite being injured in two serious accidents.

Nirupam's statement was highly defamatory and had misled voters, he said.

The magistrate deferred the hearing to Friday and issued a notice to Nirupam.

Outside court, Dutt told reporters that he had earlier asked Nirupam to modify his statement, but he had refused to do so. "Nirupam's charges have hurt and angered all the Congress workers of this constituency," said Congress General Secretary of Mumbai North-West, Krishna Hegde on Monday: "The allegations have damaged the image and stature of Dutt *saab*."

Sunil Dutt(right) with his lawyer Majeed Memon leaving Bandra Metropolitan Magistrate's Court on Monday

In a Lighter Vein

A bull was reportedly stolen from Victoria Garden shelter home in Mumbai. A complaint of theft was lodged against unknown persons at the local police station having jurisdiction. It so happened that the bull in question had, in fact, escaped from the custody of the zoo and was randomly wandering in the adjoining area. A small-time animal trader happened to see the bull unattended near his residence. He found the bull to be apparently exhausted and hungry. He, therefore, brought the bull to the open space, just outside his house and tied it to a pole there. He fed the animal, took care of it, and kept it there for a few days.

Sometime later, some cops searching for the bull landed at the place of the trader. When they found the bull, they immediately arrested the trader for theft of the animal. The police then took both the bull and trader to the police station. The trader was charged with theft of the bull and was released on formal bail.

A few months later, the trader was charged with the offence of theft, and he was made to face a criminal trial in the Metropolitan Magistrate's Court. At that stage, the trader approached MM, with a request to defend him in the case. Before the trial could commence, on every date of hearing the poor bull, which became the *muddhemal* (stolen property), was being brought before the Court in an extremely cruel manner. It used to be tied to a tree in the Court compound from 11 a.m. till 4 p.m. when the case would be adjourned. After a couple of such dates, MM observed that the poor animal was physically pulled and dragged from the Government-run animal shelter home to the court on foot, covering about three kilometers. Under the hot sun, it used to be tied for 5-6 hours, without food or water which conduct, by itself, would invoke the provisions of Prevention of Cruelty Towards

Animals Act. Having observed this on several occasions, MM told his client that if the case is adjourned three or four more times, he would succeed in his case without having to put in any effort. On each date the Magistrate would have a huge backlog of cases and this bull theft case would be adjourned to the next date.

As anticipated, on the fifth or sixth such occasion, the bull was not seen in the compound; it was reportedly dead. On learning of this development, MM conveniently pointed out to the court that the *"muddhemal"* (stolen property) in the case did not exist and, therefore, the case against his client would not proceed. Helplessly, the Magistrate ordered the acquittal of his client.

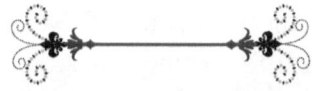

Fifteen

SAHIL ZAROO AND THE SHAHTOOSH SHAWLS

Sahil Zaroo was a co-accused in the Rahul Mahajan drug case in New Delhi. He was also wanted in Mumbai, in a case involving the sale of Shahtoosh shawls, which is illegal, under the Wildlife Protection Act. The Marine Drive police had registered a case against Zaroo, in Mumbai. He was brought to Mumbai, after a Delhi Court granted him a three-day transit remand, in June 2006

The case went back to March 2006 when the wildlife officials raided Essa Brothers, Sahil's uncle's shop, at Hilton Towers, Nariman Point, Mumbai after receiving a tip off that Shahtoosh shawls were being sold there. Under the Wildlife Protection Act, Shahtoosh deer is an endangered species and cannot be poached. During a raid on the shop, on 13 March 2006, three shawls were found on the premises. While forest officials questioned one person, Mohammed in the shop, another person, Ilyas Khan, snatched the bag containing the shawls and passed it on to Sahil Zaroo who was standing outside and ran away with the shawls. The Marine Drive police subsequently registered a case of theft, conspiracy and deterring a public servant from doing his duty, against Sahil Zaroo and Mohammed Ilyas Khan. Zaroo was the last person in possession of the shawls. The Wildlife Officials then registered a separate case against him, under the Wildlife Protection Act. The Wildlife Warden and the Assistant Conservator of Forests (Wildlife), Thane was the complainant in the case against Sahil.

As Sahil was later arrested in Delhi and brought to Mumbai, he was produced in the Metropolitan Magistrate's Court at Esplanade. I appeared for him seeking his bail. I submitted that the police have been unable to trace the shawls. My contention was that Sahil was falsely implicated in the case as the shop belonged to his uncle. He was a student and had nothing to do with his uncle's business. I submitted that he was ready to cooperate with the police in the investigation.

On this, the prosecutor took strong objection and submitted that the shawls could not be recovered, and that the accused needed to be further interrogated in the matter. He further submitted that on 13 March, the Regional Deputy Director, Wildlife Preservation Department, Meeta Banerji, following a tip off, raided the Zaroo family's handicraft shop at Hilton Towers, Nariman Point. Three Shahtoosh shawls, valued at around Rs. 2 lakhs were found on the premises. The owner of the shop, Mohammed Rafiq Ahmed, Sahil's uncle, was questioned. While Mohammed was being questioned, Ilyas Aziz Khan, an employee, entered the shop and snatched the plastic bag containing the shawls. He then passed it on to Sahil Zaroo, who was standing outside the shop. Zaroo fled the scene. Banerji then contacted the control room and the Marine Drive police arrested Khan and Mohammed immediately.

I appealed to the court that the accused had nothing to do with the shop or the sale and purchase of items there. Sahil was a student from St. Xavier's college, Mumbai. I further pointed out to the court that business rivals had tipped off the Wildlife Officer, with wrong information. As the officers who raided the shop were not in uniform, Mohammed was suspicious of them. I submitted that Sahil was not present in the shop when the shop was being raided. I further pleaded that since his uncle and an employee of the shop were already out on bail, there was no need for custody of Sahil, as he was not concerned with the business in the shop.

On my submission, the prosecutor further contended that the police had to investigate Sahil's links in smuggling Shahtoosh shawls. While hearing the prosecution and the defence, the Magistrate enquired with the police whether Sahil was wanted in any other case in the city or in the capital. In response, the police informed the court that the accused had no other case pending, other than the Rahul Mahajan drug case. After hearing both the prosecution and the defence at length, the court was pleased to order the bail of Sahil for a sum of Rs.25,000/-, with one surety in like amount. In the order, the court mentioned that as the co-accused had been released on bail, there was no reason to detain Sahil in police custody. The order stipulated a condition that Sahil would attend the Marine Drive police station, once a week.

After an exhaustive court hearing before a Magistrate and obtaining bail, the events in the courtroom took a sudden turn, when the forest officials came forward and arrested him and took him to another court, where they sought his further custody, in the case registered by them, under the Wildlife Protection Act. I opposed their action tooth and nail.

The Wildlife Warden and the Assistant Conservator of Forests (Wildlife) of Thane was the complainant against Sahil and he was personally present in the court. His contention was that three Shahtoosh shawls worth about Rupees two lakhs were to be recovered from Sahil and hence his custody was necessary. As against this, I submitted that Sahil was already arrested by the Marine Drive police for the same offence and hence he could not be remanded to police custody twice. I was at a loss to understand as to how the police could register two FIRs using the same set of facts. No person can be prosecuted twice for the same offence, according to the Indian Constitution.

The prosecutor countered my argument by submitting that the two cases were different since the Marine Drive police had only invoked the sections from the Indian Penal Code and not from the Wildlife Protection Act.

In response to the prosecutor's submission, I further brought to the notice of the court that the arrest and custody in the second case was without any legal sanctity and, therefore, the arrest itself was unconstitutional. It violated the rights of the accused against double jeopardy. I submitted that the two cases against Sahil were registered on the same day and the incident involved was the same. Charges under the Wildlife Act could be added to the first case by the police, later. I drew the attention of the court to the fact that the second case against Sahil was illegal and seeking his custody again is a violation of the Constitutional rights of the accused. My next contention was that both the complaints were incidentally filed by the Forest Officers.

After hearing both sides, the court passed a verdict ordering release of Sahil immediately on a personal bond of Rs.10,000/-. A condition was imposed in the bail order that Sahil must attend the office of the Wildlife authorities, as and when required.

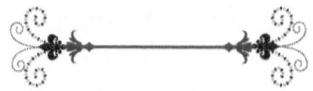

In a Lighter Vein

A Punjabi ex-army man, who ran a small business in Mumbai, had a grievance against Bombay Telephones and he approached MM for justice. His case was that he had his office unit in Veena Beena Shopping Centre, in Bandra (West), Mumbai, where two of his employees worked. His office used to function from 10 a.m. to 6 p.m., six days a week. There was a telephone line with Subscriber Trunk Dialing (STD) facility. The telephone instrument provided had a rotary dialing system.

The gentleman was apprehensive of misuse of his phone. So, he had requested the telephone department to discontinue the STD facility. His phone thus was used only for local calls. That was the pre-mobile era. The gentleman's monthly bill on an average used to be around Rs.500-700/- which he was paying regularly.

His current grievance was that he had received a grossly inflated bill showing a liability of Rs.72,000/-, for the previous month. He was shocked and surprised at such an exorbitant bill. His reasoning was that if one uninterruptedly continued to dial and make calls, the bill for the month would not reach such a high figure. Any misuse of his telephone by the office staff was also ruled out. It was with this history that he approached MM.

MM advised him that a representation should be made to Bombay Telephones setting out the facts of the case and asking them to reconsider the billing. The gentleman said that he had already made such a representation and that it was in vain. The department did not seriously examine his case. Under the circumstances, the only option left for him, he felt, was to approach the court for justice. MM advised him that the best way to get the matter heard was to file a writ petition in the High Court. However, he informed the gentleman that the cost involved in the whole process could be more than the amount he was incurring in the impugned telephone bill and, as such, it would be imprudent to move the High Court. To this the gentleman assertively replied that it was not just a question of an inflated bill, he was seeking justice on a matter of principle. MM was moved by his determination and agreed to file the writ petition.

Accordingly, the writ petition was filed in the High Court and it came up for hearing wherein the prayers were for withdrawal of the impugned bill and the notice to discontinue the telephone line for non-payment of the bill. On the date of the hearing, the petitioner himself was present in the court. When the matter was called out, the Learned Judge was in a bit of a hurry. He straightaway turned to the lady counsel for Bombay Telephones and suggested to her that the petitioner would pay Rs.20,000/- against the impugned bill and the notice for discontinuation of the line should be withdrawn. The order was passed without ascertaining the willingness of the petitioner to agree to such terms. Obviously, MM requested the court to permit him to take instructions from his client for this arrangement. It took a couple of seconds for MM to consult his client, only to inform the court that the proposal was not acceptable to him as his client was genuinely aggrieved that for no fault of his, why should he pay even Rs.20,000/- to Bombay Telephones? By this time the Learned Judge had already written his order by hand, stating, "upon payment of Rs.20,000/- by the petitioner, the respondents to waive the rest of the amount and shall restore the line." When the Learned Judge was informed of the non-acceptance of the proposal by the petitioner, his face turned red out of rage and in utter anguish he struck down what he had written and loudly uttered "Admit, no interim relief. Come after ten years." The Learned Judge then literally threw down the petition towards the bench clerk, who failed to catch it and the petition fell on the floor. This enraged the petitioner and resulted in quite a scene in the courtroom. He shouted, "Ask the judge to get up from his seat and pick up the petition by himself, or else it is gross contempt of court." The Learned Judge appeared nervous, but uttered, "next, next" indicating thereby, that the next petition in the list should be called out. There was total chaos in the court. Many advocates got up from their seats and started talking in hushed whispers. The petitioner asked MM as to whether he would take up the issue with the Chief Justice. Some senior advocates present in the court endorsed this idea.

In the next half an hour, MM and the petitioner were outside the chamber of the Chief Justice. Luckily, the CJ was available in his chamber. After waiting for about 15 minutes, MM and the petitioner were called in. It appeared that by that time the CJ had learnt about the incident in court. As soon as MM started speaking about what had transpired in the court, the CJ smiled and told him that at 2.45 p.m. (i.e., post-lunch session), he should go to the courtroom of a division bench where two Learned Judges would attend the matter. Accordingly, MM entered the appointed court, along with the petitioner. The two Learned Judges in the court there wore a mild smile on their faces, and before MM could make any submission, they said,

"We have passed the order in your petition as follows.

Rule. Returnable forthwith. Interim relief granted. The bill amount is waived. Restore telephone line immediately".

The Learned Judges read out the order and asked MM "Anything else?" When MM tried to speak about the unpleasant incident in the court hall of the single judge, the Learned Judges stopped him smilingly and said, "Only submission on petition." The petitioner was elated, having won the battle.

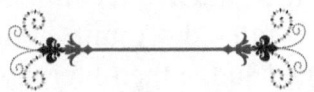

Sixteen

BOLLYWOOD AND ITS U-TURN

In the year 2002, diamond merchant Bharat Shah was prosecuted under the Maharashtra Control of Organized Crime Act (MCOCA), along with film producer Nazim Rizvi, his assistant, Abdul Rahim Allah Baksh, and another person. They were being prosecuted for their alleged nexus with the underworld don, Chhota Shakeel. The trial was going on in full swing before the designated Court for MCOCA, in Mumbai.

The allegation against Shah was that he was the financier for Nazim Rizvi's film *Chori Chori Chupke Chupke,* which he produced, at the behest of Chhota Shakeel. The proceeds of the film were attached by the Court Receiver. To bare the alleged nexus between Bollywood and the underworld, an important witness, Aarif Lakdawala, a city businessman, said that he had introduced noted film directors Abbas and Mastan to Rizvi, and Abdul Rahim at the instance of his childhood friend, Tariq Parveen, to seek their confirmation for making *Chori Chori Chupke Chupke*. The witness told the court that Tariq Parveen had informed him that Rizvi and his assistant were Shakeel's men, and that Shakeel had instructed him on telephone to introduce Abbas and Mastan to Rizvi and Abdul Rahim for directing the film. He had taken the duo to Abbas and Mastan, as they were living in his neighborhood in South Mumbai. The witness identified Abdul Rahim, sitting in the dock. He said that he would also be able to identify Rizvi but he was not present in the court, as he had been hospitalised for treatment of spondylitis.

By way of cross examination of this witness, in defence of my client, Abdul Rahim, I asked him whether he had visited the car showroom of the notorious criminal Abu Salem in Dubai, during his visit in 1995-96. He admitted that he had dealt with Abu Salem for some car purchase transaction; he added that he did not know that such an act was an offence. To another question put to him by me, the witness said that he had no personal knowledge about Shakeel's talk with his friend Tariq Parveen. The witness was not able to tell the court whether Tariq Parveen was telling the truth or was exaggerating. He was also not able to state as to when he had introduced Rizvi and Abdul Rahim to Abbas and Mastan. Asked if Parveen was the right-hand man of Shakeel, the witness replied in the affirmative and told the court that he was presently in Dubai and that he had called him on phone four months back. This witness denied a suggestion by me that he was involved with Tariq in a land-grabbing case. However, when confronted with his statement recorded by the police to that effect, the witness said that it might be correct that he had indulged in land-grabbing.

The prosecution claimed to be in possession of a recorded telephone conversation between Shah and Rizvi with Shakeel which revealed their alleged nexus with the underworld and that the underworld had targeted film personalities for their personal gains.

Another witness identified Bharat Shah in the court saying that he was the same person whose voice was recorded by the police, matching with the one figuring in the conversation with Chhota Shakeel. Surprisingly, Shah did not remember whether his voice was ever recorded by the police. Deposing before the designated court, the witness said that he was called to the office of the Crime Branch two years ago and in his presence, the cops recorded the voice of Bharat Shah. He said Shah was asked to read out a printed material placed before him, and his voice was recorded on a cassette. At this stage, Shah's advocate asked for a copy of the cassette containing his client's voice sample.

Two tapes containing alleged conversations between Nazim Rizvi and Chhota Shakeel, were played by the prosecution in the court. While one tape contained the exchange between Shakeel and Rizvi, the other tape contained a conversation between Rizvi and Faheem, a Shakeel associate. The defence advocates objected to the playing of the tapes in court saying that they were inadmissible in evidence. Besides, the contention of the defence was that the tapes were procured illegally and therefore violated certain set procedures.

As per the *panch* witness, there were discrepancies in the *panchnama*. According to him, the two cassettes were put in one envelope and not two, as recorded by the police. Besides, there was just one label on it and the cassettes were not sealed separately. The *panch* said that it was not correct to say that he had signed blank papers or that he had signed a pre-written *panchnama*, without knowing what was written on it, at the instance of the police. But he did admit that he was not familiar with the Marathi script in which the *panchnama* was written. The witness also said that he had never heard the voice in the tapes earlier and did not know whose voice it was.

During my cross examination for Abdul Rahim, the *panch* admitted that he was aware that such audio tapes could be tampered with and that he was not aware that these tapes had been sealed so that no tampering was possible. When I showed him two envelopes with a few lines written on them, the *panch* said that he could not say for certain if they were the same envelopes in which the tapes were sealed. Earlier he had said that the envelope that contained the tapes did not have anything written on it.

The next witness was a woman employee of a shop selling mobile phone SIM cards at Andheri. I questioned her on the sale of a controversial prepaid SIM card, allegedly sold to Rizvi's driver, on 5 April 2000. The prosecution's case was that the card was used by Rizvi for talking to Shakeel. While Rizvi spoke, police taped the alleged conversation with Shakeel, by using this mobile number. Replying to my question, this witness said that except for the name of Rizvi's driver, she had not entered any other particulars like the SIM card number, mobile phone number, or his address, in the sales register. She said that she had filled in these particulars for other customers on the same page. She also stated that she sold the card to Rizvi's driver when he produced a photocopy of his driving license but admitted that photocopies could be doctored. She also said that she did not ask for his original driving license. "Since it was a cash transaction, I did not seek many details," she said.

At this stage, I pointed out to the court that the two entries made on 1 April 2000 were also against cash transactions. However, in these cases the mobile phone number and the SIM card number were mentioned.

The next witness in the case was DCP Shri R.D. Shinde. He had recorded the alleged confessional statement of Nazim Rizvi in the case. I asked the officer in the witness box if he had ascertained whether Rizvi was interrogated by any other police officer, prior to his alleged confession. The DCP answered that he had not and added that he did not find out at what point in time Rizvi expressed his willingness to make a confession. DCP Shinde conceded that Rizvi was in police custody, during the 48 hours' reflection period granted to him.

The next witness in the case for me was film actor Shah Rukh Khan. During his examination, Shah Rukh accepted, having met Nazim Rizvi a couple of times in the year 1997-98. He also said Rizvi had approached him in connection with a film he was making. However, when the actor denied having spoken to Chhota Shakeel, the prosecutor had to declare him hostile. He further denied that he was threatened by Shakeel and was forced to work on the film. In a statement recorded by the police earlier, Khan had said that a person accompanying Rizvi had threatened him in Shakeel's name. He had also mentioned that there were some documents that the man had produced saying that he could tear them if Khan did not accept Shakeel's terms. However, while deposing before the court, Khan denied the incident completely. He further failed to identify Abdul Rahim, the man who had allegedly accompanied Rizvi to his house.

To a question put by me, Khan said that he could not say confidently that the person present in court, Abdul Rahim, was the person who had accompanied Rizvi when they met him. To another question put by me, he answered that many people approach him with offers and it was not possible to work with all of them.

During his cross examination by the prosecutor, Khan said he had received threatening calls at a time when they were less common but denied receiving calls from Shakeel or a call from Abu Salem, during a show in Singapore. Khan was questioned about his cordial relationship with the accused, Bharat Shah. To this question, Khan replied saying that Shah was a business associate and a producer but denied that his multi-crore bungalow in Bandra was a gift from Shah for having worked on the film *Devdas*, a film that was allegedly financed by Shah.

Khan denied telling the police during investigation that Rizvi and another person who identified themselves as Shakeel's men had made him talk to Shakeel on phone or had pressurised him to sign a film. He further said that he had never read or received the written copy of his oral statement to the police; he had no idea why the police had attributed to him statements that he denied in court.

In my cross examination, the actor reiterated that he could not identify the person who had accompanied Rizvi to meet him, nor did he know him as Shakeel's man. To another question, put by me, he said that refusing a film proposal made by producers and directors may cause displeasure to the person making the proposal.

The next important witness who turned hostile in this case was actor Salman Khan. In the court the actor disowned his statements recorded by the police on 26 December 2000, and 25 February 2001. In the statements before the police, Salman had told them that film producer Rizvi and his assistant, Abdul Rahim had come to his house and that he picked up a fight with them over the signing amount of the film and that the absconding accused, Anjum Ajlani had intervened to settle the matter. According to the police, Abdul Rahim and Anjum Ajlani worked for Chhota Shakeel and the film *Chori Chori Chupke Chupke* starring Salman Khan, Priety Zinta and Rani Mukerji, was produced by Rizvi and financed by Shah, at the instance of Chhota Shakeel.

Replying to questions put to him by defence advocates, Salman said that he was not forced by anyone into doing the film *Chori Chori Chupke Chupke*. He further said that he did the film because he liked the story and because it was directed by the Abbas-Mastan duo. On the second day of his deposition before the court, Salman, while answering the questions put to him by me, stated that he was called by the police to give his statement twice. "I was answering their questions, and they were typing my replies on a computer. As the computer screen was far away, I could not read what was being typed," he averred. To another question put to him by me that he was favouring the accused before the court, Salman said that he had no reason to favour them.

To my next question about his popularity, Salman answered that he had innumerable fans all over the world and he received calls from them. "Yesterday, I spoke to Chhota Shakeel and Abu Salem. They are my fans", said Salman. To all the vital questions put to him by the prosecution, Salman stuck to a firm denial. He denied that Nazim Rizvi and his assistant, Abdul Rahim had come to his house, when he picked up a fight against them over the signing amount of the film. He also refuted his police statement that the absconding accused, Anjum Ajlani had intervened to calm him down.

As the evidence of Salman was coming to an end, the prosecution came forward with an application to the court, praying for examination of film actor Sanjay Dutt as a court witness. The designated judge, however, held that Dutt could be examined as a prosecution witness and not as a court witness, allowing the prosecution to conduct further investigation under Section 173 (8) Cr. P.C.

A prosecution witness goes through the process of examination-in-chief, which has limitations. The right to cross examine the witness lies with defence advocates and the prosecution can cross examine the witness only if the witness turns hostile. However, in the case of a court witness, the prosecution and the defence are both entitled to cross examine the witness.

Defence advocates representing the accused opposed the prosecution plea on the grounds that Dutt could have been cited as a prosecution witness if his evidence was so crucial to the case. Responding to their objection, the prosecutor said that the prosecution's option to examine him as a prosecution witness is still open. On this point, I argued that the prosecution's plea to examine Dutt as a witness is premature as evidence was still being led. Dutt's statement was not recorded by the police. Yet, in the garb of summoning Dutt as a court witness, the prosecution was trying to fill in the lacunae in the case, I argued.

Ultimately, the court allowed prosecution to examine Dutt as a prosecution witness, as suggested by the defence team and not as a court witness, as suggested by the prosecutor.

Dutt was called as a witness to identify the voice samples of a conversation recorded by the police in a hotel in Nashik where he and his three friends stayed on 14 November. However, to the questions put to him by the prosecution, Dutt said that he could not identify any of the samples as he was too heavily drunk in Nashik.

To a question put to him by me, by way of cross examination, about dubbing of voices, he agreed that it was possible to dub a voice and replace it with another. In further explanation, he said that his own voice was dubbed in three of his films, while he was in jail for two years in the case of the serial blasts. He further said that the dubbing was so good that he was unable to make out the difference between the dubbed voice and his own voice. In reply to another of my questions, the actor said that during the recording of his voice samples at the Crime Branch, he was made to read out a script that included expletives written by the police.

After the witnesses were examined, cross examined and the final arguments by respective advocates of the accused and the prosecution were over, the matter was taken up for passing of the judgment by the trial judge. In his judgment, the trial court held that the prosecution failed to prove the case and hence all the accused were acquitted.

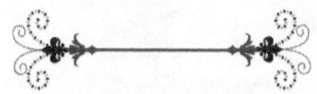

Shah Rukh turns hostile in Bharat Shah case

TIMES NEWS NETWORK

Mumbai: Actor Shah Rukh Khan on Tuesday turned hostile as a prosecution witness in the trial of diamond merchant and film financier Bharat Shah and others in a case of the alleged nexus of the accused with the underworld. He denied having ever spoken to Karachi-based gangster Chhota Shakeel or to Abu Salem.

During cross-examination by defence counsel Harshad Ponda, appearing for film producer and co-accused in the case Nazim Rizvi, the actor said there was no pressure on him either by Rizvi or by any one else to sign up any film. He said he did not know if Rizvi was Shakeel's man.

The actor was dressed in black, a v-necked black T-shirt and pants. His hair was jelled. He answered the barrage of questions put forth to him by the prosecution and defence lawyers politely and at times with his tongue firmly in his cheek. Public prosecutor Rohini Salian grilled him for over two hours after declaring him a hostile witness when he refused to support the prosecution's case. He denied almost everything the police said it had recorded as his statement in February 2001.

Shah Rukh Khan is the tenth witness out of the 49 examined so far by the state, who has refused to support the police. The police case is that Bharat Shah, Rizvi, Rahim Allahbaksh and others were allegedly involved with the underworld. Rizvi was the producer *Chori Chori, Chupke Chupke*, which was financed by Bharat Shah. The police said it had recorded alleged telephonic conversations between Rizvi and Shakeel and one between Shah and Shakeel.

Shah Rukh identified Bharat Shah, who was present in the court of special judge A.P. Bhangale,

Film star Shah Rukh Khan (in black T-shirt) leaves the sessions court in Mumbai on Tuesday after deposing in the Bharat Shah trial.

which was presiding over the trial. He told Ms Salian that he had met Rizvi in 1997-98 at a studio where he was shooting for a film. He admitted that Rizvi had asked him to do a film to which his response was that he would speak to the director-duo Abbas Mastan before deciding.

The actor denied telling the police during his probe that Rizvi and another person had identified themselves as Shakeel's men and had made him talk over the phone to Shakeel or had pressurised him to sign up a film. He said he had never read or received the written copy of his oral statement to the police. He repeatedly said he had no idea why the police had attributed to him statements he now refuted were ever his.

When Ms Salian told the actor his script rendering in films was good, the actor replied, "If I may say so, I am the best actor in the world." In response to another query, he said, Neeta Lulla, costume designer for *Devdas* was not the wife of Kishore Lulla, one of the overseas distributor of the film. When asked by Ms Salian if he would be scared if Shakeel called him, his cheeky retort was, "I would be scared if you called me." He denied that Bharat Shah had "won him over", or that he was "browbeaten" by the accused to lie in court as a witness.

When cross-examined by defence counsels Majeed Memon and Shrikant Shivade, the actor said he cannot identify the person who had accompanied Rizvi to meet him nor did he know him as Rizvi's man. He said refusing a film proposal made by producers or directors may cause displeasure to the person making the proposal.

In a Lighter Vein

An important trial was in progress in a court in Delhi. It had generated a lot of public interest due to some important people being in the dock. MM was leading the defence team, while the chief prosecutor, named by the Supreme Court of India, was leading the prosecution.

The courtroom was not very large. The presiding officer's seat was at a higher level on a raised, wooden dais. The advocates and the litigants were seated opposite the judge, at a much lower level. To add to all this awkwardness, in front of the judge on the dais was a row of thick law books. The books were so placed that the advocates and the litigants were not able to see the face of the judge. When the advocates had to address the court whilst on their feet, they had difficulty in making easy eye to eye contact with the judge. MM could clearly see that the law books, placed as they were, obstructed his access to the judge. When his turn came to address the court, he stood erect and quipped, "Let the law not become a wall between the justice-seeker and the justice-giver."

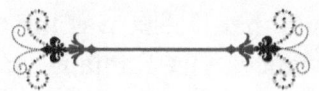

Seventeen

BIWI NO. 1 AND BIWI NO. 2

It was in the month of June 2006 that a famous Hindi film playback singer Udit Narayan Jha came to me with a request that I appear for him in a complaint filed against him by his first wife, Ranjana Narayan. Udit had received six summonses in this regard from the Women's Commission in Bihar. However, he ignored one and all. Finally, when the Commission warned him of his arrest, he came to me.

The summons was in response to a complaint filed by Ranjana before the Women's Commission in Bihar for claiming her rightful status as her husband's first wife; the date fixed for the Commission hearing was 16 June 2006.

Things had come to a head when Ranjana forced her way into Udit's posh hotel room in Bihar demanding that she be given her due status as his legally wedded wife. Udit went around teary-eyed, reiterating how Ranjana was lying, and that Deepa was the only woman in his life. It was in these circumstances that Ranjana was forced to approach the State Women's Commission in Bihar.

In her application, Ranjana averred that she and Udit were married in the year 1982 and hence she is his first wife. The Commission advised the party to bury the hatchet and live together, in true Bhartiya tradition. So, in front of the Commission, Udit accepted Ranjana and promised to provide her maintenance and upkeep.

The focus was on the legal status of the second wife. Under Hindu Law, a Hindu married man cannot have a second marriage during the lifetime of his first wife. If he does, it amounts to bigamy. The first wife can proceed against him legally. In the case of a woman who claims to be the wife of a Hindu adult, who is already married, volunteering to help the second wife is the choice of the man, since, as per the Hindu Law, she has no claim over his assets. There is no legal obligation to the second wife, on his part. The law does change where a Muslim is concerned. Muslim Law states that recognition is extended to the second wife and there is a legal obligation on the part of the husband to recognise her as a lawfully wedded wife. The husband is bound to accord her legitimate rights and claims as his wife.

How Ranjana accepted Deepa was a moot question. Traditionally, Indian women have an ingrained attitude to remain in a matrimonial bond, no matter what consequences follow. For a woman who is married to an already married man, her self-respect would be questionable. Women fear societal pressure, that of being patronised, being the object of pity, or about what they would be labelled as. Society does tend to be harsh on women in marital matters. Sometimes, a child tends to keep the marriage together. Also, the woman might not be well-off financially to look after the future of her child on her own.

In this case, the Women's Commission said that both the wives of Udit had been living under some arrangement for the last twenty years. There could have been no better solution to the problem. So, there was no question of invoking Hindu Law at that stage. Ranjana expressed satisfaction over the compromise and withdrew her complaint against Udit. Both Ranjana and Udit signed the consent terms prepared for them at my behest, in front of the Commission. The Commission said that it was a working arrangement, under which the status of his second wife Deepa and her son would remain unchanged. "I am happy that I got my honour back as his legally wedded wife," said Ranjana. Udit expressed his regrets to Ranjana for all that had happened in the past and promised that in future he would take good care of her.

Ranjana said that she had no grudge against Deepa. "Being a

woman, I sympathise with her," said Ranjana adding that she accepts Deepa as Udit's wife and will give her son a mother's love and affection.

"My client is happy with the arrangement reached before the Commission in a cordial atmosphere," said the counsel for the first wife.

The Chairperson of the Commission expressed her satisfaction over the positive outcome of her efforts. She said, "As the couple have reached a meaningful reconciliation, which the Commission wanted, there is no question of pursuing a bigamy case against the husband."

A high voltage drama thus ended by 4 p.m. on that day in the office of the Women's Commission in Bihar.

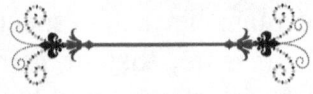

So, who's Biwi No. 1?

While it is still unclear who Udit Narayan's first wife is — Ranjana or Deepa — BT explores the second wife's legal standing

REAGAN GAVIN RASQUINHA AND PIYALI DASGUPTA
Times News Network

When Ranjana Jha forced her way into Udit Narayan's hotel room some time ago, demanding her due place as his legally-wedded wife, Udit went around teary-eyed, reiterating how she was lying and that Deepa was the only woman in his life. Ranjana then lodged a complaint with Bihar State Women's Commission, who've told the trio to bury the hatchet and live together in true Bharatiya tradition. So Udit accepted Ranjana as his wife and promised to provide for her maintenance and upkeep. Ranjana withdrew her complaint. And Deepa is busy dismissing it as a "*Ghar ka jhagda... yeh to hota hi rahta hai.* It was a big *tamasha!*"

Interestingly, while Udit's lawyer Majeed Memon has claimed that Udit got married to Ranjana in 1984, which would make her his second wife, Ranjana, in her application to the Bihar State Women's Commission, has said that she's the first wife and that they got married in 1982.

Whoever be his first wife, the focus is now on the legal standing a second wife has. "Under the law, a Hindu, already married, can't have a second wife. If he does, it amounts to bigamy. The first wife can file a case against him," says lawyer Waris Pathan. Can a third party register a complaint? "No. A third party has no say whatsoever in a case like this."

Udit Narayan and (left) Ranjana and (right) Deepa

If the first wife does not object, does the second 'wife' have a claim to the man's assets? "In the case of a woman who claims to be the wife of a Hindu adult who is already married, volunteering and opting to help her is the choice of the man. But there is no legal compulsion that he must do so."

For a woman who is not recognised legally as the wife of someone, the question of her laying claim to his assets doesn't arise," says Memon. The law does change where a Muslim is concerned. "Muslim law states that recognition is extended to the second wife and there is a legal obligation on the husband to recognise her as a lawfully wedded wife and to accord to her all legitimate rights and claims," continues Memon.

But why, then, do some wives accept the second 'wife'? "Traditionally, Indian women have an ingrained attitude that you have to remain married, no matter what. For the woman who's already married to the man, her self respect can go out of the window. And women fear societal pressure — that of being patronised, being the object of pity or about what they will be labelled as. Society does tend to be a bit harder on the woman in marital issues. Sometimes, the presence of a child tends to keep the marriage together. Also, the woman might not be as financially secure to look after the future of the child on her own," adds clinical psychologist Seema Hingorrany, who is also a marriage counsellor.

In a Lighter Vein

There was a sensational murder in Satara District, in Maharashtra, with widespread political repercussions. The case was widely publicised as parties on both sides were important people. The relatives of the accused were keen on retaining MM to defend the two accused in the trial in Satara Sessions Court. Although it was difficult for MM to go to Satara District and camp there for day-to-day trial, he agreed to take up the matter as the case was interesting and challenging.

MM, along with one of his juniors, Shri M.G.More thus reached Satara. The atmosphere of Satara Sessions Court was totally different from that of courts in Mumbai. The courtrooms were large and spacious; the Bar room of the advocates had an entirely different look too. A huge hall in which mattresses and pillows were laid was adjacent to the Bar room and it served as an additional Bar room.

When the cases were called out, the names of the parties and their advocates were also called out by the bench clerk. This was repeated and echoed by a peon standing on the door of the courtroom. The peculiarity of the arrangement was that each name was repeated by the peon in a melodious tune, as though he were singing some filmy song. MM and his junior were pleasantly surprised at this sing-song manner of calling out litigants in the court.

In good humour, MM's junior, Mr. M.G.More told him that he was keen that his name be called out in a similar manner by the peon of the court. MM told him that he could dramatise the situation suitably for the next day's hearing.

On the following day when the court was presided over, MM asked Mr. More to not enter the courtroom with him but stay outside, somewhere in the vicinity. Accordingly, Advocate More did not enter the courtroom and remained outside at some distance from the door.

When the case of MM's client was called out, Advocate More was not seen around. MM then started looking for his junior here and there, inside the court room. As Mr. More was not around, he requested the court to ask the bench clerk to call out for Mr. More. The court obliged MM. Accordingly, the bench clerk called out Mr. More's name. As wished and planned by MM, Mr. More's name was soon repeated by the peon at the door in the desired melodious manner to the joy of Mr. More, who came running inside the courtroom happily.

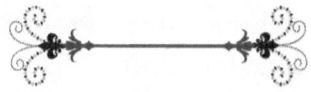

Eighteen

THE 2G SCAM

The telecommunication scam, popularly known as the 2G Scam, had rocked the nation and the United Progressive Alliance (UPA) II Central Government, headed by Prime Minister Manmohan Singh. It happened in the year 2011; the CBI had launched criminal proceedings for various offences under the Indian Penal Code and other statutes, for cheating, misappropriation, forgery etc., against over a dozen accused. They included the former Union Telecom minister, Shri A. Raja and a sitting Rajya Sabha M.P., Ms. Kanimozhi among others, who were private citizens and reputed corporate figures. The Enforcement Directorate also slapped a case against them, for offences under the Prevention of Money Laundering Act. When these powerful accused came to be arrested for non-bailable offences, there was lot of furore and publicity. Looking at the enormity of the amount involved, which in the estimation of the Comptroller and Accountant General (CAG) was several thousand crores, the offences had assumed gravity and, as such, bail, soon upon arrest, did not seem possible. All the accused remained in custody for quite some time and their bail applications before the trial court did not find favour.

The Delhi High Court had to be approached by some of the accused for bail, and in one such application my submissions in support of grant of bail for the accused were as follows:

"The Telecom industry has been rapidly growing and the endeavour of the Telecom Ministry has been to expand the reach of mobile telecommunication to every common man. While commuting from the residence to this court, your Lordship must have observed on the streets of the city, a municipal sweeper with a long broom in his hands, cleaning the street, while simultaneously talking to his wife on a mobile phone deftly balanced on his shoulder by his inclined head. Similarly, my Lord can also observe under the expanse of a shady tree, on the roadside, a poor cobbler brushing a shoe while he is talking to his little daughter at home on the phone tucked between his head and shoulder. This has been possible only because of the revolutionary growth and expansion of telecommunication facilities. Arrest of the bail seekers in the case, who have been languishing in prison for quite some time, has only crowded the jails. They wanted to increase Delhi's telecom density while what they have achieved is prison density!"

After hearing the plea, the High Court was pleased to direct the accused persons to apply afresh for bail before the trial court and bail was granted to all the accused by the trial court.

When the trial began, it captured the imagination of the whole country. High ranking bureaucrats from the telecom ministry queued up as witnesses.

The prosecutor or the Investigating Officer cannot justifiably have a conference with a witness, to tutor him to give evidence in a particular manner before he steps into the witness box. Such a practice amounts to tampering with evidence. In this important case, the demeanour of one of the vital witnesses is worth mentioning.

Soon after the process of examination of prosecution witnesses commenced, prosecution witness no. 2 stepped into the witness box to give evidence on the day fixed for him. Whilst the prosecutor was examining him, it seemed as though he was hiding certain facts and was not speaking the whole truth. After his examination-in-chief was over, the witness was now in the defence quarter for cross examination. I had to make him come out with the truth; the cross examination began which went on as follows:

Q. When and how did you come to know that you have to attend court today?

A. I received a court summons two days back while I was in my native place in Tamil Nadu.

Q. After you saw the court summons, what did you do?

A. In fact, yesterday morning I received a call on my mobile from an unknown number to which I did not respond. A call from the same number came again. Then again, I was confused and did not respond. After I had not responded to two or three such calls, a message was flashed upon the phone, which said "I am a CBI officer. Please pick up the phone."

Q. What happened thereafter?

A. The call came again within a few minutes, and I picked it up. The caller identified himself as the CBI investigating officer in the 2G scam. He told me that I should meet him in the CBI office within the next two hours. I asked him why I was being called there. The officer told me that since I must give evidence in court the next day, I must meet him. Reluctantly though, I agreed to go to the CBI office in the afternoon.

Q. What happened then?

A. I reached the CBI office at about 2.30 p.m. I was escorted to the Investigating Officer (IO) by some official inside the CBI building.

Q. Do you know that no citizen can enter the CBI building without making an entry of his particulars and purpose of visit, as also the nature of work, in a register maintained at the main entrance?

A. Yes, I am aware.

Q. Did you make such an entry before you entered?

A. No, because I was escorted by the CBI official.

Q. Did it not strike you that your entry in this manner was unofficial and illegal?

A. I partly felt so but as I had to meet the IO of the case, I went along.

Q. What happened after you met the IO?

A. The IO made me sit and showed me certain papers. He asked me to read a statement, purported to be my statement in the case.

Q. Did you see that statement for the first time, or did you have occasion to see the same earlier?

A. I had not seen or read the statement any time earlier. I went through the contents of the statement, purporting to be my statement. While going through the same, I found that some facts were wrongly mentioned, and some were missing. I told the officer that this statement is not properly recorded, and it must be corrected.

Q. How did the IO respond to this statement of yours?

A. He told me that nothing could be done now, as he could not make any changes. He told me that I had to stick to the contents as they are or else say whatever I wanted to tell the court. But no correction could be made.

Q. Were you under his fear? Were you suspecting something irregular, and illegal being done by the officer?

A. Yes. To some extent.

Q. Your statement that was given to you for reading on that day and the contents that were read by you on that day, were seen and read by you for the first time, or did you have an opportunity to see it earlier?

A. That was the first time that I saw and read my statement.

Q. Several parts of that statement were untrue and were not given by you to the IO. Is that correct?

A. Yes. It is correct.

Q. Did you report this development to his superior CBI officer or anyone else?

A. No.

Q. To sum up, it would be correct to say that the statement attributed to you by the IO is not your own true and correct version?

A. Yes.

Immediately after the evidence of this witness, an application was moved before the trial judge, stating that this was a clear demonstration of tampering with evidence and interference in the course of justice. Hence, it was prayed that notice be issued to the CBI Director calling upon him to explain as to why action should not be taken against the erring IO. The trial judge thereafter issued notice to the CBI, to show cause and the application was kept for hearing on the next date, fixed by the court. On that day the special prosecutor who was later elevated to the post of a Supreme Court judge appeared, and pleaded that it was an aberration, and that regret was expressed, with an assurance that such things would not be repeated. On this, the court asked the defence what would be the next step. Thereafter, by mutual consent, the said application was placed on record and thus the issue was closed. From then on, no prosecution witness was handled in that manner.

Ultimately, at the end of this marathon and historic trial all the accused were found 'not guilty', and they were all acquitted.

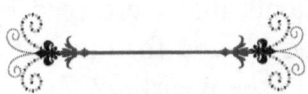

MM was invited by the Bar Association in Mumbai to give a lecture on the Art of Cross Examination. Considering his vast experience and expertise in cross examination, it was a very apt topic for MM to speak on. In the course of his talk, MM narrated an anecdote to the members of the Bar, with a view to educating them as to when and where the cross examination should stop. According to MM, the golden principle of successful cross examination is to know what is not to be asked, rather than what is to be asked. To bring out his point, MM cited the example of an eminent advocate who had to face a negative and adverse result due to his thoughtless way of cross examining a sharp witness.

In a murder trial, the prosecution case was that the accused administered poison to the unfortunate victim, who allegedly died as a result. During the trial of the accused, a chemist was in the witness stand. The prosecution alleged that the accused had approached the chemist in his medical store to buy poison on a particular day. The chemist was thus examined by the prosecutor as an important prosecution witness, to establish and confirm that it was the accused who had approached him on the said date and purchased poison. The defence was required to cross examine this witness after the prosecution's examination.

The cross examiner, a brilliant and well-known advocate of the city, began his questioning as follows:

Q. Are you a qualified chemist?

A. Yes, I hold a degree in chemistry.

Q. How long have you been working in this medical store?

A. For the last 3 years.

Q. How big is your store?

A. It is about 80' x 40' with a loft.

Q. How many sales staff attend to customers at a time?

A. We are four or five at the counter, while an accountant sits inside the store.

Q. Your store is situated at a marketplace which is always crowded?

A. Yes, true.

Q. What are the working hours of the store?

A. It opens at 8 a.m. and closes at 10 p.m.

Q. On an average, how many customers are attended to, on a particular day?

A. It is difficult to say, but roughly three to four hundred customers.

At this juncture, the advocate should have stopped and should have raised the question of the identity of the accused in the dock. Instead, he proceeded to ask a further question which he thought would be to his advantage. He continued:

Q. On that day how many customers approached the store?

A. Only one. I distinctly recollect it was a general strike day and our shutters were half down. The accused had approached me insisting that I should attend to him as he was in dire need of poison. After some argument, I obliged him due to his persistence and as such, I clearly remember his face.

This answer proved fatal to the cause of the accused and his fate was now all but sealed. The accused came to be convicted on the strength of this answer. The cross examiner was late in learning where to stop a running cross examination.

MM further enlightened the audience by highlighting the importance of cross examination in a criminal trial. He said that the witness, though under oath, tends to lie or exaggerate the events to the disadvantage of the accused facing trial. He said, "It is an art to identify falsehood or exaggeration by means of a probing cross examination." A cross-examiner must look into the eyes of the witness and make him feel that he is aware as to what the witness is hiding or where he is lying. The witness is expected to be under the influence of the cross-examiner's awe. It is only this part of the trial viz., cross examination of the witness, that is virtually relevant to extracting the truth. But it must be stressed that a successful cross examiner must be equipped with a thorough study of the facts of the case, as well as the relevant law.

Nineteen

GULSHAN KUMAR MURDER

Gulshan Kumar Dua was the Managing Director of Super Cassette Industries and T-Series and was mainly engaged in manufacturing audio and video cassettes. He was also in the business of purchasing rights of audio cassettes of Hindi movies and private albums.

Nadeem of Nadeem-Shravan fame of music composers had produced an audio album by name ' *Hi Ajnabi* 'which had songs sung by Nadeem himself. He had requested Gulshan Kumar to purchase the marketing rights of the said album, but Gulshan Kumar was reluctant to make the deal. The album did not sell well in the market due to lack of publicity, which is usually done by labels like Super Cassette Industries for their high-end products. Nadeem had visited the office of Gulshan Kumar in this regard and had exchanged hot words with him. This incident had strained the relationship between the two. After this incident, Gulshan Kumar who was well known in the market, decided not to purchase the audio rights of any works in which music was composed by Nadeem-Shravan.

It was alleged that Nadeem had approached Abu Salem and Qayum Chacha in Dubai, to put pressure on Gulshan Kumar through them. Thereafter, threats were given to Gulshan Kumar on telephone from Dubai, by Abu Salem to force him to purchase the audio rights of cassettes in which music was composed by Nadeem-Shravan. It was alleged that since Gulshan Kumar did not buckle under these threats,

Nadeem again visited Dubai, and had a meeting with Abu Salem and Qayum Chacha to hatch a conspiracy to kill Gulshan Kumar. In May 1997, another meeting was held in the office of Qayum Chacha in which Nadeem along with one Abdul Rauf Merchant and Mohammed Ali Husain Chacha was present. In the said meeting, it was decided to eliminate Gulshan Kumar. Allegedly, Nadeem agreed to provide funds required for the job to be done. After allegedly hatching the conspiracy, Nadeem, along with Abdul Rauf Merchant and Ali Husain Chacha returned to Mumbai. Accordingly, funds were collected from different sources as per instructions received from Dubai, vehicles were arranged, and the weapons for executing the plan were obtained. Two revolvers were handed over to Abdul Rauf Merchant and his gang for this purpose.

Thereafter, two teams were formed. One was headed by Abdul Rauf Merchant, who was later arrested and tried as accused no. 19, and the other was headed by one Rafiq Ahmed, who too was later arrested and tried as accused no. 2. On 27 June 1997 one Ramesh Sadhuram Taurani, who owned a music company TIPS, along with his brother and Nadeem, allegedly handed over cash amount of Rs. 25,00,000/- to one Keki Balsara, for being delivered to the persons who were hired for killing Gulshan Kumar. The said amount was handed over to accused nos. 8, 9 & 10, at Nagpada. After fully preparing to commit the murder of Gulshan Kumar, they kept a watch on his movements.

Gulshan Kumar was a devotee of Lord Shiva. He used to visit the Shiva temple at Andheri, Mumbai, twice daily, in the morning and in the evening. On 12 August 1997, Gulshan Kumar came to the temple in the morning, at 10.15 a.m. After offering prayers in the temple, he came out and walked towards his car, which was parked nearby. One Ramchandra Lavangare, a trustee of the said temple, was also with Gulshan Kumar at that point of time.

An unknown person suddenly appeared on the scene and started firing indiscriminately at Gulshan Kumar. In a few seconds, two other persons also appeared and fired bullets at Gulshan Kumar who sustained grievous injuries. On hearing the commotion, the driver of Gulshan Kumar, Shri

Rooplal arrived at the spot. Rooplal also sustained serious bullet injuries. Two other people, who rushed to the spot, on hearing bullet sounds, were also injured in the melee. Their names were later disclosed to be Madhukar Kavankar and Subhash Raundal. Thereafter, the assailants ran away from the spot. The injured were rushed to Cooper hospital at Vile Parle, where Gulshan Kumar was declared 'brought dead'. Rooplal was admitted in the Intensive Care Unit.

Police from the D.N. Nagar Police Station, Andheri, arrived at the scene and took charge of the situation. Ramchandra Lavangare's statement was recorded as an FIR and an offence was registered at D.N. Nagar Police station, vide CR No. 572, of 1997, against three unknown persons, for offences punishable under sections 302 and 307 read with section 34 IPC and section 25 (1-B) (a) and section 3 of The Arms Act. After preliminary inquiries by D.N.Nagar police, further investigation was handed over to DCB, CID Unit-VII. Investigations revealed that the offence was the outcome of a bigger conspiracy allegedly hatched by Nadeem Saifi, Abu Salem, Qayum Chacha, Abdul Rauf Merchant and other accused. During the investigation statements from several people were recorded. The assailants, who had run away from the scene of offence had forcibly taken away the taxi belonging to one Labhshankar Sharma, who was examined as Prosecution Witness (PW) No. 4, at the trial. In all, 19 persons were arraigned as accused in the case.

Accused Mohamed Ali Hussain Chacha was arrested along with other accused persons. Mohamed Ali Husain Chacha later showed his willingness to make a confession before the Magistrate and accordingly, he was produced before the Additional Chief Metropolitan Magistrate, 4th Court, Esplanade, Mumbai. His confessional statement was recorded after giving him sufficient time for reflection. Thereupon, he was granted pardon which he accepted. In his confessional statement, the accused had given minute details about the conspiracy, the means, weapons arranged to execute the murder and the funding provided by the conspirators. Thereafter, on different dates various accused were arrested.

During the trial, the prosecution examined, in all, 45 witnesses including a few eyewitnesses. However, prosecution witness no. 31, Mohamed Ali Husain Chacha (approver) did not disclose the true and correct facts, while making his statement before the Magistrate. Hence, the pardon granted to him was revoked and it was decided that he would be tried as an accused.

To establish the recovery of a motor car, one pistol and cartridges at the instance of this accused, the prosecution examined two witnesses, viz., P.W. 30 & P.W. 45. According to the witnesses, the accused led them to room number 9 in Hussain Chawl at Ghatkopar. He entered the room and took out a key from a cupboard. He further led them to a bridge where a white Maruti car was found. The accused then opened the car. From the car, he took out a white polythene bag, which contained one pistol and five cartridges. They were seized by the police. However, at the time of trial in the court the witnesses could not identify the cartridges.

To strengthen the charge of conspiracy in the case, the prosecution examined P.W. 37, who, according to the prosecution, had collected the cash amount of Rupees Twenty-five lakhs, from the absconding accused, Nadeem Saifi and accused No. 11, Ramesh Sadhuram Taurani. This witness also knew Abu Salem. In the year 1996, when he visited Dubai, he met Abu Salem. He had stayed in Dubai for about 15 days and visited Abu Salem's car show room.

According to this witness, on 27 June 1997, at about 2.15 p.m. he received a call from one Keki Balsara, (since deceased) saying that they were required to go to Juhu for some work. He further told the witness that within 5-7 minutes he would come to Bandra to pick him up. As promised, Keki Balsara reached Bandra in his white Maruti Esteem car. They then started for Juhu from Bandra and reached Juhu Tara road, near Natural Ice Cream, at about 2.45 p.m. After 15-20 minutes, this witness observed a Tata car, bearing no. MH-04 G-5120. This witness further stated that absconding accused, Nadeem Saifi was sitting on the rear seat of the car. Another person of fair complexion was sitting on the left, front seat of the car. The witness identified him in the court as accused No. 11, Ramesh Taurani. The witness said that he knew the absconding accused Nadeem Saifi and that accused No. 11, Ramesh Taurani was introduced to him and Keki Balsara by Nadeem. This witness further said in court that two boxes were removed from Nadeem's car and were placed in the car of Keki Balsara. After placing the two boxes in the car of Keki Balsara, Nadeem made a call from his mobile phone and told the person at the other end that he had given Rupees Twenty-five lakhs and added, *"Gulshan Kumar Ka Kaam Kar Do"* (Get the Gulshan Kumar job done). The witness stated that accused No.11 also called the same person who was called by Nadeem and said, *"Paise To De Diye Hain, Gulshan Ka Kaam Jaldi Nipta Do."* (Money has been paid. Get the Gulshan Kumar job done fast). This witness further said that he himself had talked to the person called by both on mobile and identified that person's voice as that of Abu Salem.

P.W. 37 further stated that thereafter, Keki Balsara and he went to Nagpada, near Cafe Sagar Hotel, at about 5.45 pm. After some time, three persons came and collected the two boxes lying on the rear seat of the car. In the court, this witness identified accused Nos. 7, 8 & 9 to be the same persons who had collected the boxes. However, according to the prosecution, the boxes were collected by accused numbers 8, 9 & 10 and not 7, 8 & 9. As such, P.W 37 had wrongly identified accused No. 7.

To wipe off the damage caused by this witness, I had to resort to meticulous cross examination. Very tactfully, I could bring on record through this witness that he believed that Rupees Twenty-five lakhs could be pertaining to some property transaction of Keki Balsara. This witness also had to agree with me that he was very close to Abu Salem, having visited him in Dubai on many occasions. However, he could not exactly remember as to how many times they had talked to each other. He further knew that Abu Salem was accused in the 1993 bomb blasts case in Mumbai. After an exhaustive cross examination of this witness, I knew I had achieved my target.

P.W. No. 1, Ramchandra Anant Lavangare was examined as the

star witness. This witness was one of the trustees of Shiv Mandir, situated at Jeet Nagar, Andheri. Deceased Gulshan Kumar used to be inside the temple for 15-20 minutes each time he visited the temple. On 12 August 1997, Gulshan Kumar arrived at about 10 a.m. in his car. After parking his car, his driver, Rooplal, had also come along with him. When the deceased came to visit the temple, this witness was standing outside the temple. After finishing his prayers inside the temple, the deceased was proceeding towards his car. At that time his driver, Rooplal was following him. This witness was behind them, about 10 feet from Rooplal. As soon as the deceased reached his car, an unknown person suddenly appeared there. He had come from the Eastern side. The deceased was proceeding towards the North. As the deceased was trying to open the front door of the car, the unknown person placed the barrel of a pistol on the back of the deceased. He, therefore, turned around. At that point of time, the unknown person started pumping bullets from the pistol. He fired bullets on the chest of the deceased. The deceased fell to the ground. He, however, got up from the ground when the unknown person fired bullets at him again. Despite being shot several times, the deceased could still manage to walk up to the door of a neighbouring house. But he fell in front of the house.

This witness further stated that in the meantime, one more unknown person arrived at the scene from the side of Siva Hair Cutting Salon. This person also fired at the deceased with a pistol. The witness further went on to state that, in the meantime, one more unknown person, standing near the auto rickshaw appeared and he too fired at the deceased. When Rooplal went to the deceased to pick him up, he too was shot at. One of the bullets hit the right thigh of Rooplal. However, he was not able to identify the assailant who fired at him. The witness rushed towards a coconut tree to save himself. While he was hiding behind the coconut tree, he observed two of the assailants running towards Bharat Nagar. However, he did not know in which direction the third man went.

As the assailants had left the spot, this witness came near the deceased and with the help of neighbours, the deceased and Rooplal were moved to Cooper Hospital in the car of the deceased. One Rajesh Johari was driving the car. The witness followed the car, in an autorickshaw. In the hospital, the deceased was declared 'brought dead'. Rooplal was admitted in the intensive care unit. The statement of the witness was recorded by the police in the hospital. The witness identified accused Nos. 16 & 19 to be the assailants, who shot at the deceased. However, he could not identify the other accused. This witness described in detail the identification aspects of the accused at the time of identification parade that was held in Thane prison, on 2 February 2001. Since he was an eyewitness to the whole incident, I had to be very tactful while cross-examining this witness. My intention was to bring on record some of the omissions and contradictions, with a view to demolishing this witness and I got apt answers to all the questions that I put to him.

"I do not remember whether I had stated before the lady police officer at Cooper hospital that the deceased got up after collapsing. I cannot give any reason as to why it has not been recorded in my police statement. The lady police officer had enquired from me whether I knew anything about the incident. There were 20-30 people in the casualty department around the stretcher. The lady officer did not ask anybody else about the incident. My statement was recorded by the lady police officer, who was sitting behind the metallic grill. I was on the other side of the grill. My statement was recorded at about 11.30 or 11.45 a.m. It took 15 -20 minutes to record my statement."

As I put up my case, the witness was in total denial. "It is not correct to say that I had not witnessed the incident, as stated by me in my examination-in-chief. It is also not correct to say that I had not identified anybody during the identification parade. It is also not correct to say that two persons were shown to me by the police before holding the identification parade. It is not correct to say that I have been tutored by the police to give evidence as required by them." Thus went the denials of the witness.

P.W. No. 2 Saherao Phuke, was a rickshaw driver, staying at Jeet Nagar, i.e., the place of the incident. His house is situated about 70 to

75 ft. away from the Shiva temple. On 12 August 1997, at about 10.15 a.m., this witness was standing near the Kamgar Nagar gate, which is 120 to 150 ft. away from the Shiv temple. While standing there, he heard sounds like firecrackers. He, therefore, proceeded towards the Shiv temple to find out what was happening. There, he had seen that two persons were firing shots with pistols at Gulshan Kumar in front of the house of Roundal. The witness, therefore, started shouting. After the incident of firing, Gulshan Kumar tried to walk further, but he could not. He soon collapsed, in front of the house. The witness then went near Gulshan Kumar and found him to be lying in a pool of blood. He further saw P.W. No. 1, Lavangare and other residents of the locality putting Gulshan Kumar and his driver in a car. Lavangare had directed Rajesh Johari to take both to Cooper Hospital. This witness was frightened due to the incident and, therefore, went back home. At about 4.30 p.m. when he came out of the house, he saw policemen on the spot of the incident. The witness then told the police that he had seen the incident of firing. He was thus called to the police station and his statement was recorded.

During his examination-in-chief, this witness identified accused Nos. 16 & 19, from amongst all the accused who were in custody. He could not identify the pistol used by the assailants. During an identification parade, held in Thane prison on 20 October 1999, this witness was not able to identify accused No. 19, though he identified accused No. 16 as one of the assailants.

However, this witness claimed to have identified accused No. 19 in an identification parade held at Thane prison on 2 February 2001. During his cross examination, this witness came up with a new version that he had not mentioned so in his statement to the police. His version was that he had seen one of the assailants five to six times in Jeet Nagar area, prior to 12 August 1997. The last occasion being about a day or two prior to the incident. However, he could not tell the court whether some other unknown persons were also visiting Jeet Nagar, prior to the incident. He could categorically state before the court that normally, the said person visited Jeet Nagar during morning hours. While witnessing the incident of shooting, he suddenly recalled that one of the assailants was the same person whom he had seen loitering in the area, prior to the incident. To a question put to him as to whether he told this fact to the police, the witness replied that he did not feel it necessary to tell this to the police. However, he did not mention this fact to the police, while giving his statement. This 'improvement' in the conduct of the witness went to the benefit of the defence.

P.W. 3, Rajesh Ramchandra Johari was a driver by profession. He was examined in court as an eyewitness to the incident. It was this witness who had driven the injured Gulshan Kumar to Cooper hospital, soon after the incident. On 12 August 1997, as he heard a commotion from Jeet Nagar area he went there and saw eight to ten people on the run. They were all running towards Bharat Nagar. This witness, in fact, took the chance of chasing one of them. When the running person realised that this witness was chasing him, he pointed a pistol at him. The witness, therefore, abandoned the idea of chasing the person. He then reached the spot where Gulshan Kumar was lying injured in front of the house of Roundel. The witness, with the help of Lavangare and other residents of the area, soon put Gulshan Kumar and his injured driver Rooplal in the car of Gulshan Kumar and took them to Cooper Hospital. The witness stated that on admission in the hospital Gulshan Kumar was declared 'brought dead'. Rooplal was admitted to the Intensive Care Unit. In the court, this witness identified accused No. 19 to be the assailant who was running and pointing the revolver at him.

This witness further claimed to have identified the assailant, accused No. 19, in an identification parade held in Arthur Road prison, on 3 March 2001. In his cross examination by me, as advocate for accused No. 19, this witness was asked about a vital omission in his statement before the police that one of the running persons pointed a pistol towards him. This witness answered that he did not feel it necessary to tell the police this fact. However, in response to a question put to him by me, on behalf of the accused, this witness stated that one assailant who was running realised that he was chasing him. He further told the court that the reason for pointing the pistol at him was that the witness was chasing him. When I put up my case to this witness, his answers were all in denial.

Several of the eyewitnesses were examined by the prosecutor and were cross examined by different advocates for different accused. Though the prosecutor did a good job, the testimony of almost all witnesses was demolished in cross examination.

Among the eyewitnesses, Rooplal Barod was examined as P.W. 7. He was the injured victim in the incident. Rooplal was working as the driver of the deceased and was accompanying him to the Shiva Temple on the day of incident. Before the court, Rooplal described in detail the happenings of the day, without exaggeration. His version tallied with the version of P.W 1 and other eyewitnesses. In the court, Rooplal identified accused No. 19 to be the person who had shot at him. Earlier, Rooplal had also identified the accused, in an identification parade held on 2 February 2001, in Thane prison.

To my questions while cross examining this witness pertaining to the parking of the car of the deceased when they reached the temple, the witness answered that he did not remember whether he had stated before the police that the key to the car was left in the car itself and the glasses were also in rolled down mode. He could not assign any reason as to why that fact was not recorded in his police statement. The witness also could not offer any reason why his version before the court that the assailants who arrived at the scene had first fired on the back of the deceased, was not appearing in his police statement, The witness also could not remember whether he had stated before the police that the car was driven to the hospital by the person who was called by P.W. No.1.The witness also did not state before the police that he had informed the son of the deceased from the mobile phone of the deceased. He further explained that he did not state this fact to the police because he did not find it to be important. This witness was not able to identify any of the assailants in an identification parade held in October 1999.

During the trial in the court, in all, 45 prosecution witnesses were examined. They were all cross examined by advocates, appearing for various accused. Among all the witnesses, the evidence of the Investigating Officer was the most vital. Here, I would like to mention some of the crucial answers I could get from the I.O. in favour of the accused.

Investigating Officer, Shri Arjun Baburao Bagadi, attached to Special Branch, Unit VII, Bandra (W), was examined by the prosecution as P.W. No. 45. Almost all advocates for the accused cross examined the officer. In my cross examination, I could successfully bring on record that the SEM who conducted the identification parade in the case was an ex-SEM and not a current one.

"I am aware that the identification parade cannot be held by an ex-SEM. I had informed my superior officers that I was requesting an ex-SEM to hold the identification parade. An entry to that effect was made in the Station Diary, as well as in the Case Diary. I did not contact other police stations to find out whether any other SEM was available in their jurisdiction. I did not try to get the list of SEMs from the Home Department."

The officer's answers went to the benefit of the accused as the identification parade was discarded by the court. When I suggested to the officer that he had fabricated evidence against some of the accused, his answer was a total denial.

During evaluation of evidence in the case to reach a verdict, the trial judge wrote in the judgment:

"With this background of P.W. 37 and certain admissions made by him in the cross examination and the highly improbable nature of evidence given by him, I am of the view that evidence of P.W. 37 needs to be rejected. At the same time, it may also be mentioned here that the evidence of this witness has not been corroborated by any other independent witness in material particulars.

Evidence of P.W. 37 is being rejected not only for want of corroboration in material particulars, but it is being rejected because it is found to be not worthy of reliance. As such, the charge of conspiracy to commit the murder of Gulshan Kumar, framed against accused No.11 also must fail."

The three accused, being accused nos. 8, 9 & 10, implicated by P.W. 37 in the charge of conspiracy, were acquitted by the trial judge.

The charge under section 120-B IPC, read with section 25 (I-B) (a) of The Arms Act, failed against all the accused. Further, the charge under section 3 of The Arms Act, for possession of firearms also failed in this respect. The trial judge made specific appreciation of my argument on behalf of accused Nos. 16 & 19 that it had come in the evidence of one of the panch witnesses that the accused who was in custody of the police was handcuffed. Taking note of this fact, I argued that the statement made by the said accused was not a voluntary statement.

After meticulously examining and evaluating the evidence on record the trial judge had to discard a greater part of the evidence as it did not support the prosecution's case. Though accused Nos. 16 and 19, both were present at the time of assault on the deceased along with a third person (absconding accused Anil Sharma), accused No. 16 was not identified by P.W No.1 and 7, on whose evidence the prosecution had placed reliance to sustain a conviction. However, the trial judge could not wholly rely upon the evidence of P. W. 1, though he could fully rely upon the evidence of P.W.7 to sustain a conviction for accused No. 19. The cumulative effect of a careful reading of evidence of P.W. Nos. 1, 2, 3, 4 & 7 led the judge to the conclusion that P.W. No.1 had not seen accused no. 16. However, he had seen accused no. 19 and the first assailant (absconding accused Anil Sharma) running towards Bharat Nagar.

The trial judge had a Herculean task in extricating the little grain of truth from the piling chaff of falsehood. However, in all fairness, he acquitted 18 accused of the charges levelled against them and convicted accused no.19, Abdul Rauf Merchant on five counts, for murder of Gulshan Kumar and he was sentenced to life imprisonment and fine.

Accused No, 19, challenged his conviction in the High Court, by filing an appeal against the verdict of the trial judge.

gulshan kumar verdict / the closing statements...

RIGHT: Defence lawyer Majeed Memon, who appeared for some of the accused in the Gulshan Kumar murder case, talks to reporters soon after the accused were let off by the court due to lack of evidence. From the 19 people accused in the murder case, one died while the remaining 17 were acquitted by court. The sessions court however, has convicted the main accused Abdul Rauf. Photographs by Gajanan Dudhalkar

In his capacity as Secretary of the Bar Association, in a particular year, MM had the occasion to invite an eminent international criminal law expert from United States to address the members of the Bar and judges in Bombay. A lecture was organised in a spacious hall where, among the audience, were eminent advocates, magistrates, judges, law students and law teachers.

The speaker spoke for a little over one hour. His speech was not merely educative and full of legal knowledge but was spellbinding and sprinkled with his extraordinary wit and humor. He said "I have a lucrative practice and worldwide fame. I live my life in my own way, unaffected by praises or criticism. I have my own standard of life, likes and dislikes. I care for none. Then he said, "Those who are with me, may raise their hands and those who are not, may raise their standards."

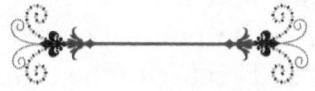

Twenty

EXTRADITION PROCEEDINGS IN LONDON

One of the most arduous legal proceedings that I have ever come across during my career was the extradition proceedings of Nadeem Akthar Saifi, in London. Nadeem was accused of conspiring to kill Gulshan Kumar by hiring the services of Abu Salem from Dubai.

After initial investigation by D.N. Nagar police and registration of FIR, for offences under sections 302, 307, 120-B read with Section 34 Indian Penal Code and section 25 (1-B) (a) read with section 3, of The Arms Act, against three unknown persons, further investigation was taken over by the DCB, CID Unit-VII. During their investigation, it was revealed that the murder of Gulshan Kumar was the outcome of a larger conspiracy. The police pointed at Nadeem as the main conspirator. This was so because of the differences between Nadeem and Gulshan Kumar, pertaining to the audio rights of Nadeem's album, *'Hi Ajnabi.'*

Nadeem was in London at the time of the murder of Gulshan Kumar on 12 August 1997. He had arrived there sometime in July 1997 for medical treatment of his wife. He was staying in King's Barry, along with his wife, Sultana, two minor children and a maid. The fatal assault on Gulshan Kumar took place much later, on 12 August 1997. Since the deceased was an important Bollywood personality, there was lot of hue and cry upon his broad daylight assassination in Mumbai. The Police Commissioner, Shri Mendonca, was under tremendous pressure from the media and Bollywood, in addition to his political bosses in power Mr. Mendonca held a well-attended press conference in Mumbai, in the beginning of September 1997, in which he claimed that the investigation clearly indicated that Nadeem had hired the services of Abu Salem's gang to eliminate Gulshan Kumar and that he had ample evidence to prove Nadeem's involvement in the murder. On the following day, the Deputy Chief Minister of Maharashtra State, Shri Gopinath Munde, also held a similar press conference in Delhi, reiterating the claim of the Mumbai Police Commissioner.

After detailed investigation by DCB, CID and the arrest of some of the suspects, the Mumbai police continued their investigation, showing Nadeem as the prime accused along with others, and filed a charge sheet in the concerned Mumbai court. Simultaneously, since Nadeem was not found in India at his known address and the police learnt that he was in the U.K., extradition proceedings were initiated against him in India. A red corner notice was issued and with the help of Interpol, Nadeem was made to surrender in London, and was forthwith released on bail, on execution of a bond. The extradition proceedings against him commenced in Bow Street Magistrate's Court, in Covent Garden, London. The learned Magistrate refused to go into the merits of the evidence and as such Nadeem's team of lawyers headed by me from India, had no option but to invite the order of extradition against him, to challenge the same, before the higher courts in London. Accordingly, the Magistrate passed the order extraditing Nadeem from London. The said order was challenged on merits in the Supreme Court of Judicature, Queen's Bench (Divisional Court).

Before the Queen's Bench, the entire evidence was examined on merits, by the Hon'ble Supreme Court of Judicature, presided over by Lord Justice Rose and Mr. Justice Newman. The justices held in their verdict that the claims made by the Mumbai police were false and without any substance.

Sec.27 of The Extradition Act 1989 provides: " (1) in any proceedings under this Act in relation to a person whose return has been requested by a designated Commonwealth Country or a colony including proceedings on an application for habeas corpus in respect of a person in custody under this Act (a) a document duly authenticated which purports to set out evidence given on oath in a designated Commonwealth country or a colony shall be admissible as evidence in the matters stated in it.

(2) A document shall be deemed to be duly authenticated for the purpose of this section (a) in the case of a document purporting to set out evidence given as mentioned in sub-section l (a) above, if the document purports to be certified by a judge or a magisterial officer in or of the country or colony in question to be the original document, containing or recording that evidence or a true copy of such a document."

In Nadeem's case, the all-important document was the English translation of a witness's testimony in Hindi before the English Magistrate, in Bow Street Court. It was the crucially different translation of an alleged telephone conversation in Hindi on 9 August 1997, between Gulshan Kumar and a newspaper editor, relating to threats made to the former. The purported English translation before the court included a reference to the applicant Nadeem, whereas the correct translation did not.

A second point vehemently pushed forth, in favour of Nadeem, before the Queen's Bench, was that as in extradition proceedings there is no opportunity to cross examine, and accomplice evidence may be sufficient to establish a case, a police officer in the requesting State can disproportionately influence the decision to commit, if he produces evidence obtained in bad faith. Therefore, the consequence of admitting improperly obtained evidence is more profound at committal than at trial. It was thus argued that the Court must have regard to its obligations under the Human Rights Act, 1998, when considering Section 78 of the Extradition Act. Furthermore, breaches of international and foreign law, and rules designed for the protection of an accused or a witness in the country where evidence was gathered, shall be considered. Regard should also be paid to the Convention Against Torture and Other Cruel Human or Degrading Treatment or

Punishment (1984). In the circumstances, it was argued that the Bow Street Magistrate should have been certain that the police did not coerce accomplice Ali Shaikh to give his evidence against applicant, Nadeem. If the Magistrate was not certain, the evidence of Ali Shaikh should have been excluded in the outline. The case of Nadeem was that Ali Shaikh was an uncorroborated accomplice, who made statements, implicating him, in return for a pardon for a capital offence which, subsequently he retracted, on more than one occasion. His statement was the result of physical and mental ill-treatment and coercion, arising during his unlawful detention between 25 and 31 August. He had also succumbed to the pressure on his family, as confirmed by sworn evidence by his wife and daughter, on 26 September 1997. Mr. Mokashi, an Advocate suggested by the police, was foisted upon him, so that he made the confession which implicated applicant Nadeem.

The Bow Street Magistrate should have made findings about several disputed facts. These included date and time of Ali Shaikh's arrest, whether he was physically tortured, whether the stress which he was under on 20 and 28 September 1997, as observed by the Magistrate at Ballad Pier, was the consequence of police activity. Whether his wife and daughter were required by the police on 21 September to change his advocate, from Sutrali to Mokashi, whether the police engineered a false confession before Magistrate Palnitkar, on or after 1 October, whether his statements of 27 and 28 November, inculpating Jawed Fawda, were falsely contrived by the police, whether Inspector Bagadi and/or Assistant Commissioner Rao fabricated evidence, thereby undermining the integrity of the investigation, whether the name 'Nadeem' was properly added to the charge sheet under the guise of a purportedly accurate translation, and whether the evidence of prison officer Wankhede and Advocate Mokashi that Ali Shaikh wrote the Hindi text in the document ABB10 appointing Mokashi as his Advocate and asking to give evidence for the prosecution is false. If the Bow Street Magistrate had resolved any of these issues, as he ought to have, adversely to the prosecution, this should have led to the exclusion of Ali Shaikh's evidence, under section 78, a consequential insufficiency of evidence and a refusal to commit.

Furthermore, a few undisputed facts were themselves sufficient to lead to exclusion of evidence, under section 78. Those were breaches of Indian Law, in particular the Police Manual and rules in relation to the keeping of a diary concerning the arrest and detention of Ali Shaikh, the lack of any written notes or statements in relation to Ali Shaikh's alleged admissions prior to 1 October up to 3 October 1997 and during a bail application on 14 September, Ali Shaikh was still protesting his innocence. The Ballard Pier Magistrate, on 18 and 20 September recorded Ali Shaikh as saying that he was in danger if he did not give a statement; the incriminating statement was given only after Ali Shaikh's advocate had been changed and his wife and daughter threatened; the offer and acceptance of a free pardon in relation to a capital offence in return for making the statement; the signs of fear and intimidation on 1 October, before Magistrate Palnitkar, the fact that despite being in judicial custody, supposedly without police contact, Ali Shaikh was brought to court without a court order on 5 November; the introduction of Javed Fawda as a co-conspirator for the first time in Ali Shaikh's evidence on 27 November; internal inconsistencies in Ali Shaikh's account, in particular as to whether he was inside or outside the cabin in which the conspiratorial conversation allegedly took place; Ali Shaikh's subsequent retraction of his evidence and the issue of a Writ Petition, not only retracting the evidence but making allegations against the police of being threatened and tortured to give the evidence implicating applicant Nadeem and Javed Fawda, and the omission of any reference in the extradition proceedings to the Ballard Pier Magistrate on 18 and 20 September. The findings of Justice Auguiar, that Javed Fawda was never involved in the murder of Gulshan Kumar but was deliberately killed by the police by a shot at close range, was also relied upon by the applicant. In relation to section 78, the applicant contended that the Bow Street Magistrate gave no reason for not heeding the Torture Convention.

As to sufficiency, it was common ground that the prosecution case against the applicant depended on the evidence of Ali Shaikh. For they describe in detail, visits by the applicant to Dubai, in May 1997, during the first of which, he says, there was a discussion among the applicant and others, to the effect that Gulshan Kumar was troubling the applicant in his business and was, therefore, to be killed. Thereafter, two guns and a car were acquired and used in the killing.

It was submitted on behalf of the applicant that it was the Bow Street Magistrate's duty to weigh the evidence before him, rejecting that which was inherently incredible or worthless. In this regard reliance was placed on R v Governor of Pentonville Prison ex parte Alves (1993) AC 284, where it was held that the Magistrate should reject any evidence which he considers to be worthless and that he should not commit.

In ex parte Alves, the House of Lords held that the retraction by a witness in extradition proceedings, previously given in the requesting country, did not, in itself discredit that evidence and unless it was worthless the Magistrate was entitled to act upon it in deciding whether there was sufficient evidence to justify an order for committal. But subsequent retraction of itself does not render previous evidence worthless, because it may be that the later retraction is not worthy of belief. The facts of the present case were different in several respects from those in Alves. In that case, the Magistrate saw the witness who had a motive to help the accused retracting his evidence. In the present case, the original evidence was motivated by a promise of pardon for capital offence, and it contained inconsistencies as to whether Ali Shaikh was inside or outside the room at the time of the crucial conversation, as to the date when he was arrested and in relation to the late introduction of the name Javed Fawda. Furthermore, his evidence against the applicant came after he had protested his innocence until the failure of his 14 September bail application, and there was sworn evidence from his family on 26 September, tending to support his claim of police coercion.

In the evidence on oath, given by Ali Shaikh, in his Writ Petition and to the National Human Rights Commission, from March 1998 onwards, he claims to have been arrested on 25 and not on 31 August 1997, to have been tortured and intimidated by the police, to have been deceitfully induced to change his advocate to another chosen by the police, to have been promised bail if he implicated the applicant, Nadeem, and to have been tortured and intimidated to introduce the name of Javed Fawda, which had not appeared earlier into his final statements to the Magistrate in late November, 1997. If Ali Shaikh had lied about any of these matters, his evidence was worthless. His evidence is confirmed in part by the evidence of his wife and daughter that they had been arrested with him and that contrary to Mokashi's evidence, they had not instructed Mokashi to represent Ali Shaikh. Furthermore, there was evidence from Mr. Vanjara, the Advocate who later represented him in the Writ Petition, that Ali Shaikh could not read or write. Even if it was not necessary for the Bow Street Magistrate to make specific findings for the purpose of submissions under section 78, it was necessary for him to do so when looking at sufficiency.

It was further argued on behalf of the applicant that the court shall order the applicant's discharge, if it appears to the court that, in relation to the offence, or each of the offences, in respect of which the applicant's return is sought and if the accusation against him is not made in good faith in the interest of justice, it would, having regard to all the circumstances, be unjust or oppressive to return him.

The applicant relied on several matters as demonstrating bad faith on the part of the police and the prosecution authorities, in relation to the applicant. First, as appeared from the newspaper report on 31 August 1997, by the Mumbai Police Commissioner and on 2 September, the Mumbai Deputy Chief Minister asserted that there was evidence of the applicant's guilt, at a time when no legally admissible evidence was available. Secondly, in relation to extradition proceedings neither the first request in November 1997 nor the second in January 1998 made any reference to the pressure and tension exhibited by Ali Shaikh and recorded by the Magistrate on 18, 20 and 26 September 1997. There was a failure to represent Ali Shaikh properly before the Bow Street Magistrate to enable proper assessment of his credibility. Thirdly, the original ABB10, the authority to Mokashi to act and the expressed wish to give evidence for the prosecution had never been produced and the explanation for its non-production never came forth. In July

2000, Mr. Nikam, the prosecutor, claimed that Mokashi had refused to hand it over.

In October 2000 Mokashi said he had never been asked for it by the police and he failed to produce it before the court. Ali Shaikh's family denied ever instructing Mokashi to act for him. Fourthly, the literacy of Ali Shaikh had been challenged by the defence, ever since a copy of ABB10 was produced, but the prosecution has refused requests for an independent investigation of his literacy. Furthermore, ABB10 was never mentioned by Mokashi to the Magistrate on 26 September, in the pardon order on 27 November, in the request for extradition, or by Inspector Bagadi on his affidavit in response to Ali Shaikh's Writ Petition in April 1998. Fifthly, there was evidence before the Bow Street Magistrate from Mr. Vanjara that Ali Shaikh signed instructions to act, in broken Urdu, did not read any of the documents which Mr. Vanjara showed him and said that he could not write in any language. There was also evidence before the court from Ali Shaikh's educated daughter, Shabnam, that her father could write his signature in Urdu, but cannot write in Hindi. In addition, there was expert evidence before the court that the signature on ABB10 in broken Urdu was not written by the educated writer of the Hindi text and was made on a blank sheet of paper before the text was written. Sixthly, there was a breach of the Maharashtra Prison Rules, in that no records were made, or if made, kept in the Crate Register or otherwise, of the visit of Mokashi to the prison and his alleged interview there with Ali Shaikh, with Prison Officer Wankhede, 10 to 15 feet away. It was also inappropriate for Wankhede to countersign ABB10, on the basis that it had been voluntarily made. Seventhly, as to the date and circumstances of Ali Shaikh's arrest, during a bail application on 14 September, it was claimed that he had been illegally detained. On 20 September he broke down in the presence of the Magistrate and said he was in danger that if he did not give a statement "he would be sent somewhere very long". He requested to be kept away from gangsters. The Magistrate recorded that he appeared to be in tremendous pressure. On 1, 3 and 4 October, he said he had been arrested on 25 August, and he did not change that date to 31 August until making amendments to his October statements on 5 November. There were also discrepancies in the remand sheet as to the time of Ali Shaikh's arrest. Finally, Assistant Commissioner Rao applied for extradition.

It was submitted on behalf of the applicant that if, on the balance of probabilities, it was established that Ali Shaikh was illiterate, or that Wankhede and Mokashi had been lying in relation to ABB10, there has been a want of good faith requiring the applicant's discharge under Section 11(3). On this point, reliance was placed on Woolf LJ in Osman on 25 February 1992.

"Good faith has to be given a reasonably generous interpretation, so that if the proceedings were brought for a collateral purpose or with an improper motive, and not for the purpose of achieving the proper administration of justice, they would not be regarded as complying with the statutory requirement. Likewise, accusations would not be made in good faith and in the interest of justice, if the prosecution deliberately manipulates or misuses the process of the Court to deprive the defendant of the protection to which he is entitled by law."

It was submitted on behalf of applicant Nadeem that it would be unjust or oppressive to return the applicant, because of the circumstances in which he came to be charged in India and the conduct of the Indian authorities in the extradition process, both in India and the United Kingdom.

As against the evidence brought on record by the defence in favour of the applicant, the prosecution vehemently argued for the return of the applicant to the Indian authorities. Mr. Paul Garlick QC did not seek to diminish the significance of the Human Rights complaints but urged that they be put in context with reference to the specific aspects of the applicant's case. He submitted that it was not an appropriate forum to determine the wide-ranging issues involved. He stressed that since the murder, there had been a change of Government in India, and in Maharashtra.

As to section 78, the QC submitted that the Bow Street Magistrate's function was to consider the circumstances and give a reasoned decision, but this did not involve an obligation to make findings of fact upon every issue, the state of the evidence might make this impossible. The Magistrate correctly drew a distinction between the terms of sections 76 and 78. He dealt with the evidence of Ali Shaikh's wife and daughter, and with the literacy issue. He was not able to make any findings because he had not seen the witness or heard any cross examination on the voir dire, or otherwise. He bore in mind the circumstances and reached a reasoned conclusion.

The QC submitted that section 27 distinguished between documents and depositions. Proceedings in India are habitually conducted in more than one language and the Magistrate was entitled to receive the evidence in the local language and to translate and record it in English. Ali Shaikh's evidence was read over to him in Hindi. He admitted that it was correct, and the deposition was then signed by him as well as by the magistrate. Accordingly, he submitted that the Magistrate's ruling on 25 February was correct.

Quoting from relevant judgments, the QC further submitted that the principal focus of the judge's attention must be upon the procedural fairness of the proceedings, the nature and reliability of the prosecution evidence and the fullness and fairness of the opportunity available to the defence to deal with the evidence which the prosecution seeks to adduce. He submitted that the Magistrate was correct in concluding that there was no obligation on the prosecution to disprove matters raised by the defence beyond reasonable doubt and that he correctly identified his role as being to carry out an evaluation of the evidence tendered by both, the government and the accused, as to the circumstances in which the evidence was obtained and ultimately to decide on that evidence, whether the admission would have such an adverse effect on the fairness of these proceedings and that he should exclude it.

The QC further submitted that it would be entirely inappropriate, in the absence of the principal witness, for the magistrate to make specific findings of facts on every issue. The disputed facts were proper for determination at trial and not on the extradition proceedings.

Accordingly, he submitted that the magistrate did not err in his approach to section 78. He did not misdirect himself and his decision was not perverse. Furthermore, the magistrate specially referred to the Torture Convention which raised precisely the same factual issues as under section 78.

As to 'sufficiency', it was submitted in reliance to ex parte Alves that retraction did not discredit Ali Shaikh's evidence. 'Sufficiency' was essentially a matter for the decision of the Magistrate, whose decision is only susceptible to challenge, on Wednesbury grounds. The Magistrate considered ex parte Alves and accepted that it was necessary to look at the evidence with great care. He commented that if the original evidence was the product of inducement by way of pardon, it was curious "that he would wish to retract his evidence, lose the offer of free pardon and place himself once again in jeopardy of the severest penalty." The Magistrate considered the possibility that it might be the retraction, rather than the original evidence, which was false, because of Ali Shaikh's fear of gangsters. He referred to the remarkably detailed account which Ali Shaikh gave over a three-day period. He concluded, applying the Galbraith test set out in Alves, that a properly directed tribunal could find Ali Shaikh's evidence capable of belief. This approach, submitted the QC, cannot effectively be challenged.

As to section 11(3), the QC submitted that there was no basis for concluding that the requisition for extradition was made for a collateral purpose or improper motive. It comes, he said, from the Union of India, not the police, the prosecutor, or the State. He accepted this did not end the matter. But the burden is on the applicant to show that the accusation was not made in good faith, and because of this, it would be unjust to return him. The QC referred to the well-known observations of Lord Diplock in Kakis v Government of the Republic of Cyprus (1978) 1 WLR 779.

"Unjust" I regard as directed primarily at the risk of prejudice to the accused in the conduct of the trial itself, "oppressive" as directed at the hardship to the accused resulting from changes in his circumstances that have occurred during the period to be taken into consideration; there is room for overlapping and between them, they would cover all cases where to return him would not be fair." He pointed out that Justice Aguiar, who had concluded that Javed Fawda was executed by the police, is one of the judges at an appropriate level in Maharashtra to try the applicant if he is returned.

He submitted that the "accusation" in the present case is made by the state of Maharashtra. He accepted that if the state were tainted this would taint the accusation. But he submitted that "accusation", in section 11(3), refers to the state, not those involved in investigation or prosecution or the witnesses. He pointed out that it was not until March 1998, after the request for extradition had been made, that the retraction occurred, and a serious allegation was made against the independent prosecutor.

There is no suggestion that the judiciary is partial, and every indication is that they are vigorous in investigating impropriety, so there will be no injustice in the trial process, this is particularly so as the applicant is very well known and there has been much publicity in relation to the case already, so the judiciary will be particularly alert to investigate matters thoroughly.

In relation to the evidence of impropriety, the QC submitted that it was far from conclusive. Ali Shaikh's statements had not been in cross examination. On the literacy point, prison officer Wankhede and Advocate Mokashi were both credible witnesses who had given evidence and been thoroughly cross examined. Their account gain says that of Ali Shaikh, and the conflict should properly be resolved by an impartial, competent, and vigilant judiciary in India. A trial, in such circumstances, will avoid any possibility of prejudice from the prior investigation and prosecution.

As to section 6(1) (d) the QC submitted in reference to the speech of Lord Diplok in Fernandez v Government of Singapore (1971) 1WLR 987 that the proper test was whether there was 'reasonable chance', 'substantial ground for thinking', or 'serious possibility' that the applicant would be detained or restricted, by reason of his religion, if returned. He submitted that there was no basis on which, it could be said that the legal system in India was unable to protect the Muslim minority adequately, or at all. He also relied upon the expert evidence of Dr. Chitnis that since the *BJP-Shiv Sena* Government was replaced in 1999 by the Government of the Congress Party and its secular allies, a Minority Commission for the protection and interests of minorities, and a State Human Rights Commission had also been formed. Furthermore, he submitted, there were pro-Muslim parties in the new Government. The high profile of the applicant would ensure vigilance by the judiciary at trial and there could be no possibility of further questioning, if the applicant is returned, because he would be taken before a Magistrate.

Accordingly, the QC submitted that the Court should take the view that there was no reason under Section 6(1) (d) for the applicant not to be returned.

In his reply, Mr. Nicholls submitted that if Mr. Garlick's (QC) construction of "accusation" in section 11 (3) were correct, the section would be sterile: the word must extend to persons responsible for presenting and maintaining prosecutions, including the police: he referred to Propend Finance Ltd. vs Singh (1998. International Law Reports) 611 where, in relation to S.14(1) of the State Immunity Act 1978, the Court of Appeal held that the activity of a Police Superintendent involved acts of a sovereign or Governmental nature.

In the light of these competing submissions, advanced by both sides, the Bench turned to a conclusion as under.

Conclusion on Section 11(3):

The Court has received evidence on the issue over and above that which was before the Magistrate. We find the following circumstances bear upon whether the accusation is made in good faith and in the interest of justice, and whether it would be unjust or oppressive to return the applicant.

There was no legally admissible material available to the Mumbai Police Commissioner to provide reasonable grounds for the statements that witnesses "quite clearly indicated that Nadeem (the applicant) hired Abu Salem gang's services to eliminate Kumar........." and "we have ample evidence to prove Nadeem's involvement... ". This Court is placed on enquiry as to what motive there could have been for such an unsubstantiated statement to be made at a press conference. Indeed, even if grounds existed for such a belief, making such a statement would raise questions about the underlying motive.

The assertion of Mumbai (Maharashtra) Deputy Chief Minister gives rise to like concern. Having regard to the vital importance to be attached to the circumstances surrounding the confession made by Ali Shaikh, the absence of any reference for his return to the pressure recorded by the Magistrate on 18, 20, and 26 September, is remarkable. This non- disclosure of such a central feature of the case has not been explained.

It is to be inferred that it was deliberate and calculated to leave those considering the case with the impression that it was stronger than the true facts merited. Equally, the failure to disclose Ali Shaikh's retraction, until part way through the committal proceedings, causes this court astonishment. No explanation has been provided. It is to be inferred that it, too, was deliberate and calculated, to leave the impression that the case against the applicant was stronger than the true facts merited.

The above circumstances have to be considered in the light of further evidence, since the committal, about the obtaining of Ali Shaikh's confession, his literacy and the genesis of ABB10. In our judgment, a pattern of events emerges, which is consistent with (a) a preconceived desire to blame the applicant when no evidence existed, and (b) the use of improper pressure to obtain a statement from Ali Shaikh to make good the allegations. Whereas the evidence of Ali Shaikh's advocates may have provided some reassurance about the propriety of what happened, the evidence of Prison Officer Wankhede and Advocate Mokashi gives added cause for anxiety. Further, so far as these two witnesses are concerned, the police plainly disregarded Mr. Garlick's direction that no approach should be made to them before they gave evidence. We infer that the police have an improper interest in interfering with the evidence of this case.

The expert evidence points to ABB10 as having been signed by Ali Shaikh, in blank. The language of the document shows that unless he is more educated than anyone suggests, it could not be his own confession. We infer that this document could not have been created without interference from those responsible for holding Ali Shaikh.

The evidence of Mr. Vanjara supports the conclusion that Ali Shaikh is illiterate. His daughter's evidence is consistent with the document being construct of another, placed above his signature after this had been obtained from him on a blank sheet of paper.

The inclusion of Javed Fawda's name in Ali Shaikh's deposition at a later stage, and where there are grounds to connect it with unlawful and unjustified action by the police requiring false justification leads us to question the role of the police in relation to the appearance of Javed Fawda's name.

The cumulative effect of all these circumstances causes us to infer that the accusation of murder and conspiracy made against the applicant is not made in good faith and in the interest of justice.

Having reached the conclusion, we are also satisfied that it would not be fair, and would be unjust to return the applicant, because of the appearance of misbehaviour by the police in pursuing their inquiries, and the significant risk that the activities surrounding that misbehaviour have so tainted the evidence as to render a fair trial impossible.

CONCLUSION:

"We, therefore, order that a writ of habeas corpus issue to procure the production before this Court of the applicant Nadeem Akhtar Saifi and that he be discharged forthwith in relation to the offences in respect of which his return is sought by the Union of India."

****** ******

On 21st December 2000, the Queen's Bench, comprising of Lord

Chief Justice Christopher Rose and Justice Newman ordered the Union of India to pay 9,20,000 British Pounds to Nadeem, being cost of litigation incurred by him for his high-profile defence advocates. The order was a great relief for me personally. I had made 23 trips to London for the conduct of Nadeem's defence. The amount was transferred by the Indian Government to Nadeem's account in London, in the month of October 2001.

City — AFTERNOON SATURDAY 29TH JULY 2000

GULSHAN KUMAR MURDER CASE

'Now the case is in Nadeem's favour'

BY A STAFF REPORTER

Music Director Nadeem Saifee's counsel from India, Mr. Majeed Memon claimed that his client's contention of innocence had now become "stronger" even as a bundle of contradictions and omissions had surfaced during examination of a key witness by a team of British lawyers before a Sessions Court here in Gulshan Kumar murder case on Thursday.

For the first time in history, the Mumbai High Court, on a request made by the Supreme Court of Great Britain, had permitted British lawyers, Mr. Clive Nicholas (Nadeem's counsel in the London High Court) and Paul Garlik (of the Queen's counsel) to examine Shabnam, daughter of Mohammad Ali Sheikh who is a key accused in the murder of the cassette king. The examination, which was for a limited purpose, pertained to the authorship of a letter (written in Hindi) and literacy level of Sheikh, who had allegedly signed the letter in broken Urdu.

Nadeem had alleged that Sheikh did not know Hindi and that the letter was false and the signature forged.

During the examination, Shabnam told Clive Nicholas that her father understood Urdu and could sign in that language only. She said her father could not read or write in Hindi.

However, Shabnam fumbled when crown prosecution counsel Paul Garlick drew her attention to her own affidavit filed in a London court wherein she had talked about receiving a letter in Hindi from her father, describing alleged torture by police to become an approver.

She had however made it clear that she had no knowledge as to whether the letter was written by his father or by someone else.

But she had latter identified her father's signature in English on an embarkation and disembarkation card although earlier she had told Nadeem's counsel that her father could sign only in Urdu.

The Session's Court Judge Mr. L.S. Deshpande had latter sent the recorded statements to the London High Court in sealed tape. These statements are likely to have an important bearing on the extradition trial of Nadeem Saifee.

Meanwhile, Mr. Memon maintained that irrespective of the other disclosures made by Shabnam, her admission that she had no idea about the authorship of the letter supported Nadeem's contention. "Our argument was for a limited purpose about the authorship of the letter and the level of Hindi literacy of Sheikh. Shabnam has made her point clear, which vindicates our claim," Memon said adding, "the case is now heavily in our favour." ■

■ Nadeem's counsel in India, Mr. Majid Memon, and his counterpart in the London High Court, Mr. Clive Nicholas, outside the Sessions Court.

BOMBAY JOURNAL

THE FREE PRESS JOURNAL ■ WEDNESDAY, MAY 22, 2002 ■ PAGE 9 ■

Nadeem got costs of extradition proceedings and not damages, says lawyer

MUMBAI

MUSIC composer Nadeem Akhtar Saifee has received from the UK government Rs 6.7 crore as costs of unsuccessful extradition proceedings initiated against him for his alleged complicity in Gulshan Kumar murder case but he had still not claimed compensation or damages from the Indian Government, has lawyer Majeed Memon clarified here on Tuesday, reports PTI.

Reacting to a report in a section of the media that Nadeem had not been awarded compensation or damages by a UK court, Memon said they had never claimed that damages had been awarded

On the contrary, Nadeem had gone on record to say that he was contemplating to file an appropriate suit against the Government of India for damages, his lawyer said.

He clarified that in the order of December 21, 2000, of UK High Court, Deputy Chief Justice Lord Rose and Justice Newman clearly mentioned that Nadeem was discharged forthwith in relation to offences in respect of which his return was sought by the Government of India. The court also provided for costs of litigation to Nadeem for the groceedings in Bowstreet Magistrate's Court as also in the UK High Court, Memon said adding that the bench had directed the master of the court to compute the actual costs.

Later, the office of the court, in consultation with Nadeem's solicitors, worked out a sum equivalent to 900,000 Pounds (approximately Rs 6.7 crore). The amount was duly received by Nadeem by cheque, Memon said.

Nadeem's lawyer, however, clarified that neither he nor the music composer had ever claimed that the Government of India had paid him Rs 6.7 crore as damages. On the contrary, Memon said, he and Nadeem had gone on record to say that they were extenuating the possibility of filing an appropriate suit for damages against the Government of India for a sum much higher than the cost of extradition proceedings. Memon said that filing of such suit would be entirely on legal merits and there will be no victimisation or vendetta against anyone for such a step.

In a Lighter Vein

Once there was a riot between two groups of people at Juhu beach, which falls under the jurisdiction of Santa Cruz police station in Mumbai. Both the groups were engaged in providing horse rides to children on the beach, for a fee. On either side, there were eight to ten young boys. Incidentally all of them were Muslims.

One fine day, a sudden and unanticipated altercation and scuffle took place between the two groups. In the melée some of them sustained minor injuries. Santa Cruz police registered a case and a cross case against the groups. In all, the police held 18 of them, as accused. All of them were arrested and arraigned as accused before the concerned Magistrate.

The dingy courtroom where the accused were produced was unusually overcrowded. All the 18 were accompanied by almost an equal number of police escorts. The presiding Magistrate had the reputation of being a follower of the RSS ideology.

One group of accused persons approached MM to apply for bail. MM was thus present in the court when the remand proceedings started. The names of the 18 accused persons were called out, one by one, by the bench clerk, to make them stand in a row. All the names were patently Muslim names. The Magistrate was surprised and in a lighter vein he uttered, "I believe I am in Pakistan."

This was heard by some of the educated youths in the group. They took serious exception to this utterance of the Magistrate. One of them shouted at the presiding officer, at the top of his voice. He asked, "How dare the judge call us Pakistanis? We don't care if you send us to jail. But we will report this to the High Court." MM tried to pacify the protesters. However, they were highly enraged and created quite a scene in the courtroom. The presiding officer appeared intimidated, seeing such disorder in the courtroom. He soon chose to withdraw from the courtroom to his chamber till tempers cooled down. MM tried to convince his clients to refrain from creating a scene in the court. From the chamber, the Magistrate then sent his orderly to call MM and the prosecutor. When MM entered the chamber, he found the presiding officer quite anxious and disturbed. He tried to explain that he did not mean to offend anybody. It was just by way of humour that he had made such a 'light comment' in an otherwise drab courtroom. He was, however, repentant for the impact it had created and requested MM to pacify his clients. He even suggested that he was ready to release all of them on personal bond.

MM brought out the message to the accused. He asked them to withdraw their protest and consent to the arrangement. The accused accepted his advice, and all were set free on bail.

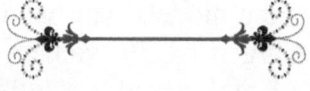

Twenty One

THE CASE OF ANAND JON IN THE UNITED STATES

It was on 6 March 2007 that Anand Jon, an India-born, noted fashion designer in the US was arrested for alleged sexual offences against various women. His arrest came about, barely days before he was to launch his multimillion-dollar denim line 'jeanisis'. A year earlier, the Wall Street Journal had evaluated his brand at 10 million dollars, and he was planning to inject another 10-15 million dollars into the company. Strangely, the first allegation of sexual assault surfaced in March, filed by one of the models with whom he had worked. Within months, Anand was charged by 30 women, aged between 14 and 27 years with 90 counts of raping and assaulting them after luring them with promises of modelling contracts for his clothing designs.

It was in this context that Anand's sister Sanjana, also from the US, met me in my office in Mumbai. She claimed that Anand was a victim of racism and professional jealousy. Sanjana stated that "all victims had admitted before the Courts that they had not suffered any physical injury, not a scratch".

Anand was a 33-year-old India-born celebrity. He was placed in a Los Angeles prison since his arrest and was awaiting trial without bail. He was facing charges of rape, indulging in lewd acts, and wrongful confinement. If convicted on all counts, he could be sentenced to life in prison. Sanjana instructed me to assist Anand's counsel in the US. It was generally felt that being brown skinned, he would be perceived as guilty. The alleged incidents occurred between November 2002 and

March 2007. But strangely, the 'victims' continued to work and tour with him even after that. Anand was supposed to have been tried in Los Angeles, Texas, and New York Courts.

Sanjana Jon visited Mumbai to proclaim to the people here that her brother had been framed by publicity seekers. On Wednesday, 2 January 2008, a press conference was held in my office in Mumbai, where she declared that her brother was innocent and that the US Government was not giving him a chance to defend himself. "He is being denied a fair trial," she said. Over 30 complainants from different parts of America had charged Anand in 90 odd cases. Sanjana said that the charges were levelled against her brother exactly two weeks before the global launch of his new fashion line 'jeanisis'. "Some of the complaints are over five years old," said Sanjana. The complainants had been hanging out with him and had even been staying in his house, as paying guests, long after the sexual harassment incidents were supposed to have taken place. "The motive behind the allegations thus ranged from seeking fame and fortune to making Anand a 'fall guy' as he was a non-American who had achieved great success in the American fashion world," said Sanjana.

The complainants claimed that he harassed them at his place. However, Sanjana said her mother and she stayed in the same house. "How could he sexually assault any woman in the same house where his mother and sister were living?" she asked.

Sanjana strongly believed that there had been a conspiracy to frame Anand. "The women who complained against him recruited supporters on social networking sites, like My Space," said Sanjana, who was in the city to gather support for Anand from the Indian community.

Sanjana met me to ensure that I would travel to the United States and fight for Anand when the matter was scheduled for hearing on 30 January 2008. Sanjana added that she feared that Anand might not get a fair trial there and "...perhaps only a reputed advocate from India would fight for him without prejudice." I assured her that by mid-January, I would place the matter before the Prime Minister and the External Affairs Ministry. It would help me get detailed information from the Indian Embassy in the US.

One of the charges against Anand was that he tried to kiss a woman. Another woman, who had accused him of raping her, said to the police that the alleged rape took place a year back. When the claims were investigated, it was discovered that nearly all of them were false charges against him. I assured Sanjana that I would make another plea to the International Human Rights Commission to get her brother justice. Sanjana informed me that Anand was kept in chains for the past seven months, which astonished me. Repeated bail pleas were unsuccessful. He was out on bail once, just for a month, but was arrested again and had been in jail since then. Sanjana made it clear before the press that her brother was a victim of racial discrimination. She further said that they had documentary evidence to show how the girls had been conspiring against Anand. However, they were not given a chance to prove their point.

Sanjana had vowed to wage a war against the US legal system for torturing her celebrity brother Anand, who had previously dressed Paris Hilton, Janet Jackson, and Bruce Springsteen. "I had immense faith in the American legal system but increasingly now, I find things are getting murky," admitted Sanjana, before the press.

She further added, "I am here to appeal for my brother, not just as a sister, but as an Indian. He is victimized and discriminated there because of his colour."

To my mind, the facts and circumstances of the case hinted at a conspiracy by some influential persons in the United States to tarnish the smart India-born youngster's hard-earned reputation. The possibility of racial prejudice could not be completely discounted. However, because the fight was mostly against false, unfounded, and irresponsible allegations with extra-legal motivations, we had to exercise restraint before accusing anyone, and get to the bottom of the truth. Sanjana said, "Being a woman, I would support and do anything for a rape victim. But if the woman is lying for selfish motives, then she needs to be duly punished. I have enough material to prove that Anand is increasingly getting buried in lie after lie. He is tied to a wall with a chain. His civil rights have been taken away. What sort of justice is this?"

According to Sanjana, an attempt to kiss and a touch here or there while trying to take measurement have been trumped up into rape charges. "Some of the girls who have filed charges against him have hung out and partied with us even after their alleged rape, which was supposed to have happened five years ago. Isn't that ridiculous?" asked Sanjana. She believed Anand's success, the funding of his company, and Wall Street Journal evaluating the business at ten million dollars, all have made the 'victims' greedy.

I felt Anand's phenomenal success and racial discrimination could be the reasons for his false implication. Some of the complaints appeared to be ridiculous: there were no medical evidence of sexual assault on the complainants. For Sanjana, I organised a meeting with the Prime Minister's office, and the External Affairs Ministry, to bring some pressure on the U.S. government so that Anand could have a free and fair trial.

I met Anand in a New York jail in 2013 and I was appalled to find that he was being kept there in inhuman conditions as an under-trial prisoner. They had chained him by his feet and hands. He had to hold a pen in his mouth to write a note to me. Later, I took part in the trial proceedings in a New York court. In a plea-bargaining Anand got a reprieve when he pleaded guilty on one count and got 48 of the total 49 cases in New York dropped against him. In New York, he was sentenced to five years' probation, and five years in jail. His jail term of five years was to be set off as he had already undergone six years in jail. But there was one case in Texas, and then there was the task of trying to overturn the Los Angeles conviction of 59 years in jail for which he was serving time in a California prison.

According to me, the entire episode against Anand was a calculated move against him "to bring down one of India's young and bright men," because the Americans, who were his rivals in business, were jealous of his success. I went through all the charge sheets filed and even back then I had my doubts like any alert mind would have. I was surprised to find that a girl in her complaint said that she was assaulted in California, then months later again in Texas, and she came to India with the same person who allegedly assaulted her, because she thought she had prospects in India. It was obviously a calculated, conspired attempt to ruin his career, when he was right at the top.

Anand Jon's plight brought up the crucial question: What did the Indian Government do? Was it supporting one of its bright young men? I have represented many Indians abroad and it is always the same. What do the Indian Ambassadors and Consul General do in such cases? The government will have to decide on a policy to help not only Anand Jon, but many others like him, who are languishing in foreign jails under false allegations without any support.

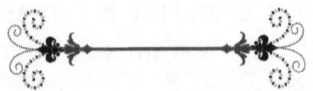

DNA

Mumbai, Thursday, January 3, 2008

Majeed to defend NRI in US

The lawyer feels charges against Anand Jon are fabricated

V Narayan & Divya Unny

Noted criminal lawyer Majeed Memon has an overseas assignment. He would take a flight to the US by the end of this month to defend NRI designer Anand Jon, who has 34 rape and molestation charges against his name. The accused has been on trial for the past seven months in the courts at Los Angeles and Texas.

Anand's sister Sanjana met Memon in the city to ensure that he would be there in the US, fighting for her brother, when the case comes up for hearing on January 30.

Sanjana said, "We fear that Anand would not be given a fair chance to defend himself. Perhaps, only a lawyer India would fight for him without prejudice."

Memon said, "I will place the matter before the prime minister and the external affairs ministry by mid-January. It will help me get de-

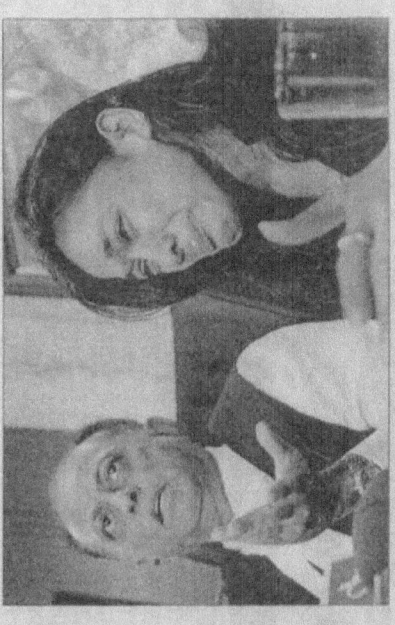

■ Sanjana Jon with Majeed Memon - Kamlesh Pednekar.DNA

tailed information from the Indian embassy in the US."

Anand was arrested on March 6 for allegedly molesting and raping 34 women. But according to his sister, the charges were fabricated. Memon said, "One of the charges against him was that he tried to kiss a woman. He has also been accused of raping a woman. But when it was checked, it was found that the victim had said to the police that the alleged rape happened a year ago. There are many such baseless charges filed against him."

The lawyer would also appeal to the international human rights commission to get Anand justice. Sanjana said that her brother had been kept in chains for the past seven months. Repeated pleas for bail went in vain. "Anand was out on bail once, just for a month. He was rearrested in May and had since been in jail," she said. Sanjana made it clear that her brother was a victim of racial discrimination. "We have documentary evidences showing how the girls had been conspiring against Anand, but we have not been given a chance to prove our point."

ADC City

Jon, a victim of his own success

Indian-American fashion designer was 'being demonised' because of his fame in the US fashion industry, his sister feels

BY A STAFF REPORTER

Indian-American designer Anand Jon, who is facing a slew of charges related to sexual assault and molestation in the United States, was 'being demonised' because of his success in the American fashion industry, his sister alleged in Mumbai on Wednesday.

"This demonisation is (happening) because he broke into an industry where Americans find difficult to break into," Sanjana Jon, his US-based sister said.

Jon, an Indian citizen, is facing complaints of either rape or molestation from 30 women in several states of the US. Since June this year, he has been in jail in Los Angeles.

"All these complaints started coming after Anand's company got funded. Some of them date back to five years. Why these girls did not file complaints immediately," Sanjana said, fighting back tears.

According to her, when the first of these complaints was filed on March 6 this year, Anand was about to launch his denim line in association with a company called Genesis.

Her lawyer Majid Memon too said there was a possibility that "Anand's phenomenal success raised a few eyebrows.... they could not digest it" and "connived" to implicate him in false cases.

"Racial discrimination could be a factor," he added. Dubbing some of the complaints as "ridiculous and absurd," Memon said there was no medical evidence of sexual assault in any of the cases.

Sanjana said complaints made no sense because the complainants continued to go around with Anand after the alleged incidents.

"Some of them came to India with us after the incident's date. Does this make sense?" she said.

Asked what help she expects from Indian government, she said she merely wanted to create awareness about her brother's predicament through the Indian media.

Advocate Memon — who is also a member of Nationalist Congress Party — added that they would be approaching the Prime Minister's Office in this regard.

Sanjana, Anand Jon's sister with her counsel Majid Memon in Mumbai on Wednesday.

Majid Memon along with Sanjana Jon and the two models

In a Lighter Vein

A senior lawyer was on his legs arguing before a trial judge vociferously. In the midst of his submission he became aggressive and his language and movement were literally bordering on indiscipline that could be objectionable. The Ld. Judge reprimanded him and said " Mr. counsel don't behave in an unparliamentary manner in the court". The lawyer promptly replied " Your Honour, thank God that I am not following parliamentary conduct, else I would be throwing papers, paper weights, shoes etc. at the chair.

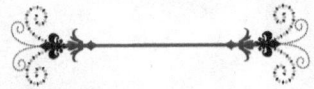

Twenty Two

THE BOMBAY BOMB BLASTS

It was on 12 March 1993 that the city of Bombay was rocked by 12 serial blasts in various parts of the city. Almost all spots where blasts took place were prime commercial centres. The blasters chose strategic points with a view to causing maximum number of deaths and heavy destruction of properties. They planted RDX filled bombs on scooters and new Ambassador cars at 10 sites, while they hurled hand grenades at 2 locations.

It was a Friday. Soon after the afternoon prayers in mosques, the city was jolted by the cold-blooded acts of a few misguided people. While rivulets of blood flowed in many areas, mutilated bodies and shattered limbs lay scattered around. The near and dear ones who accompanied their beloved ones on outings were charred in no time. The wails of those who survived even surpassed the deafening sound of blasts.

Soon after the blasts the State swung into action. Enquiries brought to light that there was a large conspiracy that worked behind the serial blasts. It was also made clear that the main conspirators were Pakistan based Dawood Ibrahim and Tiger Memon.

The conspirators had arranged for meetings with the blasters in Dubai and Pakistan. The blasters were given training in use of weapon and bomb making in Pakistan and places like Raigad, in Maharashtra. Firstly, they flew to Dubai and from there to Pakistan. Their training trip was arranged by the main conspirators settled in Pakistan. After they returned from training, they were asked to undertake surveillance of strategic spots. Later they had to oversee the safe landing of RDX, weapons like AK 56 rifles and hand grenades, at Dighi Fort and Shekadi Fort in Raigad district. Next, the RDX was to be loaded in scooters and Ambassador cars, on the intervening night of 11 and 12 March 1993. Various batches of blasters and loaders were assigned the job of parking the loaded vehicles at selected points.

On 12 March 1993, between 1.30 p.m. and 3.30 p.m. the city experienced 12 serial blasts in which 257 innocent persons lost their lives and 713 were injured. Properties worth 27 crores of Rupees were damaged and/or destroyed.

The biggest impact was by the blast at Century Bazar in Worli, where 101 people died on the spot. Reportedly, a Maruti van loaded with hand grenades and weapons like AK-56 rifles was passing through the area of Siemen's Company in Worli. It was abandoned by the occupants near Century Bazar, in the afternoon. Later on, in the investigation into the catastrophe that befell the city on that black Friday, it was brought to light that the Maruti van in question was registered in the name of one Rubina Memon, of the Memon family residing in Al Hussaini Building, near Mahim Police Station. On further enquiries by the police, it was revealed that the flats in which the joint family was residing in Al Hussaini Building, were locked, as also the garages that belonged to the family. Police learnt that the entire family had left their residence two days prior to the blast, i.e., on 10 March 1993.

Later investigations revealed that the notorious Tiger Memon was also a member of the same Memon family residing in Al Hussaini building. He had already shifted to Pakistan, much before the blast. The family's fourth floor flat was used for filling RDX and preparing bombs.

The police could initially lay their hands on 198 suspects and 28 suspects were shown as absconding. In all, 27 different cases were registered under various sections of law, including The Arms Act. Later, they were clubbed together into one single case and the charge-sheet was filed in the case by the DCB, CID. It was noted that crimes were committed in Mumbai, Raigad, and Thane districts.

On filing of the charge-sheet in the case before the designated TADA Court, the case was numbered at BBC/1/1993. Some of the suspects were discharged before filing of the charge-sheet and in all 139 accused were made to face the trial in the designated court. It was at this stage that the CBI took over the charge of the case. The CBI dropped the charge of 'waging war' against all the accused. During this time two of the accused viz., Abu Asim Azmi and Amzad Meherbux approached the Supreme Court with prayers for their discharge from the case, and the Hon'ble Supreme Court was pleased to grant them their prayers.

During further investigation it was revealed that the members of the Memon family from Mahim had played a major role in the blast. It was revealed to the investigators that after conspiring to blast the city on 12 March 1993, as planned earlier, under the directions of Dawood Ibrahim and Tiger Memon from Pakistan, all the members of the Memon family had left the country for Pakistan and Dubai. The shocking news of the involvement of the family in the worst ever bomb blasts in the country spread like wildfire. A couple of days thereafter, it was further reported that the members of the family were intending to return to the city to face the charges against them, with a view to proving their 'innocence'. The city was aghast at the news and the media waited with bated breath for their return.

It was in this context that Yakub Memon, a young Chartered Accountant, and younger brother of Tiger Memon, returned to the city from Pakistan, on 5 August 1994 with a view to 'clear' the name of the family in the case. Six other members of the family, including women, returned to the city on 15 August 1994. Yakub Memon's wife returned with a newborn baby in her arms on 5 September 1994. She reportedly returned from Dubai. On return of the members of the Memon family, a supplementary charge-sheet was drawn up after completion of investigation. The said supplementary charge-sheet was submitted to the designated court by the CBI. The charges against the Memon family were thus subjoined with the charges in the case, BBC/1/1993, for a joint trial.

Among the 139 accused who stood to face the trial before the designated court was the famous film star, Sanjay Dutt. Dutt was arrested in the case on charges of possession of arms. All the accused were in custody and were denied bail.

During trial in the court, I was requested by one junior advocate to plead for Yakub Memon before the designated Court. Professionally it was a challenging assignment and one which would require great skills and hard work if I were to do an honest job. Though my first instinct was to reject the brief, the criminal lawyer in me made me consider the offer. I was persuaded to accept the brief by one Mr. Usman Memon, who was my classmate in the Government Law College and whom I knew from the year 1970. Later, I was assigned the job of defending some more members of the family.

A special courtroom had been erected for the trial at the Arthur Road Central Prison in Mumbai. The large number of accused facing trial meant that the courtroom would be packed with the accused, their advocates, their juniors and assistants and the relatives of the accused. Every morning the accused were brought into the courtroom by the police. Their dock was at the far end of the spacious courtroom. The State prosecutor's seat was close to the witness box and seats for the defence advocates were arranged next to him. Special arrangements were made for the media in the courtroom. Each day in this special courtroom was hectic and unfolded a new drama.

During this period, I observed that the court was regularly rejecting the bail applications of the accused. It was at this time that Shri Sunil Dutt approached me to appear for his son, Sanjay Dutt, who was incarcerated. Sanjay's bail application was earlier rejected by the trial court and thereafter, even by the Supreme Court. I was also told that late Shri Ram Jethmalani had appeared for him in the trial court and in the Supreme Court. I realized that this was a daunting task before me, and I would require extraordinary legal skills to get the actor out of jail. The fact that his application was once rejected by the highest court of the country went against him. Getting bail for Sanjay Dutt was quite a challenge.

When the judgment in Sanjay Dutt vs State through CBI, Bombay (1994) 6 SCC 86 was thoroughly examined, it was found to contain that since bail provisions in TADA cases were extremely stringent and people were found languishing in prison for long, the apex court emphasized on setting up a Central Review Committee with a view to periodically examine the hardships of prisoners. This aspect was totally ignored in the case of Sanjay Dutt and others.

I, therefore, moved the High Court accordingly. Once the petition was filed by me in the High Court it became a big news and the newspapers on the following day carried the news prominently. The trial was ongoing as usual. The trial judge, having read the news, asked me to move the trial court itself instead of the High Court. On this I withdrew the High Court petition and moved the trial court.

Upon such motion the designated court issued notice to CBI for response. It was placed on record that no review was conducted by any Review Committee for the past over six months and as such the review of the situation was justified. Accordingly, the court directed the respondents to conduct review and file report thereof.

After the stipulated period was granted by the court to CBI, they filed the report in a sealed envelope before the court. When it was opened by the trial court the report contained three categories of undertrial prisoners. First, with no serious allegations who could be released on bail. Second, with serious allegation of hard-core nature and third containing the names of those accused who had not participated in actual blast but were charged with lesser offences. This last category included the name of Sanjay Dutt.

Thereafter a joint bail application for all the accused in the third category was moved before the designated judge which included the name of Sanjay Dutt. The application was highly publicized by the media and it could afresh renew the prospects of release of Sanjay

Dutt. The stake was very high and there was unprecedented crowd in the court room to watch the proceedings. The matter came up for hearing in a very solemn atmosphere. I had the opportunity to address the court on behalf of all the applicants. There was pin drop silence in the court room for over an hour as I was making my submission with vehemence. The Ld. Judge was deeply engrossed, and audience listened in rapt attention, almost mesmerized by my submissions. The spontaneously powerful language in which I argued for the restoration of the actor's personal liberty gave all those in the court room an impression that we had won the day and the judge was bound to grant him bail.

The State prosecutor opposed my bail application tooth and nail, although those who were charged with lesser offences were entitled to bail, as per the report of the Review Committee. As my arguments were concluded by the end of the day, and as the presiding officer retired to his chamber, reserving the order for the next day morning, as usual, senior journalists and reporters came forward and shook hands with me, appreciating my arguments. They described my arguments as 'extraordinarily brilliant legal submissions'. Some of the senior journalists literally lifted me up in their enthusiasm. They had all concluded that this time, the actor would be out. They were awestruck with my performance in the designated court. My colleague advocates too were equally hopeful. The morning papers reported my pleadings highlighting the vehemence of my submissions. Asian Age, dated 6 October 1995 reported as follows:

"After the arguments, where Majeed Memon had, rather uncharacteristically, presented a brilliant argument, the feeling was that bail was inevitable. What could possibly be the reason enough for denying bail now? was the general feeling. A group of journalists thumped him on the back after the day was up."

To the shock and dismay of one and all, the designated court rejected the application and refused to release Sanjay Dutt on bail though he was not charged for participation in any blast but only for possession of arms. Thereafter, Dutt approached the Supreme Court, and got a favourable order on the strength of the Review Committee Report. As soon as the designated court learnt about the order in favour of Sanjay Dutt, the court asked me to file bail applications on behalf of all other similarly placed accused. The court insisted that I did it on the very same day and I was obliged to do it. Soon, on filing of the applications, after a brief hearing, the court granted bail to all those similarly placed accused who applied for bail. It was pertinent to note that the other similarly placed accused were physically released from custody even before Sanjay Dutt could avail of the order obtained from the Supreme Court. That was the promptness with which the trial court acted.

I knew that the trial in BBC/1/1993 was going to be a marathon one, involving months and years. The trial in the case started on 30 June 1995. In the trial, I was appearing mainly for Memon family members including women. I was also appearing for a few other accused before the court. For the sake of this case, I had to take leave from my busy daily schedule in other courts. During the year 1996, trial judge Shri J.N.Patel was replaced by Judge Shri P.D.Kode, as Shri J.N.Patel was elevated to the position of a Judge of the High Court.

Confessions of Accused:

Of the 139 accused, 89 of them confessed to the crime at the initial stage of investigation. Their confessions were recorded by SPs at Raigad and DCPs at Mumbai. 23 confessions were recorded by DCP Bishnoi, which included those accused who had taken part directly in the blast. He had also recorded the confession of Sanjay Dutt. DCP Sanjay Pandey recorded 16 confessions.

Out of 89 confessions, 78 were accepted by the court during trial. The other 11 were discarded by the trial court. Even the confessions of those accused who had implicated the co-accused about their role in the crime were accepted by the court. The special clause of TADA {P} Act provides that confession of a co-accused is valid and can be accepted against the named co-accused, though that accused has not confessed.

The Trial:

With a view to sustaining certain conviction in this case, the State prosecutor used a ruse by turning two out of the total 139 accused to be approvers.

According to the prosecution case, two of the accused who were earlier arrested sought pardon under the scheme provided in the Code of Criminal Procedure, 1973. There is an underlying principle in the Code under which, a request for pardon can be put up by an accused through the Investigating Officer before the trial judge, in cases where the facts and allegations show that such an applicant accused is an offender who has not played any major role in the crime but displays remorse for the happening at his behest. Contrary to this principle, accused Zamir Sardar Khan (name changed), approver No. 2. who had played a prominent role in almost all the components of this mega crime, was put up by the State prosecutor for pardon and the same was granted to him at the initiation of the prosecutor, He was examined in the trial as prosecution witness No. 2.

The other accused approver Mohammed Ali (name changed) was granted pardon by the court on initiation of the prosecutor, and he was later examined as prosecution witness No. 1. This approver No.1, Mohamed Ali had taken the name of only one accused and narrated his role in the blast. He was cross examined by the advocates of the concerned accused.

Since the prosecution did not have any direct or satisfactory evidence against many accused in the dock, the CBI desperately sought reliance upon the approvers to depose before the court, for establishing this mammoth case against several other accused who were facing trial. Approver No. 2, Zamir Sardar Khan was thus the star witness in this historic trial. There used to be a literal drama in the courtroom when his evidence was being recorded by the first trial judge Shri J.N.Patel. This approver was in the witness box for a fairly long time. He had to be extensively cross examined by the team of defence lawyers.

The evidence of P.W No.2, Zamir Sardar Khan was extraordinarily lengthy as it involved the examination-in-chief by the state prosecutor, followed by cross-examination by various advocates for their respective clients. He was quite dramatic in his presentation and in answering questions at cross-examination. He narrated the prosecution story as if he was saying it by-heart. In the witness box, he could describe flawlessly the role of each accused who was implicated by the prosecution. This was so as he himself was the main accused in the whole operation. While standing in the witness box, he even went to the extent of demonstrating the operation of an empty AK 56 rifle. To the court, he gave names of 37 accused in the dock and verbatim described the role attributed to each one of them by the prosecution. This approver narrated in detail as to how the conspiracy to blast the city, with a view to avenge the demolition of Babri Masjid was hatched in Pakistan, under the aegis /auspices/ supervision of Tiger Memon.

Zamir Sardar Khan was cross examined in detail by almost all the advocates. I cross examined him continuously on 23 dates. It may be of interest to note that during my cross examination he was literally trapped telling lies. He soon pretended that he was sick, with a view to avoiding some of my crucial questions. He informed the court that he was unwell and needed rest. I realized that it was an excuse on his part because he understood that I was about to expose his mendacious ways.

As he complained of stomach pain, a doctor was summoned from the adjoining prison. The doctor rushed to the court within minutes and the 'patient' was examined in the witness box itself.

Injured Witnesses:

Many injured witnesses were examined in the court. Their injuries were proved through their deposition, as well as through the injury certificates, and the examination of the doctors in the court. This was apart from scores of independent witnesses examined by the prosecution.

Panchnamas:

Recovery of weapons at the instance of the accused was proved through *panchas*. The *panchas* in the witness box could identify the concerned accused, from amongst the 139 accused in the dock.

Police Officers:

The officers who recorded the confessions of the accused were examined by the prosecution and cross-examined by almost all the defence advocates, in detail. In all, scores of officers were examined by the court. They included investigating officers from DCB CID and investigating officers from CBI.

Doctors:

Doctors from various hospitals in Bombay were examined by the court, with a view to proving the injuries to the victims. The postmortem report on the dead bodies proved that the particles found on them were of RDX and nothing else.

All the above cited witnesses were extensively cross-examined by me and the team of defence advocates who represented various accused in the dock. The collective effort of the advocates was to demolish the prosecution case at the very root itself.

Coming back to the case of the Memon family and their alleged role in the blasts, I had a difficult time convincing the court about their innocence. Except for the fact that a flat in Al Hussaini building in Mahim was used for the purposes of filling RDX by some other accused at the instructions of Tiger Memon, my clients had no role in the whole operation. Apart from this, a Maruti car used by the blasters was registered in the name of a woman called Rubina in the household. At the relevant time, however, she was not in the country, and she had no knowledge about what was happening here. Whatever happened here was in her absence without her knowledge or consent. The only crime the other members of the family committed was that a flat and a garage in the building were registered in their joint names. Therefore, the court concluded, under the TADA (P) Act, that they had knowledge about what was happening and there was a conspiracy to cause blasts in the city.

The court had taken note of the fact that Yakub Memon was an educated member of the family, an upcoming Chartered Accountant. He was held guilty, along with three other members of the family, whose names were shown as joint owners of the flat and a garage in Al Hussaini building.

I advanced my final arguments only for the mother of Yakub Memon, Smt. Hanifa Memon, and Yakub's young wife, Raheen, from the family, though I argued for a few other accused. I had withdrawn my appearance for Yakub Memon and some other family members while the trial was halfway through. My argument for the two women, Hanifa and Raheen from the family was appreciated and upheld by the court. My point was that these two women were *pardahnashin* (wearing veils) women, and they do not have any knowledge about what their husbands do outside the house. They are orthodox Muslims and could not question their husbands. These women could not be, therefore, held for any vicarious liability of their husbands' activities. Amongst the other points in my argument for these two women, Judge Shri P.D.Kode appreciated this point in the open court.

After hearing the final arguments in the case by the advocates for various accused, the court passed the historic judgment awarding death sentence to ten of the accused who had played prime roles in the whole operation. Yakub Memon was held guilty by the court and awarded death sentence. Three other male members of the family were also held guilty by the court and awarded life imprisonment, as they were joint owners of a flat and a garage in Al Hussaini building. A female member of the family viz., Rubina, whom I did not represent, was also convicted for life sentence, as she was the owner of the Maruti car used in the crime. She had 'lent' her name to the family to purchase the Maruti car involved in the crime. Their aged father, Razak Memon, expired while the trial was on.

The Court further passed varying terms of imprisonment including life imprisonment to many other accused. I must mention here that my contentions for the two women, Hanifa and Raheen, mother and wife respectively of Yakub Memon, were upheld by the court, and the court was pleased to acquit both the women.

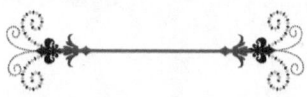

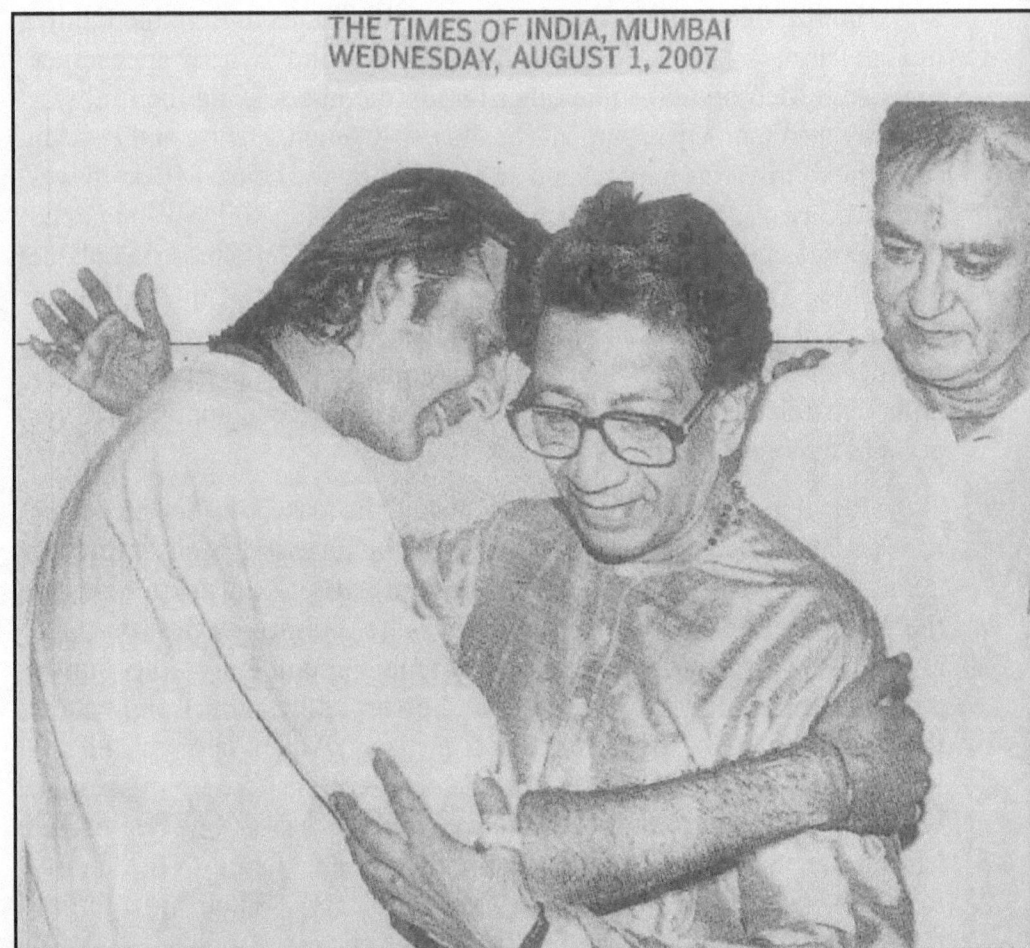

BAL BAL BACH GAYE: After initially creating a ruckus about Sanjay's 'anti-national' behaviour, the Shiv Sena did a volte-face. Sena supremo Bal Thackeray is said to have played a role in extricating Sanjay from the mess he was in and, the actor's first stop on the way home was perforce Thackeray's bungalow, to touch his feet. Sanjay later said that the only three people he had thus bowed to were his father, Thackeray and criminal lawyer Majeed Memon, who got him bail

Sanjay's Wall of steel and faith in God

asked specific question. There was a lot of apprehension on how damaging the things he would say.

His first bail hearing after the trial started began on September 8. The morning before, he was fairly optimistic, perhaps due to the fact that his lawyers had possibly told him that with the Central Bureau of Investigation deciding not to oppose the motion, there was no reason for the court to deny him bail this time. After the arguments where Majeed Memon had, rather uncharacteristically, presented a brilliant argument, the feeling was that bail was inevitable. What could possibly be reason enough for denying bail now?" was the general feeling. A group of journalists thronged him on the back after the day was up. When Justice Jai Narayan Patel denied Sanjay bail, he was strong in his acceptance. He grinned and said, "I have had so much disappointment in life, that I've come not to expect too much.

"Is he scared Jindrcc, he told me. "Do you know what I would give to get out of here? This has become the bloody story of my life."

Though it was very disappointing for him, the fact that the Supreme Court decided to consider his letter as a writ plea lifted him again. "They have felt it serious enough to hear it," he said. But what pleased him most was the fact that the letter was entirely his own. Neither his lawyers nor his family had any hand in the Supreme Court agreeing to consider his plea. After his plea was dismissed in the Tada court and quashed in the Supreme Court, he was extremely morose. "He is not in court today," said his friend Mohammed Jindran. "Uska to man hi uth gaya hai."

But this carried on only till the time that the Supreme Court asked him to file an appeal against the Tada court order. Then Sanjay Dutt was sure he would be free. Even when he told people, "Let us see how it goes from here," he knew what the outcome would be himself. He refused to speak on the matter after The Asian Age printed an article quoting him on the similarities between his case and the case of O.J. Simpson. After that his lawyers said that if he spoke of anything to the press other than "God

that day, October 4, he never spoke on details of the case.

The day that he finally got bail, he said he was too stunned to react. He just held his head in his hands and cried in court. Then he hugged all the accused, all the lawyers, all the journalists that were present. I told him I was sorry if he thought the arrest caused him any damage. He just smiled and told me to forget about it.

I cried as he is in drawing large crowds, even he was surprised at the number of people that turn ed up for his release. The atmosphere at Siddhi Vinayak temple where he went to offer pay was near-hysterical. As he entered the temple, there was something visibly different about him. The shuffle the he had in the jail was gone. Even though the tears were streaming down his cheeks, his face had a solemn serenity that was not there when he was in jail. A woman standing near the door screamed his name and started crying. He turned toward her even with around 100 people tunnelling him toward the temple idols and walked up to her, putting a hand on her shoulder and taking the garland she offered him. As he finished his obeisance and came out toward the bus, a hundred photographers kneeled down and blocked his way to get a shot of him leaving the temple. He stood there, crying, the *rupa thali* in his hand, his hair all over his face and still full of repose. He climbed out through the sunroof of the bus and acknowledged the crowd with hands folded above his head. He pointed toward the bronze dome of the temple. Nobody followed his gaze, he was too powerful a sight to look away from. I tried to wave but he didn't see me. I don't think he was really seeing anybody, just a crowd of people.

As I walked away, my lasting memory of him was our final meeting. He was about to leave jail and I commented on the fact that he had so many religious charms on his body; *mala* rings, amulets. "Of course, man. I have come to believe in God," he said. "Don't you believe in God?" I shrugged. He squeezed my hand and said, frowning, "You start believing, man." "... is very hard to believe how anybody could dislike this man.

God bless you Sanjay Dutt.

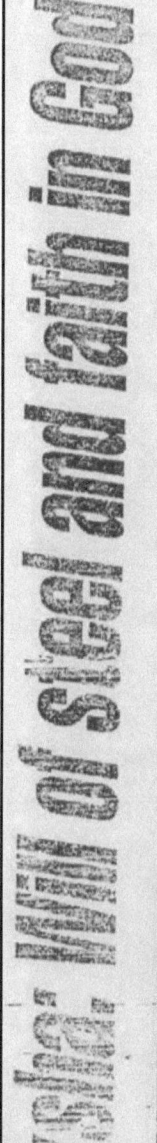

MID-DAY, SATURDAY, JUNE 29, 2002.

Mid Day   www.chalomumbai.com

Bomb blasts trial

Defence disputes confession by quoting Bertrand Russell

The trial into the Mumbai serial bomb blasts began on June 30, 1995. Mid Day's courts correspondent **PRASAD PATIL** brings you exclusive daily reports of the proceedings as they enter the final stages, with the defence presenting its arguments

AFTER raising doubts over the recording of the confession of the accused, the identification parade procedure and the filing of the First Information Report for the 1993 bomb blasts at Fishermen's Colony, Mahim, defence advocate Majeed Memon, continued his arguments yesterday by borrowing a quote from Bertrand Russell's Taming of Power.

Memon quoted from the book, "A police officer, who is investigating the case, is interested in gathering evidence which may bring a conviction for the accused and result in his promotion. It is never safe to rely on such evidence."

The advocate was clearly taking a dig at Deputy Commissioner of Police I. K Bishnoi, who had recorded the accused's confession.

"Equity, fair play and rationality forbids a police officer, who is investigating the case, from recording the confession of the accused," he said. "Bishnoi in his statement admitted that he was part of the investigation. Yet he proceeded to record the confession of the accused without realising it would be unsafe," added Memon.

To support his argument, Memon cited a past Supreme Court judgement where the court had observed that the superintendent of police, who was part of the investigation, was compelled to record a confession because the other superintendents had refused to record his confession. It was permitted in that case as an exception, said Memon.

According to the prosecution, on March 12, 1993, at 2.45 pm, seven people in a blue Maruti van came towards Fishermen's Colony and hurled hand grenades at the colony. Six people — Bashir Usman Gani, Firoz Amani Malik, Salim Rahim Shaikh (driver), Moin Kureshi, Abdul Akhtar and Zakir Hussain — were arrested. The prosecution had presented three eyewitnesses. Memon argued on behalf of Gani and Malik, both of whom confessed to the crime. Memon contended that even if Gani's confession is accepted by the court, despite it being given to the investigating DCP, it can be shown that he had changed his mind at the time of the plan's execution.

In his confession, Gani said that he was unable to remove the pin of the bomb and so put it back into the bag carried by co-accused Kureshi. "Gani did not remove the pin because he didn't want to and at the same time he wanted to show others that he tried," Memon said. Memon will continue his arguments today.

prasad@mid-day.com

In a Lighter Vein

A short statured counsel was making submissions before a High Court judge for grant of bail to his client in a rape case. While on his legs, he realized that he could not be seen by the judge easily. He was therefore, gesticulating with both his hands. Incidentally he had minor injuries on two of his fingers on the left hand, on which he had put a band-aid. His submissions, though legally not effective, were humorous and laughable. On merits, he did not have a good case for grant of bail and his bail application was once rejected earlier.

The Learned Court asked the counsel to show what was the change of circumstance that entitled his client to be granted bail. As the counsel was not ready with an apt answer, the Court adjourned the hearing, and told the counsel that he should prepare and come after a week.

On the next date of hearing, his manner of submissions was almost the same. This time while literally throwing his fingers into the air to suit his submissions in a dramatic manner, his left-hand fingers were distinctly visible to the Judge who noticed that there was no band-aid on his fingers.

The Learned Judge questioned the counsel as to what the changed circumstances were this time, to which he could not again give a satisfactory reply. At this, the Learned Judge in a jovial manner told the counsel that for him the only change in circumstance was that there was no band-aid on his fingers this time, and hence he was granting bail to his client.

Twenty Three

THE AGED MAID AND THE STOLEN GOLD

One Rashida Banoo, a senior citizen, was working as a domestic servant at the household of a Sindhi family in Navjeevan colony at Mahim. She was a trusted maid to the family for several years with a clean record. One day, the lady of the house found that a gold necklace and two gold bangles were missing from her cupboard. The lady suspected Rashida Banoo to be the thief.

A complaint of theft was recorded at Mahim Police Station. On her complaint the maid was arrested and was kept in custody for sustained interrogation. The investigating agency somehow recovered the stolen ornaments and attributed the same to be recovery at the instance of Rashida Banoo. A strong case was thus made out against her, including offences triable by the Court of Sessions. The accused had to remain in prison for a few months till she was released on bail to face the trial. Years thereafter, when Rashida Banoo got older and more fragile, her trial in the Sessions Court began. I was engaged by Rashida Banoo to defend her.

During the trial several witnesses were examined, and the prosecution made it a prestige matter to get her convicted. The defence conducted a tight case and by the end of the trial succeeded in creating a reasonable doubt regarding the guilt of the accused.

I was conscious of the fact that an accused cannot be held guilty unless the charges against him/her are established beyond all reasonable doubts. Towards the end of any criminal trial, if there are two probabilities, one in favour of the accused and the other against him, the one against him is to be discarded and the one in favour of him is to be accepted.

A date was fixed for pronouncing the verdict by the Sessions Court. It was a Friday and the last working day of the week. Everyone was keen to know the result. The court did not pronounce the judgment in the first half of the day, so anxieties were writ large on face of every one concerned including Rashida Banoo, her family members, and the whole defence team. The working hours of the Court were till 4.45 p.m. The time was well past 4 p.m. It was precisely 4.10 when the case was called out at the fag end of the day. Rashida Banoo was made to stand in the dock when her case was called out. The Judge pronounced the operative part of the order, holding Banoo guilty of the offences and sentencing her to jail with quantum of imprisonment to be decided later, after hearing both the sides.

Consequently, an aged lady as she was, Banoo, had to be physically taken into custody at the end of the court's working day. This situation created a furore in the court and the guards in the court were about to whisk her away into a waiting jail van to be taken to prison within the next few minutes. The Court time left was barely 30 minutes. The trial judge had no power under the Code to suspend the sentence and release her on bail. The accused and the whole defence team were left high and dry.

I was upset, not only because Rashid Banoo was held guilty but primarily because the trial judge pronounced the order at the last hour of the last working day. There was no time left to write down or type out any application/prayer to be made forthwith, to grant her any relief.

In an emotionally charged atmosphere, I waved out to the accused and her family and left the courtroom without any papers in my hands. My team of juniors followed me as I marched up to the Bombay High Court building where I straight away barged into the courtroom of the judge who had power to give instant relief. When I entered the courtroom, some proceedings were on and there were just 15 minutes left for the court to rise. Every second was precious. I interrupted the sitting judge which shocked everybody around. The sitting judge looked at me and asked what the matter was. At this I gently roared and said, "My Lord will pardon me for my somewhat uncivilised way of interrupting this Hon'ble Court, but without this act, irreversible injustice would result and, therefore, I am compelled to seek urgent attention of the Hon'ble Court. An elderly female accused facing a criminal trial has been ordered to be taken in physical custody, by a Learned Sessions judge, under the very nose of this Hon'ble Court in the last hour of the last working day of the week ".

This impressed the presiding judge, and he asked me to give the case number of the Sessions Court case and the title of the case to the judicial officer sitting below his dais and directed the officer to go to the Court of Sessions with an oral order of stay of the order of the Sessions Court till the next working day morning.

"Justice prevails," I said to myself. Rashida Banoo was thus prevented from being taken into custody on that day. On the following Monday, a proper application was made, and the sentence and conviction of Banoo was stayed till the hearing and disposal of the appeal. However Banoo did not live long to receive the final verdict of the appeal as she passed away at the age of 76 years.

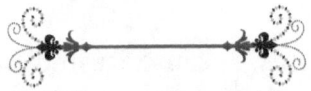

In a Lighter Vein

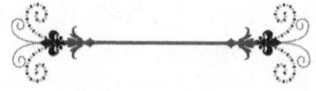

Once MM was arguing a criminal appeal in Bombay High Court. As the ld. Judge saw MM in the court he was surprised and asked " Mr. MM I have heard that you went to the U.S. for heart treatment. How come you are here before me this morning". On this MM replied " My Lord's information is fallacious on three counts. Firstly, by the grace of Almighty I have no heart ailment. Secondly, even if I were to have any such problem I would get treatment from competent local doctors rather than rush to the U.S. Thirdly, my Lord, I possibly will not have any heart problem as my heart is not here, it is elsewhere".

Twenty Four

THE TRUTHFUL LOVER

A well-placed businessman with Indian roots had established a reputed business with a lavish outlet in the prestigious New Bond Street in Central London. Married and having three children, he lived with his family in London. While developing his business, he got into a love affair with one of his lady staff members which went to the extent of them having a physical relationship. When his wife learnt about the clandestine affair of her husband, she filed a criminal case of adultery against him for which he had to execute a bond and face accusations in court.

Much disturbed as he was, he could afford a team of the best of local solicitors and attorneys to defend him against the charges. However, being of Indian origin he preferred to engage one of his countrymen. He invited me to come over to London and help him get out of the criminal charges. I advised him to send the charge-sheet, to enable me to understand the gravity of the accusations, prepare the case and then go to London. The papers were immediately sent to me in Mumbai and after carefully reading them, I decided to fly to London to proceed in the matter.

Thus, in the following week, I reached London, and was taken to his office/showroom. There were a couple of local lawyers with whom he discussed the case threadbare. From the charge sheet it was evident that the only star witness against the accused was his own employee, the lady with whom he allegedly had an illicit relationship.

I understood that the outcome of the case would depend upon her testimony. Anxiously, I asked the accused where the said lady was and, to my surprise, I was informed that she was on those very premises working upstairs. I was wonderstruck because in my country when an accused is on bail, till the trial concludes, he is forbidden from contacting the witness to avoid any tampering of evidence. And here in the UK, the accused, and the most important witness against him in a criminal case, continued to work together despite the pendency of the trial.

In these circumstances, I asked the accused if I could meet the witness. "By all means," was the reply. Thereafter, arrangements were made for me to be seated in a separate chamber. Within minutes, a young lady entered the chamber. We greeted each other, and I asked her to take a seat. The young lady was aware that I was an attorney from India. She paid her respects to me. Reluctantly, I began the conversation with some formal questions, and thereafter I came to the subject proper. Our conversation is reproduced herein below:

Q. Miss, since when have you known Mr. X, who is your boss?

A. About two and a half years I have been working in this showroom, almost since then.

Q. The accused is your boss. How do you find him?

A. He is a fine gentleman, fairly soft spoken, and very noble.

Q. Do you know his family?

A. Yes, I am aware that he is from India and is a married man, with three children.

Q. Please be frank to tell me about your relationship with the accused, your boss.

A. We have a very cordial relationship. In fact, we are good friends.

Q. Will you kindly elaborate to what extent does your friendship extend?

A. (Reluctantly). We have been good friends for quite some time.

Q. Kindly elaborate. Do you have physical relationship with him?

A. I love him, and I believe he also does. We have an intimate relationship.

Q. Do you know that he is a married person, and to have a physical relationship with him would amount to a criminal offence.

A. Unfortunately, yes.

Q. Do you know that his wife has filed a criminal case against him?

A. Yes

Q. How much do you love him? Or care for him?

A. My feelings and love for him are intense. I am prepared to give my life for him. (This answer encouraged me to ask some further questions).

Q. I believe you know that you are a witness against him in the prosecution case.

A. Yes

(I was hinting at the idea of help from her, by supporting him in the court, if possible. So, I framed the next question)

Q. Miss, you can help him in the court.

On hearing this, her complexion and looks changed. She firmly replied to me saying "Once the court issues summons to me, and I have to depose in the court, I will have no option but to speak the whole truth."

This principled stand of the lady made me wonder about the comparative situation prevailing in my country, where the witnesses turn hostile at the drop of a hat. In the courts in my country, my vast experience has been that there is no solemnity in an oath taken. People lie with impunity and the courts are misled in their quest for truth. "In the UK even today, there is respect for truth, and criminal trials are meaningful," I concluded.

In a Lighter Vein

In a robbery case, that was heard in the Court of Sessions at Mumbai, MM was representing some of the accused, who were charged with train robbery. The case of the prosecution was that the accused pulled the emergency chain of an express train and made it stop at a pre-determined spot. They then decamped with valuable textile materials and precious diamonds, that were being smuggled in the train. All the accused were young men, in the age-group of 25-35 years. The trial judge in the Sessions Court was a brilliant and judicious person, whereas the State was represented by an extremely incompetent and poor prosecutor. It was quite difficult for the court to keep on helping the prosecutor to get on with the case, within permissible limits. On several occasions, during the trial, the prosecutor created problems for the court which, at times, were adversely affecting the interest of the State, as well as the cause of truth and justice. Such instances even antagonised the judge, too often.

During the trial, the alleged recovered stolen property, viz., diamonds were produced by the prosecution for identification and the same were taken into the custody of the court, till the disposal of the trial. Since the diamonds were precious stones, the learned judge called the Registrar of the court and cautioned him to preserve them properly, in safe custody.

At the fag end of the trial, the defence enjoyed the lapses by the prosecutor, which served as a great advantage to the accused. The evidence, in its totality, could not persuade the learned judge to believe that the offences were established against the accused beyond all reasonable doubts and, as such, he had to pronounce the order of acquittal of all the accused.

The established law is that, in such situations, the property produced before the court must go back to the person from whom the same was recovered, during investigation. In the present case, admittedly, the diamonds were recovered from one of the accused persons. The court was obliged to hear both sides, before passing an order.

MM strongly submitted that the diamonds must be returned to his client, because the same were recovered from him. The learned prosecutor was also given an opportunity to make submissions on the point, and he ended up outraging the court by making irrelevant and inconsequential submissions. The learned judge was aghast. Turning to MM, the judge said "MM, don't you agree that the court is entitled to keep the diamonds, for tolerating this prosecutor all along?" On this, MM quipped, "Sir, these diamonds would be too inadequate a compensation for the torture suffered by the court for so long".

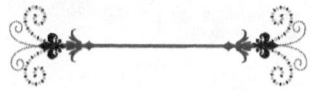

dna.

MAJID MEMON

by shrikant bhat

Leading criminal lawyer. Poet. Thinker

Legal Eagle

Majid Memon is a ruthless opponent, but a loyal friend. He fights his cases hard, but leaves the acrimony back in the courtroom. He's versatile, constantly varying his style. He is unafraid of unpopular causes. I admire his oratory and his sense of humour.

Very few know that his wife is a Christian.

BHAT IS A CRIMINAL LAWYER

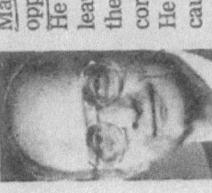
Rajan Chaughule

49

Poetic Stance
Has published a book of poems called *Saaye-e-Gul*

Fan male
Is a great fan of ghazals sung by Mehdi Hassan and Ghulam Ali

>> legal eagle

Man With An Iron Will

He is one of the best criminal lawyers in India with a successful career to boot. His devil-may-care attitude and his knack for picking infamous cases, has made him more enemies than friends—a recent attack on his life created an uproar in the legal fraternity. *Society* meets Mumbai's tough criminal lawyer, Majeed Memon

Accomplishment

LEADERSHIP EXCELLENCE AWARD FOR OUTSTANDING ACHIEVEMENT AS A LAWYER AND LEADER

Majeed Memon
Senior Advocate

Majeed Memon is a top eminent legal luminary with a notable expertise in the fields of Criminal, Constitutional & Human Rights Laws. With an impeccable reputation and formidable knowledge base, Mr. Memon is one of India's illustrious criminal lawyers with a rich experience of over four decades in legal practice. Mr. Memon is associated with the 'Nationalist Congress Party' (NCP) of India and has been its National Secretary for the past 10 years. He is presently a Member of Parliament (Rajya Sabha). Mr. Memon has appeared in several high profile matters both nationally and internationally. Mr. Memon has been responsible for conducting successful defense in numerous high profile trials before the Courts in South Africa, UAE, United Kingdom, United States of America, Portugal and the ECHR in France. A favorite of the media both print & electronic alike, Mr. Memon is sought-after for his expert opinion and comments on leading contemporary legal and political issues. He is an active speaker in several Law colleges and has been a great source of inspiration for aspiring lawyers all over India.

Senior Advocate Majeed Memon with Justice A. K. Sikri (Supreme Court Judge)

Part 2

As People's Representative

A PARLIAMENTARIAN

After completing twenty years in the legal profession, I felt the need to venture into politics to expand my sphere of influence and to be able to serve the people more effectively. I joined a secular party, the *Samajwadi* Party, under the leadership of Shri Mulayam Singh Yadav in the year 1996. I was given an opportunity to contest the Lok Sabha seat from South Mumbai constituency, as a joint candidate of *Samajwadi* Party and Nationalist Congress Party, against *Shiv Sena's* sitting M.P, Mohan Rawle.

It was a three-cornered contest in which I was the main contender against Shri Mohan Rawle. Had it been a straight fight, there was a possibility of my winning the seat against the right-wing *Shiv Sena* candidate. Congress fielded the third candidate which caused the upset, and I lost the election.

I distinctly recall that Shri Mulayam Singh, *Samajwadi* Party supremo and Shri Sharad Pawar, the Chief of NCP, both attended my election campaign. I was honoured and moved to find that Shri Sharad Pawar in a public meeting, spoke very highly of me. He said, "I have thrown a major challenge to two big National leaders, Atal Bihari on one side, and Sonia Gandhi on the other. I required immense strength to fight both together and therefore we have fielded 'the ocean of knowledge' (referring to me), as a candidate of this constituency. You all must whole heartedly support him." After polling, when the results came, as expected, we found that *Shiv Sena's* Mohan Rawle had polled exactly the number of votes that I and the Congress candidate together did. The opportunity was thus lost, and I could not enter the august House of Parliament in the year 1999.

In 2006 I joined the Nationalist Congress Party, under the leadership and guidance of eminent National Leader Shri Sharad Pawar. It did not take much time for Pawar Saheb to recognise my potential as an effective leader, both as a successful advocate as well as a representative of the minority community. He immediately appointed me the National Secretary of NCP, and in 2014 he was gracious enough to offer me a seat in the Rajya Sabha. I had the good fortune to file my nomination form for the Rajya Sabha on 24 January 2014 along with Shri Sharad Pawar himself who was also entering the Rajya Sabha for the first time in his long political career.

On 2 April 2014, I was elected unopposed to the Rajya Sabha. In the House, right from day one, I had opportunities galore to highlight a whole range of problems. There were critical issues faced by the nation, which remained unattended by successive governments. These ranged from oppression and suppression of women and children to rampant corruption among highly placed government officials, all of which, I felt, needed urgent attention of the government and if not attended to would subvert the very course and cause of justice.

I was soon inducted into the Parliamentary Standing Committee for Law and Justice, as also in the Parliamentary Consultative Committee for Ministry of Law and Justice. This gave me an opportunity to suggest ideas and reforms for the improvement of our justice system. In fact, the Secretariat of the Rajya Sabha deemed it fit to ask me to address fresh Members of Parliament and guide them on the law-making process, though I was myself a first timer and new in the House. In addition to membership of these committees on law and justice, I was given an opportunity by my party to speak in the House on different subjects. Our party did not have many members in the Rajya Sabha and therefore our allotted time to speak on any subject used to be very short. Yet, I made every minute count, and spoke vociferously whenever an opportunity came my way. A few of the speeches which I delivered in the House are worth reproducing here.

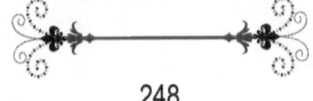

One

ON THE ISRAEL-PALESTINE CONFLICT

The first speech which I delivered on the floor of the House was on 21 July 2014, soon after my election to the Rajya Sabha. This was the period when an Israel-Palestine conflict was going on and the matter was taken up for discussion in parliament. The focus was on the killings of innocent people in Gaza. I was asked by my party to speak on the subject. The allotted time was only five minutes as per the practice in Parliament. Therefore, my endeavour was to make a short and meaningful speech which would touch the hearts of the audience.

In my brief talk, I condemned the rampant killings of innocent people including women and children in Gaza. During my speech I quoted Martin Luther King Jr, "The ultimate tragedy is not the oppression and cruelty by bad people but silence over that by good people." I further asked why India did not raise an objection all this while to the civilian killings of Palestinians by Israel. I suggested that a very strong-worded resolution be passed, condemning every single human killing. Towards the conclusion of my speech, I quoted in Urdu, the couplets of Sahir Ludhianvi on war, emphasising the grave need to avoid war at all costs.

While giving my speech, I was greatly disturbed by a report of the Shifa Hospital Director, Shri Nasir, wherein he stated that on the very previous day (Sunday, 20 July 2014) 17 children, 14 women and 4 elderly persons were among the 87 killed. As we were talking about humanity, in my view there was no room for differentiating among victims. When we were condemning this sort of massacre, I was sorry to hear what had come from the Treasury Benches. They said, "... well, this sort of bloodshed is going on all over the world. Why do we not discuss other things?"

My appeal to the ruling party members at this juncture, was that we should not be silent spectators to what had been happening in Gaza for the past couple of weeks.

Towards the conclusion of my short speech, I had the occasion to quote Abraham Lincoln. When the civil war was going on in America, centuries ago, Abraham Lincoln was asked by the wife of a Field Marshal, "Sir, you say that war is evil, and you can stop the war in a minute. How?" Abraham Lincoln replied, "It is the weakness, jealousy, and folly of man, that makes a thing so wrong possible, we are all weak, jealous and foolish, that is how the world is, and we cannot outstrip the world".

I said, "It was so long ago. Now the whole world has progressed so much over the past few centuries. We are no longer that weak, we are no longer that jealous and we are no longer that foolish. We must stop war at all costs at once."

Here, I urged the House to rise for the Palestinians, the victims and the oppressed. Our silence was becoming culpable. I urged the House to adopt a resolution, with absolute majority, condemning every killing. I further urged the House to condemn the aggressor and stand up firmly on the side of the victims.

Several of the veteran members, including those in the opposition, appreciated my suggestions. The External Affairs Minister, Smt. Sushma Swaraj had to reply to the House, on behalf of the Government. In her reply in Hindi, she said, "What should be done in the given situation? I am sure, what is to be done is what our NCP member Majeed Memon Saheb has said." She then referred to the couplet of Sahir Ludhianvi, which I had quoted earlier in my speech. Thereafter, she told the House that we need to do exactly what message was conveyed by me. She suggested that we should urge the parties to sit across the table and through discussion sort out differences and disputes and avoid war.

Two
ON OUR CONSTITUTION

On 30 November 2015, there was a discussion in the House on the nation's Constitution. When my turn came, I recalled the invaluable services of great Dr. Baba Saheb Ambedkar, not only for the formation of the Constitution but also for taking up the very challenging mission of coming to the rescue of the Backward and Scheduled Caste people. I went thus:

"Sir, the discussion is on the Constitution and, I have heard since Friday, from both sides, long speeches being delivered about the history of formation of Constitution. Sufficient time was given by this Hon'ble House and the Hon'ble Chairman in hearing speeches about the formation of Constitution, which is an old story now, 65-70 years old. I think the little time that I have, I would rather not go to the past, but would speak about the Constitution as it is seen and felt today and the Constitution which inspires us and guides us in the light of the future of India.

The Constitution of India is a sacred document, the longest written one in the world, of which every Indian citizen is proud. The Constitution is the compendium of apex laws that regulate the conduct of individuals, institutions and the three vital organs of the State, namely the Legislature, the Executive, and the Judiciary. Since the Constitution is the law of the highest order, any other law, rule, regulation, or notification issued by any authority within India, including the State Governments and the Centre, which conflicts with the constitutional provisions, is struck down always.

The Constitution that came into operation on 26 January 1950, which is celebrated as Republic Day every year, was given to us by ourselves and those who drafted and framed the Constitution cherished the dream of each citizen of the nation. The governments in India were to be 'of the people, by the people and for the people'.

Over the past 65 years or so, the Constitution had to be amended over a hundred times, and this was due to the practical experimentation of the provisions, and the changing needs of the growing Indian society. The Constitution has all along been under strict interpretation of the apex court and at no point of time its subversion in any form or shape by any authority has been sustained.

The leader of the House, in the opening discussion to this debate, referred to Article 21 of the Constitution, and lamented its suspension during the brief emergency period. It is true that between 1975 and 1977, various provisions of the Constitution of India were suspended, due to proclamation of an Internal Emergency by the then Prime Minister. The Leader of the House was explaining how it was done and what really happened. That period in the constitutional history of India is marked as "black days." The political decision to proclaim an Internal Emergency, for whatever reasons was a monumental blunder, for which the then otherwise extremely popular Prime Minister had to face the wrath of the people. A massive negative mandate was handed down to her in 1977, and she was thrown out of power, the lesson being that posterity would never ever think of proclaiming an Emergency for internal reasons. We are glad that the Hon'ble Prime Minister in his speech on Friday, specifically mentioned that amending or tampering with the core values of the Constitution by any Government would be suicidal. I fully support this statement.

Article 21 is the soul of all Fundamental Rights, guaranteed under Part III of the Constitution. I would draw the attention of people in authority today that right to life does not mean mere existence. Over the years, the apex court has dealt with this right in a series of decisions from A.K. Gopalan's case to the judgment in Unni Krishnan's case. The courts have expanded this right to include within it, the right to live with dignity, the right to live fearlessly and the right to enjoy life with a sense of security. If we ask ourselves a question as to whether today, a large section of Indian citizens comprising of Dalits and Muslims and backward tribals etc., enjoy this Right to Life, the answer by our conscience would be a big 'NO'.

The Preamble to the Constitution assures justice, social, economic, and political, liberty of thought, expression, belief, faith and worship, and equality of status and opportunity to all the citizens of India, and to promote among them, fraternity, assuring the dignity of the individual and unity and integrity of the nation. During the present rule of the last one-and-half year, social and economic justice is visibly not being made available to the people, and liberty of thought, expression, belief, faith, and worship has been severely and constantly under attack, not to talk of phrases like Love-Jihad and Ghar-Wapsi. The brutal killing of Govind Pansare and M.M.Kalburgi, the inhuman assassination of Akhlaq in Dadri, and the burning of Dalits in Haryana, are some glaring instances of absence of liberty of thought, expression, faith, belief and worship, as assured by the Constitution. This is a tragic violation of their fundamental rights.

The Dalits and minorities have been a soft target for onslaughts by a powerful section of society, with implied sanction of those in authority. Highly objectionable statements made by the Union Ministers and MPs from the Ruling Party, which tend to adversely affect the amity and integrity of the nation, and create an atmosphere of hatred, fear, and suspicion, as also a sense of insecurity among many Muslims, Dalits, and other backward sections, have gone unchecked.

Our leader, Hon'ble Shri Sharad Pawar and our Party, the Nationalist Congress Party, have always stood firmly whenever the occasion arose, on the side of Dalits, minorities, and socially backward people, to fight for their rights and ensure them justice and liberty guaranteed under the Constitution.

Several eminent people who have excelled in various fields have chosen to return their well-deserved awards, in anguish and disgust, when they found that deprivation of liberty and justice, and consequent unrest in the Indian society is visibly growing. It is unfortunate that we attributed motives to their action and failed to receive and register their views and take concrete steps to convince them. They were faulted, and called anti-national, traitors and even terrorists by some in power. Mind you, they have not criticised India, their motherland. They have drawn our attention to the present atmosphere of fear, hatred and suspicion between two major communities in the Indian society which needed to be attended to and cured.

While in the Constitution we talk of equality, social and economic justice and fraternity, we are anguished to find the widening gap between the rich and the poor. A report suggests that one hundred Indian families own 25 per cent of the Indian wealth. This concentration and mal-distribution of wealth needs to be cured through aggressive fiscal policies.

A huge number of youths are unemployed, common people are reeling under price rise, many farmers commit suicide, not just due to betrayal of nature but due to abject poverty. On the ground thus, where is liberty, equality, and fraternity? Learned Hand once said about liberty, and I quote him:

"Liberty lies in the hearts of men and women; when it dies there, no constitution, no law, no court can save it; no constitution, no law, no court can even do much to help it."

While both liberty and equality have more to do with legal rights, fraternity belongs to the sphere of moral obligations, rather than rights, bonding rather than statutes, harmony rather than contract, community rather than individuality, and it is in this area that we have lagged behind the most. Legislation can provide the right to ensure liberty and equality, but fraternity is a feeling of brotherhood. It has to be felt; it cannot be imposed. It is a bonding. We have to create a society where everyone, the weakest members - the Dalits, the minorities - feel secure and confident and for this, the Government may need to take positive steps, affirmative action and doing that is not appeasement. It is rather reaching out which is required and that is what is wanting. Instead of reaching out to these weaker sections, we find those in offices and positions of power making statements to spread hatred, fear, and violence. This must stop if we talk of good governance. Else, our tall claims to possess and follow an outstanding document called the 'Constitution of India' would seem hollow and an instance of self-deceit. With my own Urdu couplet, I would end my speech.

हक़ है चाहें जहां वतन में रहें,
यह अलग बात है फु.टपाथ हो घर,
हक़ बराबर है सबको जीने का
खू.न देकर जीएं या खूं पीकर,
हक़ है चाहें सो कारोबार करें,
पैसा हक़ का हो या हो चोरी का,
घर में मज़दूर के न हो रोटी,
पेट भरता रहे तिजोरी का,
हक़ यह है, हक वह है, सभी हक है,
हक़ तो यह है कि हम असीर हैं आज,
कल थे हाकिम हमारे कुछ अग़यार,
चंद अपनों ही में अमीर हैं आज,
खोखले इन हुक़ूक़ को लेकर,
जश्ने जम्हूरिया मनाते रहें,
भूख से तिलमिलाएं तिफ़लो ज़ईफ़,
हम तर.क्की. के गीत गाते रहें"

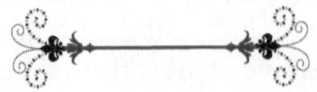

Three

LAW AND JUSTICE

One of the most memorable, much applauded, and result-oriented speeches that I delivered in the House was on 29 April 2016, when I had an opportunity to address the House on the subject of Law and Justice. At the very opening of my speech, I made it clear that the issues connected with the judiciary and the administration of justice are so vast that it would require at least an hour, even to skim through a few of the aspects of its vast range. "Since I am allotted a short time, I will be able to touch only the tip of the iceberg," I said.

I began by saying that a country's civilization can be best gauged by the effectiveness with which its criminal justice system functions. To assess the extent of success of the system one must turn to prisons of the country. If we apply this yardstick by looking at our prisons, we will find that our prisons are overflowing with inmates, the majority of whom are under-trial accused persons. By this standard our criminal justice system is far from successful and as a result we cannot boast of being a civilized country.

Among the foremost commands of the constitution to the state is to provide 'inexpensive and speedy justice' to every citizen of India. We have miserably failed to achieve the goal of dispensing inexpensive and speedy justice. The pathetic situation today is that poor litigants and poor accused persons are not able to get free legal aid. Therefore, they languish in prisons for years, due to the snail-paced movement of criminal cases in our courts.

We have to put our heads together to see what best we can do, with limited resources and means to ensure that justice visits everybody, including those who are unfortunately placed in society, as stated above. We have villagers who cannot even afford to travel to the court. When we talk of inexpensive justice system, we will have to ensure that free legal aid, as provided under the Constitution of India and Criminal Procedure Code, is provided to the needy. However, during my practice as an advocate throughout the country, unfortunately, I have seen that the concept of free legal aid remains only a paper tiger.

Hardly ever is any worthwhile assistance extended to the needy poor who, in its true sense, requires legal aid. It is time for us to examine the mandate of the Constitution and the Code of Criminal Procedure, in providing free legal aid to the less fortunate litigants, who succumb to injustice, either in the lowest court or in the first appeal court. Seldom are they able to reach the apex court, for want of means and funds. Such unfortunate litigants outnumber the fortunate ones.

Delay and backlog of cases are equally important aspects which I do not want to include in my short speech, as time is not enough even to touch on the topic roughly. However, with a view to summarise this subject in a few lines, I must confess that when we talk of speedy justice, we look upon this issue with a sense of guilt. We are guilty that we are not able to deliver justice in time. Thus, we invoke the dictum 'Justice delayed is Justice denied'. The latest and the most unfortunate example, which made me put my head down out of utter shame, is the 1987 massacre in Meerut. The trial ended in the year 2015. You can imagine, for a case of 42 multiple murders, it took 28 years to wind up, in just the trial court. As many as 19 accused persons, who were all members of Provincial Armed Constabulary had to be acquitted because it was very difficult to get evidence in establishing a case or reaching the bottom of the hidden truth, after more than two and a half long decades. This is purely a case of 'justice denied'.

Apart from the cited above case, there are many cases in the trial courts, where trial in murder cases, rape cases and dacoity cases, are waiting for disposal, for 10 to 15 years. This is nothing but mockery of justice. Our prisons are overflowing with many prisoners who cannot afford bail. How, then, do we call it equality before law? How can we claim that we are doing justice to everybody, when a poor man cannot afford bail because he does not have the money needed? It is a sad aspect that even in this twenty-first century, we have to buy bail, while we talk of free legal aid, dispensing justice to everybody and equality before law.

I appeal to the Law Minister to make note of the very serious fact that our prisons are overflowing with under-trial prisoners. I further appeal to the Hon'ble Minister that he might make a serious note of the reality and check for himself, how many under-trial prisoners are languishing in custody even beyond the period prescribed for ultimate punishment, even if they are found guilty. Is it not a matter of national shame? I place my brief suggestions to decongest the prisons as below:

'As far as bail applications are concerned, we need a relook at our procedure. Bail, in other words, restoration of personal liberty to a presumably innocent person, is the mandate of the Constitution. We must all assure that an undertrial prisoner's stay in prison waiting for justice has to be minimal. How can we do that? I am sorry to inform this House that in many courts all over the country, bail applications are not being taken up for hearing for long periods of time. They are kept pending for months together and at times, for years. This is a very sad aspect. Also, it is a shameful side of our so called 'speedy justice system'.

I, therefore, suggest that in offences which are not punishable with death or imprisonment for life and for all other lesser offences, there must be a mandate of law that bail applications must be decided within a short spell of time, say two to six weeks, or some reasonable period. For any genuine reason, if bail applications cannot be taken up for hearing within the stipulated time, the prisoner should be given interim bail, if the administration is unable to dispose of his petition. His bail application may thereafter be heard on merits, as time permits.

I am afraid that unless we take effective steps to ensure that our prisons do not have any more overflow of under-trials, we cannot be called a 'civilised society'.

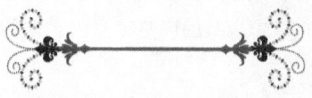

Four

ATROCITIES AGAINST DALITS

On 21 July 2016, I had an opportunity to speak in the House about the atrocities against dalits (backward classes) in the country. My speech went on as under:

Sir, let me begin with the remembrance to the Constitution of India, under which we all, all the Members, have taken oath, before entering this House. The Constitution opens with 'We, the people' and that 'We, the people' phrase, I believe, and I firmly believe, includes 170 million dalit Indians. They cannot be distinguished or discriminated against, as far as all the facilities of the country are concerned. Article 14 of the Constitution talks of equality before law but when two people are placed before a court together, one dalit and the other non-dalit, basically they are not equals when they are before the court because they are socially unequal, they are economically unequal, they are educationally unequal and, therefore, the whole spirit of equality before law gets wounded. So, it is the society which must treat a dalit and a non-dalit equally - socially, economically, and educationally, which unfortunately is not happening.

Now there are several other provisions regarding protection, and a helping hand has to be extended to dalits, because admittedly, they are left behind from the mainstream. Dr. Baba Saheb Ambedkar, way back, had said that we need to bring them up in the mainstream of our society, for which extra efforts are required to be taken. Under the Constitution, we find that we have National Commission for

Scheduled Casts and Scheduled Tribes; we have 'Appointment of a Commission' to investigate the conditions of Scheduled Castes, under Article 341; we have various provisions under the Constitution, and I am afraid that when today, we are discussing atrocities on dalits and Scheduled Caste people, we are believed to be violating those Constitutional provisions.

We are infringing upon the Constitution, and I am afraid that some of us may even have an introspection to consider that we are committing breach of oath that we have taken in this House and, more particularly, those who are in power. Now, I would say that as far as the present incidents are concerned, caste-related violence has occurred and occurs in India in various forms. According to a report by Human Rights Watch, the dalits continue to face discrimination, exclusion, and acts of communal violence. Laws and policies adopted by the Indian Government provide a strong basis for protection but are not being faithfully implemented by local authorities. For the last few days in Gujarat, the dalit community has been seething with anger, over the public flogging of a group of dalits, who were skinning a dead cow, in Mota Samadhiyala, a village near Una town, in the Saurashtra region, on July 11. Four of them were brutally beaten with steel pipes and iron rods, stripped, tied to an SUV vehicle, and paraded in the main market near the local police station in Una, by members of the local cow vigilante group, Gau Raksha Samiti (Cow Protection Committee). The flogging was filmed and posted on Facebook, as a warning to other dalits to show that if they repeat such acts, they would be treated like this. The video went viral filling the community with anger and led to an eruption of protests across the State in which more than 20 people attempted suicide, dozens of vehicles were torched or vandalised, highways were blocked, and one policeman died of injuries sustained during stone-pelting. What transpired in Una was only the latest atrocity on the Scheduled Castes, which form around 7.5 percent of the total population in the State of Gujarat.

Earlier in July, a dalit famer was killed by villagers when he tried to cultivate a common grazing land in a village near Porbandar, also in Gujarat. Only in April this year, a 31-year-old dalit, Ketan Koradia, a clerk in a local court in Ahmedabad (Gujarat), committed suicide alleging discrimination in the workplace where he had constantly faced caste abuse.

According to a leading social activist, Martin Macwan, whose organisation, Navsarjan Trust is the largest dalit body and which works in 3,000 villages in Gujarat, dalits face rampant discrimination at all levels in Gujarat. "Most of them (dalits) are not allowed entry into temples in villages. They have their own cremations because upper castes don't allow dalits to be cremated in common crematoriums," said Mr. Macwan.

In 2012, three dalit youths were killed in police firing in Thangarh town of Surendanagar District. The State Government, then headed by the Chief Minister, the present Hon'ble Prime Minister Shri Narendra Modi, had set up a three-member committee to inquire into the incident and submit a report. To date, the government has not made that report public. According to Mr. Macwan, atrocities against dalits in Gujarat are committed "...with impunity." However, there is one difference this time. "Social media has made the difference and for the first time after 1985, Gujarat is witnessing such a strong protest by the dalit community in the State".

According to the National Campaign for Dalit Human Rights, every year 13,000 - 15,000 cases of atrocities against dalits and 3,000 – 3,500 cases of 'untouchability' are registered in India. Even after the abolition of the caste system, dalits or 'untouchables' continue to face caste discrimination.

Over one sixth of India's population, about 170 million people, lead a precarious existence, shunned by much of Indian society, because of their rank as 'untouchables' or dalits, literally meaning 'broken' people, at the bottom of India's caste system. Dalits are discriminated against, denied access to land and basic resources, forced to work in degrading conditions, and routinely abused at the hands of police and dominant caste groups that enjoy the State's protection.

Historically, the caste system has formed the social and economic framework for the life of the people of India. In its essential form, this caste system involves the division of people into a hierarchy of unequal social groups, where basic rights and duties are assigned based on birth and are not subject to change.

Dalits are outcasts, falling outside the traditional four classes of Brahmin, Kshatriya, Vaishya and Shudra. Dalits are typically considered low, impure, and polluted, based on their birth and traditional occupation. Thus, they face multiple forms of discrimination, violence, and exclusion from the rest of society. Dalit women face the triple burden of caste, class, and gender. Dalit girls have been forced to become prostitutes for dominant caste patrons and village priests. Sexual abuse and other forms of violence against women are used by landlords and the police to inflict political "lessons" and crush dissent within the community. Less than 1% of the perpetrators of crime against Dalit women are ever convicted.

The plight of India's 'untouchables' elicits only sporadic attention within the country. Public outrage over large scale incidents of violence or particularly egregious examples of discrimination fades away quickly, and the state is under little pressure to undertake more meaningful reforms. Laws granting dalits special consideration for government jobs and education, reach only a small percentage of those who are meant to benefit. Laws, designed to ensure that dalits enjoy equal rights and protection, have seldom been enforced. The police refuse to register complaints about violations of the law and rarely prosecute those responsible for abuses that range from murder and rape to exploitative labour practices and forced displacement from dalit lands and homes. Laws and government policies on land reforms, and budget allocations for the economic empowerment of the dalit community remain largely unimplemented.

Dalits who dare to challenge the social order have often been subject to abuse by their dominant-caste neighbours. Dalit villages are collectively penalised for individual 'transgressions', through social boycotts, including deprivation of employment, and access to water, grazing lands, and ration shops. For most dalits in rural India, who earn less than a subsistence living as agricultural labourers, a boycott may mean destitution. Dr. Baba Saheb Ambedkar brilliantly said long ago, which is so relevant even today, and I quote "My final words of advice to you are: educate, agitate and organize, have faith in yourself. With justice on our side, I do not see how we can lose our battle. The battle, to me, is a matter of joy. The battle is, in the fullest sense, spiritual. There is nothing material or social in it. For, ours is a battle not for wealth or for power. It is a battle for freedom. It is the battle of reclamation of human personality. It is in the fullest sense, spiritual."

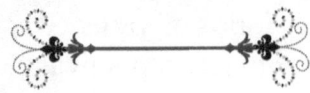

Five

THE POWERLOOM INDUSTRY

On 25 July 2016, I raised a point before the House which was the burning issue in Maharashtra at that time. According to me, the issue I raised was of urgent public importance, involving the interests of thousands of micro scale powerloom employer-cum-employee weavers.

People in the powerloom sector had become jobless and were facing severe financial crisis in the year 2014-2015, because of imposition of anti-dumping duty on Purified Terepthalic Acid (PTA), and sudden and unexpected skyrocketing prices of raw cotton and cotton yarn. The shortage and lesser sowing of cotton seeds had adversely affected the most employment generating decentralised powerloom sectors of Malegaon, Bhiwandi, Ichalkaranji and Solapur in Maharashtra. Apart from this, Surat in Gujarat, Varanasi in Uttar Pradesh, and Erode and other such centers in the South and elsewhere in India, were also facing the same problem.

These hapless people were heavily in debt. Lakhs of people lost their jobs owing to lack of support from the Government. Those who were termed as employer-cum-employee weavers turned jobless overnight. In this scenario, I emphasised the need for urgent measures towards solving this acute problem. I placed heavy reliance on the concerned State Governments and the Central Government, to rise up to the occasion, and take urgent and suitable remedial measures.

I had learnt that approximately nine lakh people were dependent on Bhiwandi powerloom alone. In my humble opinion, the powerloom industry was virtually in the intensive care unit, dying a slow death. Major part of the labour force came from Malegaon itself. They opened the looms for three to four days a week, solely with a view to supporting themselves for their timely survival. It had to be a serious concern for the Government that the strike would ensure less cloth being sent to the markets with the result that it might attract higher prices.

I further appealed to the powerloom owners to make their disclosure through the Hindu paper. Finally, I appealed to the Government on behalf of my party to kindly consider the gravity and emergency of the matter and take immediate corrective steps to save the dying powerloom sector.

On my initiative, the Hon'ble Minister of Textiles was kind enough to have a meeting of the powerloom weavers from Maharashtra, which was attended by a large section of persons from the powerloom industry in Maharashtra. Needless to mention here, that this step of the Union Minister of Textiles was the result of raising of the matter by me in the zero hour of Rajya Sabha, earlier, on the same day. On the next day, I accompanied the members of the delegation to meet the Union Minister of Commerce and Industry, followed by a communication to Hon'ble Union Minister of Finance for taking suitable steps to remedy the problems being faced by them. Their grievances had also been raised by me in Rajya Sabha, through a question, on 12 August 2016. The Hon'ble Textile Minister had also called a meeting of the powerloom weavers in which workers of the industry from all over the country participated, along with me, on 22 August 2016, in New Delhi. This meeting was also attended by concerned members of Parliament.

On 27 July 2016, I had written a letter to the then Finance Minister, Shri Arun Jaitley, for financial relief to a large section of people connected with powerloom industry from Maharashtra. I suggested financial relief for the affected people, in the form of grants-in-aid, as an immediate step, which, I was sure, could help the survival of the powerloom sector, eradicate massive unemployment and bring the weavers out of bankruptcy. On 3 February 2017, in my speech, again on this point, I had to draw the attention of the Hon'ble Finance Minister and the textile minister to a very disturbing aspect of the matter. I brought to their notice that though the budget for the year 2017-18 was presented as pro-poor it does not have even a mention of the sinking powerloom industry in the country. Almost all the hubs in Maharashtra, Surat in Gujrat, Varanasi and Erode are literally on the brink of total collapse and closure.

I drew the attention of the ministers to the fact that in July 2016, through a zero-hour mention on this point, the textile minister did convene a couple of meetings with the powerloom workers from various parts of the country. Thereafter, a delegation was brought from various quarters of the country, by the commerce minister. The matter was heard but unfortunately, in the budget we found that there was not even a modicum of relief given to the people working in the sector. I had to thus request the Government, through the Rajya Sabha, to convey to the Hon'ble Prime Minister that this particular industry which is dying a slow death needs to be revived. Else, thousands will be thrown out of employment which may result in utter starvation. Here, I expressed my fear that in that event, some of them may choose to commit suicide, like in the agricultural sector.

I also brought to the notice of the Government that most of the employees in this sector belong to the minority community, particularly to the Muslim minority which has been certified to be backward, in the sense of their economic condition as well as in academics. Unless the Government gives a helping hand to these people to come back to the mainstream, the slogan *'sabka sath, sabka vikas'* becomes meaningless an d remains only on paper. I drew the attention of those in authority, urging them that they should immediately consider their problems and protect these people. The probable suicide of these hapless workers should be averted.

I further drew the attention of the Hon'ble Finance Minister to a letter dated 26 July 2016, addressed to the minister by one Mr. Mufti Mohamed

Ismail, concerning the extremely miserable condition of the employer-cum-employee weavers of Malegaon, Bhiwandi, Surat, Varanasi, and other powerloom centers of India, for the past two years, causing unemployment and bankruptcy to thousands of them. The letter suggested that a notification vide no. 28/2016, dated 5 July 2016, issued by the Ministry of Finance, Department of Revenue, has proved fatal to the powerloom sector due to lack of any Government support, particularly to the micro scale units. The letter, therefore, suggested immediate withdrawal of the said notification. Alternatively, the Government may impose duty only on the fabrics. The letter further suggested that to avoid massive unemployment in the sector, which is an employment generating sector, the Government needs to consider immediate Free Trade Agreements (FTAs) with the U.K, the U.S.A etc.

The letter suggested that due to severe recession that existed for the past two years, the bonafide weavers have lost their entire working capital, and most of them have been exposed to starvation. It was, therefore, necessary to arrange for a grant-in-aid of Rs. 50,000/- per unit, besides extending soft loans on a subsidised interest rate of 2%, per annum.

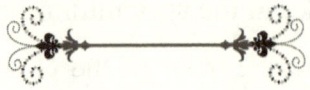

Six

PROBLEMS OF RAILWAY COMMUTERS

On 3 February 2017 in the House, I brought to the notice of the Hon'ble Minister for Railways, the difficulties faced by commuters on the railway platforms in a city like Mumbai. On the occasion, I convinced the Railway Minister, Shri Suresh Prabhu, that disabled commuters, elderly women, and sick commuters are finding it difficult to climb up the stairs to go from one platform to the other. I suggested that elevators should be provided on the platforms, with a view to help the disabled and the needy. It must be mentioned here that in a couple of meetings with the General Managers of both Western Railways and Central Railways I raised the serious problem of platform levels for ascending or descending from rail compartments. The height of the platform needed to be raised to facilitate comfortable entry and exit from the rail compartment. This was extremely necessary for women, children, elderly persons and disabled or handicapped people. In cities of London, Singapore, and Dubai, etc., care is taken to regularly announce through public announcing system "mind the gap between the trains and the platforms," to warn the passengers about the possible accident. Respecting human rights, we need to attend to this problem expeditiously.

Moreover, on many an occasion, it happens that the railways would announce at the eleventh hour their decision to bring a particular train to a platform other than the one it was scheduled to arrive on as per schedule. For example, often there will be a sudden announcement on loudspeaker in the city of Mumbai that a train which was due to reach platform No. 5 would be reaching platform No. 3, on a particular day, at the appointed time, during peak hours. This announcement causes jitters among passengers who were to board the train on platform No. 5. Commuters have to run and catch the train from the newly announced platform, as they have to reach their workplace on time. This sort of mismatch causes great inconvenience and confusion, among hundreds of commuters, mainly the disabled, elderly, women and sick as stated above. I, therefore suggested to the Hon'ble Minister of Railways, Shri Suresh Prabhu, that the platforms of railways should be divyang (physically challenged) friendly. The Hon'ble Minister informed the House that in December 2016, i.e., just about five weeks back a huge sum of Rupees fifty-five thousand crores had been sanctioned by the Government for upgrading the infrastructure of railways in Mumbai city alone. This, he said, was for the first time in the history of India that such a huge amount was sanctioned only for the railway upgradation in a city.

The minister thereafter informed the House that the railways had already started working towards the target. All new stations and new coaches which are getting built, would be divyang friendly. All the major stations, wherever there is a need, would be made divyang friendly. In fact, the railways have invited some experts in the field to advise on how the design should be and how the project should be executed.

I further invited the attention of the hon'ble Minister to a version of one of the members, Shri Narendra Jadhav, on the condition of a railway platform, for a Mumbai local train. The member said, "If any local train reached the platform 30 or 40 seconds later than usual, during peak hours, the situation of the platform turns to such a condition that it will not be possible for anyone to keep his balance."

I must mention here that after the discussion in Parliament on this subject, the railways have started systematically installing elevators in almost all stations in Mumbai, apart from various facilities for the divyang.

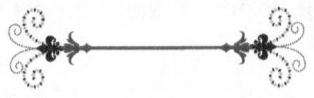

Seven

ONION FARMERS IN MAHARASHTRA

On 22 March 2017, I raised a very serious issue in the House, pertaining to the onion farmers in Maharashtra. My point was to provide these farmers with financial assistance for redress of their various problems. I brought to the notice of the House that the onion farmers of Maharashtra are getting very low prices for their produce. I pointed out that in that year onion prices in Maharashtra had touched a five-year low. The average price that farmers had been able to fetch for a quintal of onion was Rs.450/- Some farmers had set their stock on fire since they were not getting even their basic input.

While onion is being sold for less than Rs.20/- per kg. in the market, they are not getting even the basic cost per quintal. That year there was a bumper crop of onions and needed at least 40 wagons to transport the products to other parts of the state or the country. But the fact was that they were getting only 15-18 wagons. This lethargy, on the part of the authorities, had resulted in non-clearance and piling up of the stock in mandis (markets). I had information that the railways had agreed to give more wagons for transporting onions, but being the peak harvest season, inflow of the produce was not slowing down. According to reliable information, in the month of March, production will slow down, and the prices will stabilise. This might give some relief to the farmers who already suffered an accumulated loss of about Rs.200 crores.

I, therefore, urged the Hon'ble Minister of Railways, through the august House, to provide maximum number of wagons for clearing the piled-up stock, and its transportation to other parts of Maharashtra and the rest of the country immediately, and save the growers from the acute, mounting financial crisis that they had been facing. I further urged the Government to take serious note of the situation and offer the farmers substantial financial assistance which may, inter alia (among other things), include a loan waiver for their survival.

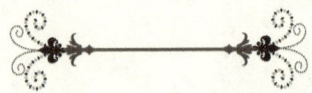

Eight
JUDICIAL VACANCIES

On 5 April 2017, I was asked to speak on judicial vacancies in the country and speedy justice. I started my speech by highlighting the lethargy of the successive Law Ministers in filling up the vacancies in various High Courts of the country.

The Allahabad High Court in Uttar Pradesh is the largest High Court in the country, where approved strength of judges is 160, while there are 75 vacancies existing today. The cases pending are 9,25,000. The Madras High Court has an approved strength of 75 judges whereas there are 20 existing vacancies. In the case of the Kolkata High Court, the approved strength is 72 judges and there are 35 vacancies. Bombay High Court has a strength of 94 judges, and it has 32 vacancies. The figures in respect of some other High Courts are as follows:

In the case of the Punjab and Haryana High Courts, the figures are 85 and 39. In the case of the Madhya Pradesh High Court, it is 53 and 16, while in the case of the Andhra Pradesh and Telangana High Courts it is 61 and 34. In the case of the Karnataka High Court, it's 62 and 31. In the case of the Rajasthan High Court, the strength is 94 and vacancies are 32. In total the strength of judges in these High Courts is 712 and the vacancies are almost 300 which is 42 per cent of the sanctioned strength. In the Allahabad High Court alone 9.25 lakh cases are pending, which is over 23 per cent of the total 40 lakh pending cases in all the High Courts in the country.

The Hon'ble Law Minister has been heard saying that we have record appointments this year. This verbal announcement of the Minister would not do. The number of judges must be proportionate to the ever-growing number of justice seekers. Why is the sanctioned strength not revised periodically as per the number of people who approach the courts for justice? Why do Courts not work with full strength? Will the Law Minister explain why these vacancies have not been filled with a sense of expediency to improve the justice delivery system? Everybody chants, 'justice delayed is justice denied'. It is a fact that both the Supreme Court, as well as the Law Ministry, have all the records available with regard to future vacancies that may accrue during the next three years. The process of filling up of vacancies should begin and conclude even prior to the occurrence of vacancies, so that we have judges available in stock. This will help avoid vacancies.

Coming back to the point of inexpensive and speedy justice, I must say that it is the solemn duty of the State under the Constitution, in co- ordination with the judiciary, to provide inexpensive and speedy justice to the people. People are fast losing confidence in our justice delivery system due to inordinate delays in the delivery of justice. When we talk of inexpensive justice, we have to bear in mind that there is a provision under the Code of Criminal Procedure to provide free legal aid to the needy. However, it has been my experience that the provision is hardly utilised towards achieving the goal for which it was incorporated under the Code. Hardly any worthwhile assistance is being extended to the needy under-privileged who need, in its true sense, legal aid. I am sorry to tell you that in various courts, throughout the country, the concept of free legal aid remains only on paper. It is high time that we examine the mandate of our Constitution and the Code of Criminal Procedure, in directing us to provide free legal aid to the less fortunate litigants.

A letter dated 3 April 2017, from Hon'ble Minister for Law and Justice, was issued to all members of the Consultative Committee. But I was the only member who responded to that. In my reply I raised certain issues relating to strengthening of federal governance by appointing best talents, inclusion of competent persons from underprivileged and marginalised communities in the judiciary, consideration of the useful purpose for creation of an All India Judicial Service, for better administration of justice, difficulties of officers from different States, language barrier, apprehension regarding control of State High Courts, pay and other service conditions, uniform eligibility criteria, etc. It is often found that regional balance is sought in selecting judges, which does not, in my view, serve the needs of the administration. We need not compromise on talent, competence and honesty of the incumbent judge, over regional representation. From that angle, representation to minorities has been dismally poor.

Another letter, dated 25 April 2017, from the Minister of State for Law and Justice, was also issued to all members of the Consultative Committee, with a request to provide suggestions for the agenda for next meeting of the Consultative Committee. However, I was the only member to respond to this letter too. In my reply letter dated 3 May 2017, I supported the agenda on speedy and inexpensive justice. I further suggested items on exploring causes for delay, possibility for enhancing strength of judges, functioning of Legal Aid Apparatus, Lok Adalats (People's Courts), cutting down expenses of litigation, and other relevant issues, with the permission of the Chair.

A meeting of Parliamentary Consultative Committee, attached to the Ministry of Law and Justice was held on 30 March 2017, in the Parliament House Annexe, to discuss All India Judicial Service, under the Chairmanship of Hon'ble Minister of Law and Justice. In the said meeting, only a single agenda viz., All India Judicial Service (AIJS), was taken up for discussion due to paucity of time. The Hon'ble Minister welcomed all members of the Committee and informed them that the Government was keen to constitute All India Judicial Service, under the constitutional provisions. He explained that there are brilliant law students in the country passing out from National Law Schools who should be given good career opportunities to serve the country. He also said that there are several boys and girls from SC/ST and backward communities, who are also equally brilliant and should get equal opportunities in becoming part of the judicial system.

After explaining the brief proposal of AIJS, the Chairman requested the Members of Parliament to offer their views and suggestions in the matter.

In my suggestions I expressed that this was an excellent opportunity for good law graduates. I appreciated the steps taken by the Government for mooting the proposal of AIJS. I supported the proposal of setting up an AIJS and asked the Government to get consensus from the High Courts. There were seven High Courts opposing the proposal, while three had agreed. Seven High Courts had agreed with conditions, and two had reservations. The rest of the High Courts were yet to respond. Therefore, I suggested that the Ministry should go back and discuss with the High Courts that are opposing creation of AIJS and they should be convinced. My concern for the large number of vacancies in the High Courts could not be looked into as AIJS is only for district Judges.

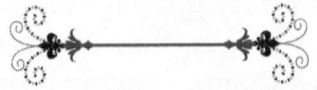

Nine

ELECTORAL REFORMS

On 3 July 2019, the subject of my speech in the House was Electoral Reforms. When I stood up to deliver my speech, I had to face a lot of interruptions from several members. Even the Hon'ble Chairman did not allot me enough time to speak on the subject. My allotted time was just four minutes. I made it clear to the Hon'ble Chairman that within four minutes, it will not be possible for me to touch the subject even roughly.

'Electoral Reforms' is a vast subject which needs in-depth study. It is a genus under which half a dozen species exist. If we are serious about having free and fair polls as mandated by the Constitution of India, we will have to attend to all these items or the captions which I am giving, because of lack of time.

Number one, how the conduct of polls can be free and fair? Whether the breach of model code of conduct is being fairly implemented? Whether the election expenditure is being properly accounted for? Then comes undue advantage given to the ruling party, interference of the ruling party in holding of the elections, use of electoral bonds and the possibility of corruption seeping in by such an issuance. Simultaneous poll itself is a vast subject. Then there is use or misuse of media. These are all various captions. Each one of them deserves to be discussed at full length. It is only then that we can reach free and fair electoral reforms.'

I then informed the Hon'ble Chairman that I could only take one of these subjects and not all.

The one subject which I chose was about Electoral Voting Machines (EVMs). I pointed out that advanced countries like England, France, Germany, Netherland, and the United States, have banned the use of electoral voting machines. Now it is necessary for India, for my country, to examine the causes under which these developed countries had to ban EVMs and why we should not.

When I finished in my time, the Hon'ble Chairman commented 'we could have discussed this before election, unfortunately we are discussing it after elections'. To which I answered, "Electoral reforms are not only for elections, we can still discuss it."

I informed the House that the question was raised before the German Constitutional Court and the question was whether Electronic Voting Machines were legal for use of conducting elections. The Chairman opined that every country has its own system. Here I got the opportunity to place my opinion before the House. I said in answer to the opinion of the Chairman, "The simple, correct answer is 'No'. The answer is 'No', because it does not have all the essential steps in the elections, which are subject to public scrutiny. Now if public scrutiny is not there, we can't have EVMs".

The constitutional mandate of holding 'free and fair polls' cannot be lost sight of. What is the meaning of a free and fair poll? Free and fair poll to the satisfaction of the ruling party, or election commission is not what is meant by free and fair. It is free and fair poll from the point of view of the people who exercise their right and it is their satisfaction which is fundamental.

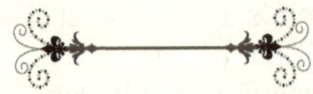

THE ORIENTATION PROGRAMME

On 5th August 2018 I was asked by Rajya Sabha Secretariat to participate in an orientation programme and address a group of fresh Parliamentarians and guide them on the process of Law making in the House. My lecture was for about 40 minutes and was attended by most of the Members of Parliament including some of the then prominent Parliamentarians. The Secretary General of Rajya Sabha, Shri Desh Deepak was also present during my lecture.

In my speech I emphasized the necessity of educating fresh law makers to understand the sanctity of the law-making process. A civil society governed by 'rule of law' must be provided appropriate laws to govern the civil society. The needs of the society keep on changing with the passage of time and accordingly, the laws also need review. In this regard, I pointed out that the Constitution, which is the apex law, has neither to be too rigid nor too flexible. When the government introduces a Bill in the House for enactment, the same becomes law only after it is passed by both the Houses. Before such a bill is passed it needs to be thoroughly discussed by the Members of the House. The laws are made for regulating the conduct of the people of the Country and the Authority of the State.

In my lecture I urged the Members that they have a great responsibility as law makers and, therefore, they must take their job seriously. The position of a Member of Parliament is not just an ornamental or honorary post, but a position of great responsibility towards the society, the country, and the people of India. The Members must study each subject by good homework. The Parliament campus has a rich library where books on all subjects are readily available to the Members. While enacting laws, the contribution of each Member can be of great utility. Whether the Member is from the Treasury Benches or from the opposition, the Member must equip himself/herself with deep study of the subject and put forth his/her views.

When you speak in the House, you must be articulate and impressive. While you address the Chair you need to respect the Chair and use decent language. You are permitted to express yourself in your regional language as well, so that you can express your thoughts with greater clarity. There are Parliamentary Committees on various subjects and as a member of a Committee your contribution can be of great value.

Do not take your job as a part-time hobby. You have a very serious assignment in running the country even if you are not a member of the ruling party.

After the lecture was over some of the Members present had doubts in their minds. I told them to ask any questions they had and many of them posed questions on law to me, which I answered to their satisfaction.

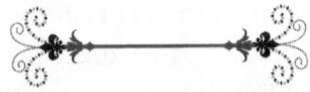

ACTING CHAIRMAN OF THE PARLIAMENTARY STANDING COMMITTEE ON PERSONNEL, PUBLIC GRIEVANCES AND LAW & JUSTICE

On 27th August 2018, Parliamentary Standing Committee on Personnel, Public Grievances, Law and Justice visited Chennai and held meeting with Chairmen and Managing Directors of important Public Undertakings. Chairman of the Committee Shri Bhupendra Yadav could not reach Chennai to conduct the meeting on account of some personal contingency although members of the Committee such as D. Raja, Bhagawant Mann and Vivek Tankha and all other members of the Committee were present for the meeting. The Rajya Sabha Secretariat was informed by the Chairman to request me to chair the meeting in the absence of Shri Bhupendra Yadav. Accordingly, I chaired and conducted the meeting as an officiating Chairman. Throughout the day, there were deliberations regarding the working of Undertakings and public grievances amidst interactions with heads and high-ranking officials of Public Undertakings. The meeting concluded with thanks to the Chair.

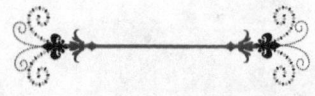

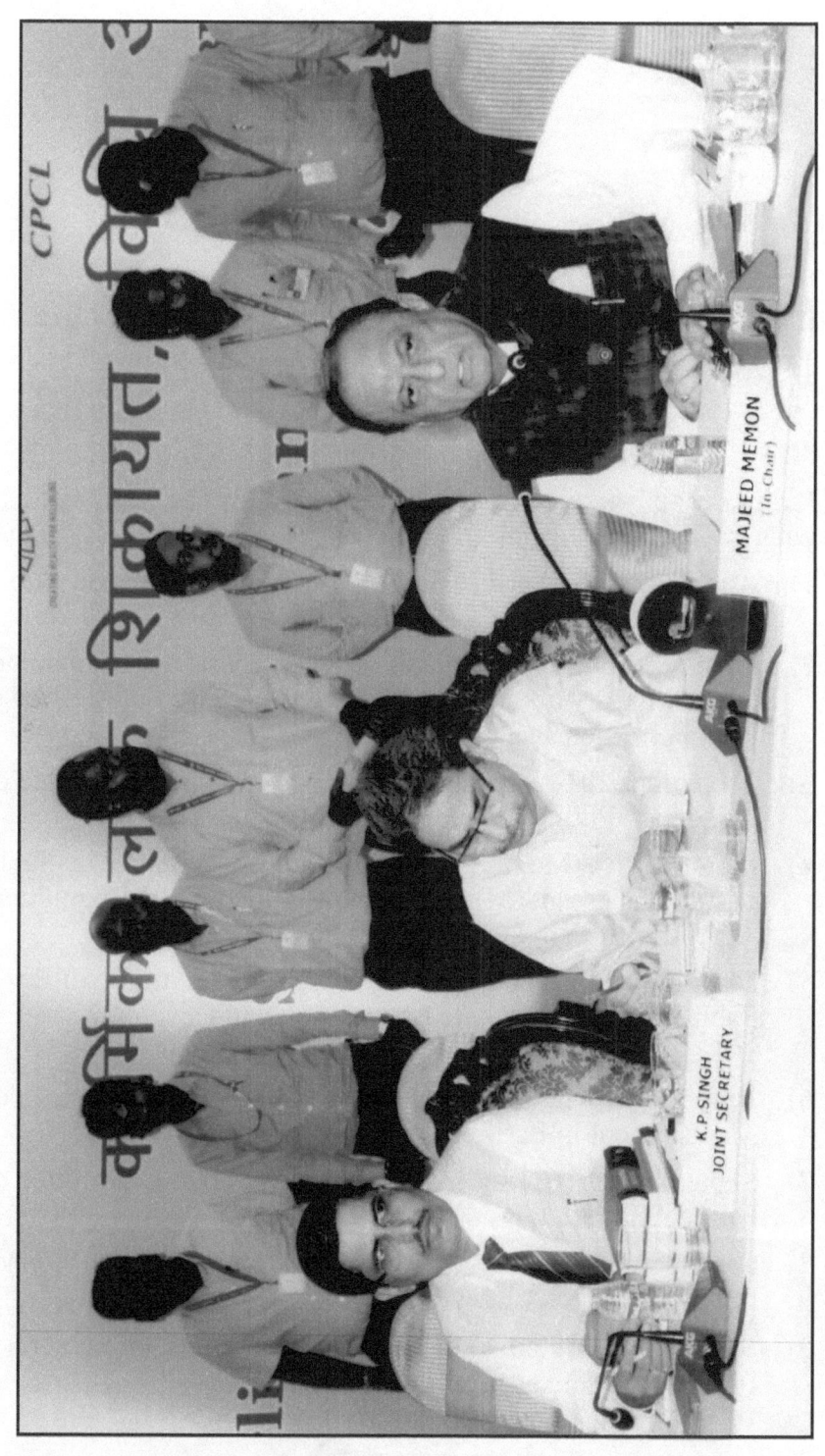

On 27th August, 2018 at Chennai chairing meeting of Parliamentary Standing Committee on Personnel, Public Grievances and Law & Justice.

POSITIONS HELD IN RAJYA SABHA

During my six years' term as a Member of Rajya Sabha, I held the following positions.

1) August 2014 - April 2015, Member, Committee on Public Undertakings.
2) From September 2014 onwards Member, Consultative Committee for the Ministry of Law & Justice and the Ministry of Electronics and Information Technology.
3) September 2014 - September 2016, Member, Committee on Personnel, Public Grievances, Law & Justice.
4) March 2015, Member, Select Committee of Rajya Sabha on the Mines and Minerals (Development and Regulation) Amendment Bill, 2015.
5) May 2015 - July 2015, Member, Select Committee of Rajya Sabha on the Real Estate (Regulation and Development) Bill 2013.
6) June 2016 - May 2019, Member, Joint Committee on Food Management in Parliament House Complex.
7) September 2016 - September 2017, Member, Committee on Home Affairs.
8) September 2017 - May 2019 Member, Committee on Personnel, Public Grievances, Law & Justice.
9) September 2019 onwards Member, Committee on Personnel, Public Grievances, Law & Justice.

www.ingramcontent.com/pod-product-compliance
Lightning Source LLC
LaVergne TN
LVHW091627070526
838199LV00044B/972